TRANS CANADA TRAIL
NORTHWEST TERRITORIES

Official Guide of the Trans Canada Trail

TRANS CANADA TRAIL
NORTHWEST TERRITORIES

Official Guide of the Trans Canada Trail

Jamie Bastedo

Fitzhenry & Whiteside
www.fitzhenry.ca

Published in Canada by Fitzhenry & Whiteside,
195 Allstate Parkway, Markham, Ontario L3R 4T8

Published in the United States by Fitzhenry & Whiteside,
311 Washington Street, Brighton, Massachusetts 02135

10 9 8 7 6 5 4 3 2 1

All recommendations are made without guarantee on the part of the author, Fitzhenry & Whiteside,
Trans Canada Trail (TCT), and Northwest Territories Recreation and Parks Association (NWTRPA).
These parties disclaim any liability in connection with the use of this information. Fitzhenry and
Whiteside, TCT and NWTRPA do not review or endorse the contents of the websites listed in this
book and assume no liability for any content or opinion expressed on those websites nor do they
warrant that the contents and links are error or virus free.

Every reasonable effort has been made to find copyright holders of quotations.
The publishers would be pleased to have errors or omissions brought to their attention.

Fitzhenry & Whiteside acknowledges with thanks the Canada Council for the Arts, and the Ontario
Arts Council for their support of our publishing program. We acknowledge the financial support of the
Government of Canada through the Book Publishing Industry Development Program (BPIDP)
for our publishing activities.

Library and Archives Canada Cataloguing in Publication
Bastedo, Jamie, 1955-
Trans Canada Trail : Northwest Territories / Jamie Bastedo with Trans
Canada Trail.
Includes bibliographical references and index.
ISBN 978-1-55455-158-3
1. Trans Canada Trail—Guidebooks. 2. Trails—Northwest
Territories—Guidebooks. 3. Northwest Territories—Guidebooks.
I. Trans Canada Trail II. Title. III. Title: Northwest Territories.
FC4157.B38 2010   917.19'3044   C2010-900226-1

U.S. Publisher Cataloging-in-Publication Data
(Library of Congress Standards)
Bastedo, Jamie.
Trans Canada trail : Northwest Territories / Jamie Bastedo with Trans Canada Trail.
[304] p. : ill., col. photos., maps ; cm.
Includes bibliographical references and index.
ISBN-13: 978-1-55455-158-3 (pbk.)
1. Trans Canada Trail—Northwest Territories—Guidebooks. 2. Trails—Northwest
Territories—Guidebooks. 3. Northwest, Canadian—Guidebooks. I. Trans Canada Trail. II. Title.
917.12043 dc22   F1060.4B37. 2010

Design by Kerry Designs
Map design by Charles-André Roy of the Trans Canada Trail
Cover images copyright © Jamie Bastedo
Printed and bound in China

I have travelled far, across rivers, in the mountains and down rivers...
Life in the bush made me very happy.
The land is so beautiful and you can see so far.

Jimmy Bonnetrouge, Fort Providence

*To my parents who instilled in me
a love of human-powered locomotion.*

CONTENTS

AUTHOR'S ACKNOWLEDGEMENTS

When I talk about this incredible project – to be given the opportunity to explore and document the longest and wildest stretch of the Trans Canada Trail – I tell people that, "If you're lucky, a job like this comes along about once every fifty years!" My store of gratitude for this work is at least as big as the land we journeyed through. None of the stories that follow could have been told without the support of my field expedition mates, including, in order of appearance: Jaya Bastedo, Nimisha Bastedo, Brenda Hans, Julian Tomlinson, Myles Woodman, Geoff Ray, Mike Mitchell, Andrea Bettger, Diana Ehman, Alfred Moses, Chris Bennington, Carrie McGown, Ron Cook, Wendy Lahey, Mellissa Wood, and Julie Rouette. Major supporters of our two-year expedition were the NWT government departments of Municipal and Community Affairs, Industry, Tourism and Investment, the NWT Recreation and Parks Association (NWTRPA), and of course the Trans Canada Trail. As for all the people in the 17 communities along the route that housed, fed, informed, and entertained us, their names are truly too numerous to mention. To all of you I extend my deepest thanks for opening up your hearts and homes to us. Some of their names appear among the many voices that enrich the pages to follow. Lastly, I thank the terrific team that helped create this beautiful guidebook, especially NWTRPA's Geoff Ray and his staff, Fitzhenry & Whiteside's Richard Dionne and Amy Hingston, plus Jane Craig, Charles-André Roy, and Carolyn Ring-Ade of the Trans Canada Trail.

My daughters tuck into chocolate cake after battling headwinds on the Slave River

MESSAGE FROM THE PRESIDENT AND CEO

The Trans Canada Trail is the world's longest and grandest network of trails. It is linking communities from coast to coast to coast and is inspiring Canadians and international visitors to experience Canada's majestic natural beauty and learn more about our rich history and diverse cultural heritage.

Covering more than 22,000 kilometres, the Trail offers countless opportunities for exploration and discovery. You can experience Canada's legendary wilderness, canoe the routes of early explorers, visit our national and provincial/territorial capitals, cycle historic rail trails, travel northern highways, and enjoy communities large and small.

The Trail was initiated in 1992 as a project to celebrate Canada's 125th anniversary. Today almost 75% of the Trail is developed. Our goal is to complete it by 2017 as a celebration of the 25th anniversary of the Trail and the 150th anniversary of Canada's Confederation.

The Trans Canada Trail is one of the largest volunteer projects ever undertaken in Canada. Each trail section represents the hard work and commitment of dedicated volunteers, local trail builders, partner organizations, municipal leaders, provincial/territorial and federal governments, businesses, corporations and individual donors.

The route of the Trans Canada Trail through the Northwest Territories is unique. This guidebook is essential for people who are planning to explore this vast northern territory and who want to learn more about the local history, culture, and special attractions of the NWT.

On behalf of the Trans Canada Trail, I want to thank author Jamie Bastedo and the many individuals and organizations that have supported the TCT project, including our territorial partner, the Northwest Territories Recreation and Parks Association; the government of the NWT; local recreation and tourism promoters; and the people in NWT communities along the entire route of the Trail.

Deborah Apps,
President and CEO of the Trans Canada Trail

FOREWORD

The creation of the Trans Canada Trail was inspired by a dream to bring together diverse groups of people and places across our country. The Trail connects new Canadians with Aboriginal Canadians; urban centres with isolated, remote communities; three coasts; major waterways; and everything and everyone in between. The Trail is a representation of everything that is and can be in Canada, and a great way to travel across a vast country.

In the Northwest Territories, as it is across Canada, the Trans Canada Trail is all about connections. The trail connects 17 communities across the NWT and links distinct cultural and linguistic groups as it passes through the traditional lands of the Dene, Inuvialuit, and Métis. By travelling past a Canadian capital city, through regional centres to remote, traditional communities, the Trans Canada Trail links the past, present and future of northern lifestyles. I hope that everyone who is able to travel the Trail can take the time to savour the experience while respecting the land and learning from the people they meet along the way.

The NWT Recreation and Parks Association is a non-profit organization dedicated to building healthy communities through recreation. Our mission is to increase public awareness of recreation and parks, and to enhance the quality of life of residents in the NWT by promoting and supporting the development of recreation and parks services throughout the North. We are proud supporters and builders of the NWT portion of the Trans Canada Trail and are thrilled to be involved with the creation of this guidebook.

In the winter of 2005, I sat down with Jamie Bastedo and our Trails Committee Chair Julian Tomlinson to brainstorm the idea of documenting the NWT portion of the Trans Canada Trail. Two summers of paddling, hiking, cycling, and countless hours of planning and follow-up ensued and I could not be more excited to now see the publication of this guidebook.

I would like to thank the many individuals, organizations, businesses, and communities that helped us, encouraged us and hosted us during our travels and work on the Trail. Without the support of these individuals and groups, we would not have been able to publish such a comprehensive guide to the Trans Canada Trail. I would also like to thank the Government of the Northwest Territories Departments of Industry, Tourism and Investment, and Municipal and Community Affairs for their financial contributions and on-the-ground help in creating this guidebook. Finally, we could not have chosen a better person to work with than Jamie Bastedo. Jamie's determination, patience and thoughtful approach to writing this guidebook have inspired us all to explore our northern landscapes and communities.

I hope that you enjoy this book, and should you find yourself travelling this magnificent portion of the Trans Canada Trail, experience a safe and fun trip!

Geoff Ray,
Executive Director NWT Recreation and Parks Association

AUTHOR'S NOTE

Just hours after returning home from 95 days of field research I did in order to write this book on the Northwest Territories portion of the Trans Canada Trail, I received a call from *News North* reporter Mike Bryant. I had e-mailed him some images from a 3,000-kilometre canoe, bike, and van expedition that took me from one end of the Northwest Territories to the other, and he needed a smidgen of text for a photo spread he was putting together.

"Can you sum up your trip in about six words?" he asked. "I'm afraid that's all we have space for. I need it right away."

"Sure Mike," I said. "Give me two minutes."

I thought about Mike's outrageous request for about ten seconds. Then, these words popped into my head: "An awesome, multi-layered journey of discovery." Six words.

What did I discover?

I discovered that I could bicycle 110 kilometres over six and a half hours and not take a pee once.

I discovered that if a one-ton bull bison parades its body sidewise at you, raises its tail, and nothing comes out the back end, you'd better give him lots of space.

I discovered that the Mackenzie is too big to be called a river and, months after paddling its entire length, that it magically continues to flow inside of me.

I discovered muscles in places I had never imagined. I learned that my body was built for long, steady, rhythmic motion — as I believe all human bodies are — and that swinging my feet over a trail, pumping my legs on a mountain bike, or thrusting my paddle into the water thirty thousand times a day is one of the greatest and cheapest and safest highs around. It's just *so* good for the body, mind, and spirit.

I discovered that a human-powered pace — whether paddling, hiking, or biking — can help you find magic in even the seemingly dullest stretches of river, lakeshore, or road. As one member of our expedition, Alfred Moses, said as we biked along a stretch of road between Providence and Behchokò that runs laser-straight for over 35 kilometres, "You've got to slow down and take it in to really see the beauty." With equal passion after several hours of biking, Alfred was also heard to say, "Oh … *my butt!*"

I discovered that, just beyond the back door of all our northern communities is a lot of wild country that looks and behaves as it has for thousands of years. At the same time, I learned that the notion of wilderness as an unpeopled landscape is a faulty view of the North, where the signs and stories of human use are everywhere if you know where to look or who to talk to.

I discovered that the Northwest Territories Trans Canada Trail takes you through a treasure trove of rich history—from the imagined armadas of birch bark canoes migrating north after the last ice age, to the tangible evidence of explorers, fur traders, and gold-seekers who wove vibrant threads into the unique fabric of northern society. For instance, on the south shore of Great Slave Lake, just a few hours east of Hay River, we discovered the rusting spokes from the stern paddle-wheel of a great steam-powered ship that stopped plying up and down the Mackenzie Valley over 50 years ago. It all comes alive out there on the land and in the communities that are strung like shining pearls along this glowing thread of history.

And the camps and cabins and fire rings along the way remind us that the land is never empty, that people know, use, and love this land and perhaps feel more at home out there than anywhere else. John B. Zoe, one of the grand architects of the Dogrib's historic Tlicho Land Claim Agreement, calls it "The Source"—the source of countless stories, of knowledge, of healing and strength, and of that special joy you can't find anywhere but on the land.

One still summer evening, while watching a spectacular sunset over Great Slave Lake, I scribbled in my field book, "If anyone does even a small part of what we have done along this trail, their lives will be immeasurably richer."

Jamie Bastedo,
Yellowknife January, 2011

Trans Canada Trail
From Coast to Coast to Coast

Land route
Water route

Tuktoyaktuk
Inuvik
Dawson City
Normen Wells
Whitehorse
Mackenzie River
Watson Lake
Fort Nelson
Vancouver
Victoria
Fort St John
Peace River
Banff
Edmonton
Calgary
Fort McMurray
Athabaska River
Yellowknife
Fort Smith
Saskatoon
Regina
Winnipeg
Kenora
Thunder Bay
Sault Ste. Marie
Sudbury
North Bay
Iqaluit
St. John's
North Sydney
Charlottetown
Fredericton
Halifax
Quebec
Montreal
OTTAWA
Toronto
Hamilton
Windsor

WorldSat
INTERNATIONAL INC
© WorldSat International Inc. 2000

ROUTE HIGHLIGHTS

The Northwest Territories portion of the Trans Canada Trail has its roots in northern Alberta, starting as a water trail in the community of Athabasca. Heading north down the Athabasca River, the Trail shifts to land at Fort Fitzgerald, where it follows a traditional portage around four sets of mighty rapids above Fort Smith, which lies on the Alberta–Northwest Territories border.

The Trail winds through the Northwest Territories (an area of 1.17 million square kilometres), spans an amazing variety of ecological regions (four of Canada's 15 major ecozones), and connects all eight of the Northwest Territories' major Aboriginal groups (Métis, Cree, Chipewyan, Tlicho, South Slavey, North Slavey, Gwich'in, and Inuvialuit). This Trail includes a 2,155-kilometre traditional water route beginning at Fort Smith. From there it winds north down the Slave River to Fort Resolution, then west along the south shore of Great Slave Lake to the

Paddling paradise in northern shield country

Mackenzie River. The Trail continues down the Mackenzie all the way to Tuktoyaktuk on the shore of the Arctic Ocean. Two additional overland legs totalling 577 kilometres include the Great Slave Highway from Fort Providence to Yellowknife plus the Dempster Highway from Inuvik to the Yukon border.

This primary route intersects with local trails within many communities along the way. Seven of these communities have already registered their trails as part of the Trans Canada Trail, totalling 59 kilometres. More communities are working with the Northwest Territories Recreation and Parks Association to register their local trails or develop new ones.

GUIDE OVERVIEW

The main purpose of this guidebook is to help you journey safely along one of the wildest and longest stretches of the Trans Canada Trail while discovering the natural and cultural riches it offers. This guide provides the kind of nuts-and-bolts information needed for unfamiliar country — route maps and conditions, community facilities and services, distances between major landmarks and access points, camping options, points of interest, and precautions. This information is complemented with details on local history and cultures, natural features, special attractions, and recommended side trips. Such practical guidance provides the main "flow" of the route description.

Another important purpose of this guide is to encourage you to look for greater depth and meaning in your experience by conveying the spirit of the land and people encountered along the way. This was our greatest challenge. Given the vast distances, the wildness and variety of landscapes, and the richly textured cultural fabric traversed by this Trail, achieving this goal would have been next to impossible without including the voices of the people who know this land best, namely those who live along the way. By including a diverse range of local contributors—through their own words and images—this guide captures something of the unique character of each featured place by grounding it in the life experience of the people who call it home. Their stories provide "tributaries" to the main flow of text, evoking a unique narrative perspective on featured locations.

The collection of both practical and cultural information was inspired by the book's overriding goal: connecting people, land, and stories through traditional trails.

USING THIS GUIDE

While paddling from Fort Smith on the Alberta–Northwest Territories border to Tuktoyaktuk on the Arctic Ocean, we met a couple of intrepid travellers for whom this immense water route was a mere fraction of their much grander trans-Canada tour. We also met a handful of bikers for whom the overland routes described in this guide barely registered on the scale of their own epic journeys. Such people are few and far between. In fact, it is the rare traveller who would attempt to cover all the water and ground described in these pages, a journey which, if you include a couple of nights in every community along the way, took us 95 days. If you have that kind of time, then go for it! We broke the route up over two summers.

This guide subdivides the entire Northwest Territories component of the Trans Canada Trail into bite-sized route descriptions that are roughly 200 to 300 kilometres long and connect convenient community access points. For instance, the first water leg of the Trail describes the Slave River between the communities of Fort Smith and Fort Resolution, a distance of 325 kilometres. These two communities are connected by road, facilitating logistics at both ends if you choose to explore only this portion of the Trail. In a canoe or kayak, this could take you anywhere from four to eight days, depending on weather conditions and travelling style. Similarly, the overland portions that branch east and west from the water route join major communities or landmarks.

You may choose to do the whole route, and then some. More likely, you will choose one or more of the ten routes described in this guide. Or you might combine these with one of the many featured side trips that would take from a few hours to a few days to explore. Although the guide systematically describes the Northwest Territories Trans Canada Trail from one end to the other, it is organized to help you customize your journey, depending on your available time, budget, skills, and interests.

Because much of the Northwest Territories Trans Canada Trail follows rivers or lake shores, the main body of this guide is written primarily for people travelling by canoe

Chillin' after a long day's paddle on the Slave River

or kayak during the open-water season, generally June to September. Boaters will also benefit from the rich detail provided along these routes. Overland portions follow major road systems and are aimed at those travelling on bicycles or in vehicles during the same time of year. People interested in hiking will find lots of ground to cover in the guide's descriptions of community trails and recommended side trips.

Be sure to check for updates to the Guide on the NWT Trans Canada Trail at www.tctrail.ca/nwtguide. You can help keep the information current by reporting on your travel experience and bringing changes to our attention.

A field-tested legend flagging features of special interest is used for all land and water route descriptions. The symbols used throughout the guide are listed alphabetically below with examples.

LEGEND

⚐ Access Points

Community launch points (recommended for safety, convenience, or respect of private property), remote access routes (rivers, trails, or abandoned roads connecting with the Trans Canada Trail), and emergency access or rescue points

⚑ Community Attractions

Community trails, parks, museums, cultural centres, visitors centres, historic buildings, special events, unique shopping opportunities, and outdoor recreation businesses (e.g., guiding, equipment rental and purchase)

▢ Cultural Feature

Places of special significance to local Aboriginal cultures (traditional gathering areas, travel routes, or sites tied to particular stories of the land)

▲ Campsite

Suitable campsites along the river, lakeshore, or road (either specific sites or general guidelines for finding a good site); established sites and facilities found in or near communities; and tips on site characteristics to look for or avoid (e.g., forest type, soil conditions, topography)

🏠 Current Use

Backcountry cabins, commercial or industrial developments, and government operations

☠ Hazard Area

Dangerous currents or potential water level changes, unusual wind patterns, unstable slopes, wildlife hazards, and traffic hazards

☺ Historical Feature

Structures or sites associated with significant events related to post-European exploration, fur trading, and missionary work

☷ Lunch or Rest Stop

Attractive places to lunch, loaf, rest, or generally smell the flowers

⛰ Natural Feature

Interesting geology, topography, plants, and habitats

🔍 Route Tip

Recommendations for the most efficient, sheltered, or scenic water route

🏔 Side Trip

Recommended jaunts branching off from the Trans Canada Trail route, from hour-long hikes such as climbing the Caribou Hills in the Mackenzie Delta to a multi-day trip such as paddling the North Arm of Great Slave Lake from Behchokò to Yellowknife

📷 Viewpoint

Lake or riverside lookout, hills, or cliffs offering outstanding vistas of surrounding landscape

🦫 Wildlife

Opportunities to see mammals, birds, or fish (in the latter case, maybe even catch one for supper)

SELECTING A ROUTE

With about 2,300 kilometres of water route and 600 kilometres over land, the Northwest Territories Trans Canada Trail offers many exciting options for you to customize your trip. Some travellers know exactly what they are looking for or perhaps have a life-long dream to follow a specific route—to paddle the Mackenzie to the Arctic Ocean or to bicycle the Dempster Highway from Inuvik to Dawson City. For others, the choice may involve poring over maps, gathering information, and zeroing in on an enticing part of the Trail. Much of the Trail follows traditional travel corridors

used by the Dene or Inuvialuit for thousands of years and later used by European explorers, traders, and missionaries. On many portions of the Trail, travellers can be virtually guaranteed weeks of solitude. The Mackenzie River courses through an amazing variety of northern communities and cultures. Some portions offer opportunities to see particular

Navigating the big waters of Great Slave Lake

kinds of wildlife, such as peregrine falcons, grizzly bears, and beluga whales. Rockhounds can choose from a wide array of geological treats along the Trail, from giant ammonite fossils to volcanic pillows dating back to the planet's earliest days. Want to catch an arctic grayling? Stroll on the tundra? Swim in the Beaufort Sea? Visit a Gwich'in culture camp? Follow in the wake of the voyageurs? Paddle across the Arctic Circle? Bike through a herd of wild bison? May your dreams come true on the Northwest Territories Trans Canada Trail!

Your paddling, biking, and wilderness experience will be an important consideration in choosing which parts of the Trail you should cover. For instance, although none of the water route requires whitewater skills, there are several stretches where high winds or rapids have proven fatal for novice paddlers. Also, there are portions of the overland route that will challenge the most seasoned of backcountry bikers.

Then there is the matter of time and money. This guide is geared as much for day-trippers as travellers seeking a summer's worth of adventure. Some people prefer to barrel down rivers and roads from one community to the next, putting 10 to 12 travel hours in each day. Others build in extra time for hiking, fishing, loafing, rockhounding, bird-watching, or flower-sniffing. The major expense of wilderness trips in the Northwest Territories is transportation. Since you're not about to paddle back upstream to your launch point, or bike the same route in two directions, you are likely looking at air travel. Most trips will end in a community with scheduled air service, making costly charter flights unnecessary. Paddlers must deal with the costs of shipping their canoes or kayaks back home by barge and/or truck.

An alternative to organizing everything on your own is to sign up for a guided trip with an experienced northern operator. Many of the businesses listed in Appendix F, Outfitters, Tours, and Equipment Rentals, offer tour packages that cover portions of the Trans Canada Trail and rent watercraft, bikes, and associated outdoor gear.

CAMPING AND ACCOMMODATION

Comfortable hotels, lodges, and bed and breakfasts are available in all of the communities along the Northwest Territories Trans Canada Trail. All route sections in this guide include a brief description and contact information for accommodation options in every community. For more details or information on other options, visit ww.nwt.worldweb.com/WheretoStay/HotelsMotels. If you like a roof over

Jaya hunts for berries by a snug cabin, Slave River

your head at night, non-motorized travel from community to community in a day or less is possible for small portions of the Trail, for instance biking from Behchokò to Yellowknife or paddling from Jean Marie River to Fort Simpson. But you should expect to camp for most of the route since, under your own steam, communities can be anywhere from 2 to 12 days apart, depending on distance, weather, and skill levels.

Well-serviced areas for camping are found in most communities as well as along major road systems. The Government of the Northwest Territories (GNWT) has an excellent Web site on all parks and campgrounds (http://www.iti.gov.nt .ca/tourismparks). Here you will find lots of useful information on both government-run and private campgrounds, such as contact numbers, campsite booking procedures, visitor information centres, fishing and hunting regulations, and local attractions. You will also find some very practical links on making travel plans, selecting equipment and clothing, bear safety, bug protection, and my favourite—no-trace camping.

Parks near larger communities or major roads offer electricity, showers, kitchen shelters, RV sites, and serviced tent sites. More remote sites offer a bare minimum of tent sites, picnic tables, firewood, and outhouses. Territorial parks are open from May 15 to September 15. Services such as toilets, firewood, and garbage removal are not provided outside the open season. Camping fees are usually $10 for tent sites, $15 for non-serviced RV sites, and $20 for sites with electricity.

Pre-booking for small groups is usually not necessary except for major centres such as Hay River, Yellowknife, Norman Wells, and Inuvik. If you plan to arrive during a long weekend or have a larger group, visit www.campingnwt.ca to make a reservation. If you are paddling, keep in mind that strong winds or bad weather may throw a wrench into your carefully made plans. In this case, set up your tent, roll out your sleeping mat, and take a nap. Most serious wilderness accidents occur when people do not adopt the pace of nature and rush toward disaster.

For most of this portion of the Trans Canada Trail, however, there are no lodges, hotels, parks, or campgrounds. You'll be on your own in the bush. This guide recommends specific campsite locations that take into account such factors as easy access, suitable tent sites, adequate shelter, bug protection, features of special interest, and great views. Where specific sites are identified, they are anchored to some clear landmark, such as a distinct beach, point, or bay, and should be easily recognized in the field with or without a GPS.

Specific campsite locations are not identified for some portions of the route where long stretches of river or lakeshore are relatively homogeneous. Instead, each route description includes general guidelines on what to look for when choosing a place to camp in a forest or on a riverbank or shoreline. You may think you are "in the middle of nowhere," but you will often find evidence of others having used the same site, such as a fire ring or crude bench. To the people who have traditionally used this landscape for generations, there is no "nowhere"; everywhere is home. You too may soon feel this way after spending many days in the northern wilds, befriending the landscape and honing your ability to recognize good campsites. Fortunately, firewood is plentiful throughout the route, even in tundra portions of the Mackenzie Delta and Beaufort Sea coast, which are blessed with abundant driftwood. Fresh water is available throughout although filtration is recommended where silt is an issue—in other words, for most of the water route (see the "Water" section in "Respecting the Land," page 30).

Whether using an existing campsite or creating a new one, always leave the site as you found it—with one exception. If you found a mess, make it better (see "No-Trace Camping" in "Respecting the Land," page 32).

As your travel day winds down, always allow yourself enough time to find or build a suitable campsite. Travellers who fail to do so often resort to setting up camp late at night on poor or unsafe locations, leading to needless damage to the land or harm to themselves.

RECOMMENDED EQUIPMENT AND SUPPLIES

Food

For paddlers, there are, believe it or not, no portages anywhere on the main routes in this guide, so you may want to sneak in a few extra luxuries or carry more produce than you would dare on a portage-laced whitewater trip. On the other hand, you don't want to load down your boat so much that there is the risk of swamping in big waves. Long days of paddling call for quick-energy foods such as granola bars, gorp, and dried fruit. A fishing rod is a definite bonus for supplementing or diversifying your protein intake. Leave space for a few of your favourite sweet and savoury spices, which can breathe life into the most utilitarian meals.

Midnight sun over the Mackenzie River

You can count on resupplying basic food items in any of the communities along the route, although be prepared to pay premium prices in more remote centres. Weight and space will be much more of an issue for bikers, so before hitting the trail, try dehydrated recipes at home to find ones that are both power-packed and tasty.

Water

With steady exertion, drink at least two litres of water a day, one in the morning and one in the afternoon. Because of high levels of silt in the Slave and Mackenzie rivers and parts of Great Slave Lake's south shore, water filtration equipment, preferably matched to your container, is essential for most of the water routes. Many clear-water creeks and rivers feed into these systems, but you can't plan to be at one every time you camp. Some people are content with letting silty water settle for a few hours or overnight. You should also consider bringing purification tablets or drops, especially for use in waters where there is evidence of beavers — well-known carriers of giardia, or "beaver fever."

Cooking System

It's a burning question: how to cook your food? Although a firewood-based system is possible for the entire route, a reliable backup stove is recommended for those wet, cool days when a hot meal is needed most. Some travellers use a simple campfire ring and grill. Collapsible fireboxes offer a more stable and efficient option while creating virtually no impact and reducing the potential spread of fires. Fire pans, often fashioned from a metal garbage can lid, are lighter and allow for a more traditional fire. Fireboxes or fire pans also make garbage burning easier. After removing non-burnables such as tin foil, cans, or glass, you can dump your ash into the water, erasing all fire signs and food smells. Some stoves are notorious for having two settings: off and high. Boiling water is easy, but simmering rice or beans for ten minutes can become a battle between keeping the stove lit and avoiding scorched food. As for fuel, white gas is recommended since it burns hot and clean, can be used as its own priming agent, and is available in just about all communities along the route.

Shelter

Tents come in many shapes, sizes, styles, and weights. Bring one that can stand up to lots of rain and strong, prolonged winds. A big tarp dedicated for use as a rain shelter over your cooking area is essential equipment. You may want to bring some extra rope (we used throw bags) to anchor the corners of your rain tarp. Prop each corner with a paddle or driftwood, add a tall central pole, and you'll be well protected.

> **Different Strokes**
>
> Juneva Green, *Summer on the Water*
>
> *Besides good food, lots of sleep, a waterproof tent, a Therma-rest, and a warm sleeping bag, a sense of humour is essential on a long paddling trip. The bow paddler, in particular, must be able to smile no matter what. It's useful when the guy in the stern asks, "How are you feeling?" Well, you think, my elbows ache, my shoulders are killing me, I want a tall cool glass of Old South orange juice, and I don't feel like paddling any more. You smile and say, "Just fine, thanks." Or when the stern paddler interrupts your thoughts to pass along this earth-shattering information: "We're doing about 34 strokes a minute, which makes 2,040 per hour or 16,320 in eight hours. Grand total for 16 days of paddling: 261,120 strokes." You smile and say, "That's nice." Why does he have so much time on his hands, anyway? Smile. YES "Sorry, what was that you said?"*

Clothing

You probably have your own laundry list of preferred wilderness wear. In selecting articles for this trip, keep in mind that the weather in Canada's North can change quickly from one extreme to another—from hot to cold (even snow), calm to windy, or dry to sopping wet. So be ready for just about anything. Cotton is great when days are hot, but a liability in cool, wet weather. Synthetics, like polyester or polypropylene, and wool provide the best qualities for warmth and protection. These fabrics wick moisture away from the skin, provide good insulation, dry quickly, and can be worn while wet. This applies from head to toe—

from toques to socks and everything in between. The fashion statement for all trips and weather conditions is *layers*. Bring clothes that are easily peeled off or thrown on so you can optimize your heat and sweat output in response to changing weather conditions or activity levels.

The quality of your rain gear can make or break your trip. Gore-Tex® or durable nylon that is both breathable and waterproof is the way to go (anything labelled "water-resistant" is useless in a serious downpour). The more you are prepared for rain, the more you can enjoy it in comfort. Also bring a complete wind layer (jacket and pants) for those days when you may be dry but wind-bound. Always be prepared for the worst possible weather and you'll be ready for anything.

Bedding

A good sleeping bag and mat can be a source of great comfort and joy at the end of a long, active day. Even midsummer nights in this region can be cool, so a three-season bag is recommended. On the other hand, you'll want a bag that zips open for the odd heat wave. Bags that zip together are a bonus for the romantically inclined. Ensure that you have a watertight storage system for your sleeping bag. Don't scrimp on a sleeping mat, as you can expect to sleep occasionally on cool or uneven ground. A small waterproof groundsheet can protect your tent floor and bedding from condensation.

First Aid Supplies

Weather extremes, cold water, strong currents, bears, unstable terrain, fires, and above all, remoteness, dictate that you bring a top-notch first aid kit. The exact contents should be tailored to match your own needs and length of your trip. If you are starting from scratch, just search online for "first aid kit" to get some ideas. Here are a few guidelines to help put together the right kit for you.

Make sure all basic categories are covered. Many pre-fab first aid kits include little more than a box of adhesive bandages and a bunch of tablets. Your kit should contain supplies from all of the following groups: antiseptics (something to kill germs to prevent infection), injury treatment (items to deal with injuries, such as butterfly closures and cold compresses), bandages (a variety to dress and cover different kinds of wounds), instruments (tweezers, barrier gloves), and medicines (analgesics at a minimum).

Kit organization. With a serious injury, a rapid response is absolutely critical. A well-organized, clearly labelled kit will help you quickly find just the right supplies you need with the minimum of time, stress, and/or blood loss.

Quality components. When dealing with an emergency, the last thing you need is adhesive bandages that don't stick, poorly shaped bandages, or a case that falls apart. Go for top quality supplies stored in a durable, waterproof case.

Instructions. A first aid kit isn't much good if you don't know how to use it. Most kits include some kind of guide, but their usefulness varies. Make sure the guide is from a credible source, contains the latest medical advice, and is laid out in a way that instructions can be quickly assimilated when

> **Be Prepared**
> Canadian Red Cross Society, Wilderness and Remote First Aid
>
> *The wilderness environment is always unpredictable and at many times will catch you off guard. Gaining as many skills and as much knowledge as possible to deal with emergencies before heading out on a trip is important. It can save lives. When venturing into the wilderness … the equipment carried and your personal preparation will affect your ability to survive.*

under stress. You may want to supplement this information with a compact wilderness first aid guide.

Navigation Tools

I know some people who have paddled all 1,600 kilometres of the Mackenzie River with no other navigation tool than a 1:5,000,000 tourist road map. I met boaters navigating almost half this distance with no map at all. While this may be all right for the cyclist doing overland portions of the Trans Canada Trail, if you are planning to cover remote sections of the water route—which means most of it—you should have at least 1:250,000 topographic coverage from start to finish. This will not only enhance your appreciation of the surrounding terrain and shoreline, but will also help you find campsites, avoid hazards, and seek emergency help if necessary. If you prefer to carry standard topographic maps, you may purchase them directly from the Canada Map Office in Ottawa (http://maps.nrcan.gc.ca/ distribution_e.php) or from a regional distribution centre (http://maps.nrcan.gc.ca/distrib_ centres_e.php). Though much of the route is on water, official marine charts are not necessary and provide little information about the land.

Be sure to take a compass along to help with orientation and bearings. If you are considering purchasing a GPS unit for this trip, a map-based system is strongly recommended. We travelled with a combination of paper maps, compass, and map-based GPS, and found all tools useful in various situations.

Other Recommended Gear
- Compact binoculars
- Fishing gear and licence (see www.enr.gov.nt.ca)
- Machete (handy for making tent sites in thick shrubbery when necessary)

- Guitar or other musical instrument
- Compilation of your favourite campfire songs
- Playing cards, compact games
- Natural history field guides
- Writing and sketching materials
- Needle and thread
- Bear deterrents (bangers, pepper spray)
- Satellite phone
- Headlamp
- Throw bag (one per boat)
- Repair kit
- And, of course, duct tape

GETTING THERE

If you're a paddler, boater, or biker and want to use all of your own gear for your trip, the most practical way to get there is to drive. Compared to trucking or air travel, this is the most economical but also the most time-consuming mode of transportation. Northwest Territories communities along the Trans Canada Trail with road access include Fort Smith, Fort Resolution, Hay River, Fort Providence, Jean Marie River, Fort Simpson, Wrigley, Tsiigehtchic, Inuvik, Behchokò, and Yellowknife. The Liard and Dempster highways have long stretches of gravel road, few services, and basic camping facilities in widely scattered campgrounds. Make sure your vehicle is in good condition before you leave and carry at least one full-size spare tire and some basic tools. Get in the habit of slowing down when another vehicle approaches you to reduce any risks caused by dust clouds and flying rocks. The highways joining communities south and north of Great Slave Lake are generally in much better condition, but regular reconstruction and poor weather call for reduced speed and extra caution.

If you are planning to ship canoes, kayaks, or bikes north, send them well ahead of time. Shipping them back home from communities with no road access, such as Tuktoyaktuk and Norman Wells, will require making arrangements with a barging company such as the Northern Transportation Company Limited (NTCL) based in Hay River (www.ntcl.com).

Major airports with regularly scheduled service are found in Fort Smith, Hay River, Norman Wells, Inuvik, and Yellowknife. Most smaller communities offer both scheduled and charter air services. If you need to charter, be sure to organize your flight as early as possible. Such arrangements are possible after you arrive, but during the busy summer season you may find yourself waiting a day or two for a plane.

2 THE LAND AND ITS PEOPLE

WEATHER

Northern summers generally bring clear, sunny weather with not much rain. Temperatures typically range between 10 and 20°C although anything from below zero to above 30°C is possible. August is definitely the testier of the summer months with stronger winds, cooler temperatures, and more rain. Expect to wake up to a snowstorm any month of the year. Knee-knocking winds are not uncommon so build in ample time to be windbound. The good news is that the wind usually dies down by evening, and the Northwest Territories' long summer twilight makes for delightful paddling, boating, or biking.

> **The Finest Climate in the World**
> Ernest Thompson Seton, *The Arctic Prairies, 1911*
>
> *This country has, for six months, the finest climate in the world ... I never knew a land of balmier air; I never felt the piney breeze more sweet; nowhere but in the higher mountains is there such a tonic sense abroad; the bright woods and river reaches were eloquent of a clime whose maladies are mostly foreign-born.*

ECOLOGY

The Northwest Territories represents a huge part of Canada, covering approximately 1.2 million square kilometres. This makes it Canada's third largest jurisdiction, after Nunavut and Quebec. To grasp the tapestry of habitats in this immense land, it helps to view it as a composite of ecozones — distinct natural regions characterized by relatively uniform landforms, geology, vegetation, and wildlife. The Trans Canada Trail winds through four of the six ecozones found in the Northwest Territories. From south to north, these are the Boreal Plains, Taiga Shield, Taiga Plains, and Southern Arctic.

Boreal Plains

In the Northwest Territories, the Boreal Plains ecozone encompasses the Slave River Corridor. It lies between the Buffalo River and the Taltson River, much of it within Wood Buffalo National Park. Bigger than Switzerland, this park is home to the world's largest herd of wood bison, a threatened species, and the only known nesting site of the endangered whooping crane. Waterfowl from all four North American flyways funnel into this ecozone's abundant wetlands and use the productive deltas of the Athabasca and Slave rivers as key staging areas along the way. In addition to bison, this area supports over 40 other species of mammals, including an abundance of moose and black bear plus the relatively rare fisher.

The Slave River has been an important travel corridor and hunting area for the Dene for thousands of years. It later became a vital fur-trading route when posts were established along the Mackenzie River and Arctic coast. Besides ongoing

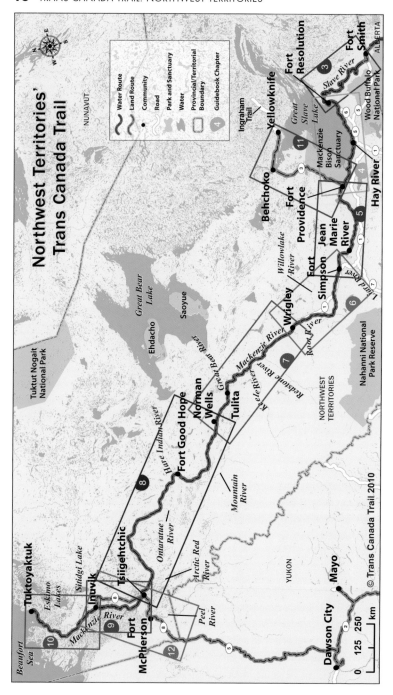

Northwest Territories' Trans Canada Trail

Legend

~ Water Route
~ Land Route
• Community
— Road
Park and Sanctuary
Water
Provincial/Territorial Boundary
Guidebook Chapter

NUNAVUT

Fort Resolution

Fort Smith

ALBERTA

Slave River

Yellowknife

Wood Buffalo National Park

Ingraham Trail

Great Slave Lake

Mackenzie Bison Sanctuary

Behchoko

Fort Providence

Hay River

Jean Marie River

Great Bear Lake

Willowlake River

Fort Simpson

Liard River

Saoyue

Ehdacho

Wrigley

Redknife River

Mackenzie River

Great Bear River

Red River

Redstone River

Keele River

NORTHWEST TERRITORIES

Nahanni National Park Reserve

Norman Wells

Fort Good Hope

Tulita

Hare Indian River

Mountain River

Tuktut Nogait National Park

Tsiigehtchic

Ontaratue River

Arctic Red River

Beaufort Sea

Tuktoyaktuk

Eskimo Lakes

Sitidgi Lake

Inuvik

Mackenzie River

Peel River

Fort McPherson

YUKON

Mayo

Dawson City

© Trans Canada Trail 2010

km
0 125 250

hunting and trapping, the area has become a centre for small businesses, including tourism, sport hunting, and lumber production.

Taiga Shield

Dominating the eastern part of the Northwest Territories, this ecozone occurs where the northern boreal forest, or taiga, and the Canadian Shield overlap. As an ecological crossroads between two very different biomes—the boreal forest and the tundra—this ecozone offers a relatively wide variety of habitats for wildlife. Here, boreal lakes, wetlands, and spruce forests are interwoven with open shrublands and sedge meadows more typical of the tundra. At the southern limit of their summer range are such arctic species as the common redpoll and Arctic tern. A host of water birds and forest species reach their northern limit here, including the common tern and white-throated sparrow.

Mammals in this ecozone include the barren-ground caribou, which winter here. Hundreds of thousands of caribou from the Bathurst, Beverly, and Kaminuriak herds make this journey each fall and return to the tundra to calve each spring.

The first settlements grew up around trading posts and later, around mineral deposits. The area is rich in hardrock prospects and has been described as Canada's "mineral breadbasket of the twenty-first century."

Taiga Plains

The Taiga Plains ecozone is a region of low-lying valleys and plains dominated by Canada's largest river, the mighty Mackenzie, and its many tributaries. It is bounded to the east by two huge lakes—Great Bear and Great Slave—to the west by the rolling foothills of the Mackenzie Mountains, to the north by the Mackenzie Delta, and to the south by the denser spruce forests of the boreal plains.

On the nutrient-rich alluvial flats bordering rivers, white spruce and balsam poplar may grow to an impressive height and girth, rivaling the largest of trees found anywhere in Canada. Riparian willow and alder habitats support abundant moose. Barren-ground caribou from the Porcupine Herd overwinter in the northwest corner of this ecozone, while scattered groups of wood-

Remnant ice lines the mighty Mackenzie River well into June

land caribou are found throughout the area during all seasons. In summer, fish-eating raptors such as bald eagle, peregrine falcon and osprey are familiar sights as they soar above the shorelines. Hundreds of thousands of ducks, geese, and swans use the region's many lakes, rivers, and wetlands as staging or nesting areas. The Mackenzie River valley forms one of North America's most well-travelled migratory corridors for waterfowl breeding along the Arctic coast.

The Dene have hunted and trapped throughout this region for centuries. Most communities along the river grew up around fur trading posts established in the 1800s. From Fort Liard in the south to Inuvik in the north, much of the ecozone has significant potential for oil and gas development.

> ### Spring Wildlife on the Slave
> Olive Fredrickson, pioneer trapper, 1923
>
> *Muskrat sign was plentiful along the river, and there was lots of old beaver work, lodges, and the evidence of dams, but nothing recent. The beaver had been trapped out of that country then, but have since made a comeback and are abundant again now. We saw deer and moose tracks on the sandbars, and flocks of ptarmigan fed in the willows on the river bottoms. Wherever there was green grass along the shore, snow geese pastured by the hundreds. We were rarely out of hearing of their wild voices, either by day or during the half-light of the short arctic night.*

Southern Arctic

For thousands of square kilometres, the pattern of habitats in the Southern Arctic barrenlands is the same: sprawling shrublands, wet sedge meadows, and cold, clear lakes. Superimposed on this pattern are impressive glacial landforms, such as giant esker trains and kettle lakes, patterned ground formations created by intense frost action in the soil, and occasional outcrops of bald Canadian Shield.

This ecozone is bounded to the south by the treeline, a broad ecological frontier between the taiga forest and the treeless arctic tundra. Over a belt that may be 100 kilometres wide, small scattered clumps of stunted spruce trees grow on warmer, sheltered sites.

Grizzly bears, arctic ground squirrels, and muskoxen are among the distinctive wildlife species inhabiting this ecozone. Moose are also present, particularly within water courses that support "fingers" of trees or thick shrubs that extend out into the tundra. Polar bears roam the coastal areas during the summer and follow the growing pack ice north as winter sets in.

Like barren-ground caribou, willow ptarmigan migrate only as far as the taiga forest to find food and shelter during the winter months. In summer, the broad silhouette of the rough-legged hawk is a familiar sight as it scans the mossy hummocks and shrublands for abundant voles and lemmings.

The Southern Arctic is rich in mineral resources, including gold, base metals, and diamonds. This ecozone's many wild rivers, abundant large mammals, and world-class fishing attract a growing number of ecotourists, hunters, and anglers from all over the world.

PLANT LIFE

Cool temperatures, a short growing season, frequent forest fires, and thin acidic soils underlain by permafrost are among the many challenges faced by plant life in the northern boreal forest, or *taiga*, a Russian word meaning moist, spruce forest. Its open, stunted forests are

Fireweed thrives in the wake of a monster forest fire

dominated by a few highly adaptable tree species, such as black spruce and jack pine. These forests are mixed with innumerable bogs and other wetlands, and scattered stands of paper birch and trembling aspen. Close inspection of the seemingly bare rock outcrops that dominate this landscape reveals a colourful array of lichens, wildflowers, and ground-hugging shrubs.

Forest fires add to the distinctive "mosaic" appearance of the forest by leaving in their wake a patchwork quilt of plant communities that vary widely in species composition and age. Although fire often destroys large areas of forest and occasionally threatens human activities or property, it also has a renewing effect on the landscape by triggering fresh plant growth, purging old-growth forests of insect pests and disease, and increasing the variety of habitats available to wildlife.

Permafrost is another major influence on the plant life of this region, especially in low areas where the soggy ground or "active layer" above the permafrost regularly freezes and thaws. Growing in these ever-shifting soils, trees are often tipped in random directions, creating the impression of a "drunken forest."

North of the tree line, summers are too short and soils too cold for normal tree growth. The tundra is dominated by knee-high shrubs such as dwarf birch, willows, and Labrador tea, and by sedges, heath, lichens, and moss.

Though life is challenging for plants in northern Canada, they are a hardy lot, each of which has its own unique character and charm. Whether exploring a rocky shoreline, padding through a spruce-feathermoss forest, bouncing over a bog, or taking your first stroll on the tundra, take time to befriend the plant species of this region and you will discover a wonderful variety of colours, shapes, and textures. Berry-pickers will be especially rewarded since few places on earth offer such a variety and abundance of berry-producing plants.

WILDLIFE

The ecological challenges faced by plant communities are, in turn, reflected in wildlife communities with low productivity and species diversity. Northern food chains are relatively short and fluctuations in numbers of one species can profoundly affect another. Dramatic population cycles,

Moose cow and calf, Slave River

such as those of the snowshoe hare and lynx, are common. Slow growth rates are characteristic of other species, such as marine mammals and freshwater fish. Still, the opportunity for the wildlife experience of a lifetime awaits you in this vast and untamed land.

The explosive return of ducks, loons, geese, and swans during spring migration is nothing short of spectacular. This well-watered landscape attracts hundreds of thousands of birds that nest or stage here, concentrating especially along the Slave and Mackenzie river valleys. The overlap of arctic and subarctic bird species gives the Northwest Territories a special richness in bird diversity.

Bison or Buffalo?

Mike Keizer, Communications Director, Wood Buffalo National Park

What's the difference between a buffalo and a bison? My usual answer is: spelling. What does a father buffalo say to his boy when he's leaving? Bison! We had both wood and plains bison here when the park was established. Many years ago, plains bison were shipped in here by the thousands from a bison ranch in Wainwright, Alberta. They knew there were diseases, they couldn't do eradication, and they let them go. We now have interbreeding, hybridization, and of course, the diseases—brucellosis and tuberculosis. The Mackenzie bison came from here many years ago before there was much hybridization so they are relatively pure wood bison.

Physically, wood bison tend to be darker brown. Stained by coffee, not tea. They tend to be more flat-backed than the more bulldog-shaped plains bison with their sloped backs. Wood bison tend to be taller and oval-shaped while the plains are stockier and more barrel-shaped. One theory is that if you spend your time moving around in the tangled boreal forest, moving around as a large barrel would be difficult, as a thinner oval is easier. Out on the bald prairie, who cares how big around you are?

The hump of a mature wood bison bull could stand at six feet with a weight of over a ton. It's a pretty spectacular animal up close.

You will see barren-ground caribou, which migrate south from the tundra to their winter range in the taiga forest. They make this journey each fall and return to the tundra to calve in springtime. During the winter months, it is not unusual to see small groups of caribou within the city limits of Yellowknife — sometimes even within sight of the mayor's desk! Larger herds of several hundred have been viewed without venturing far from town.

Lake trout, lake whitefish, arctic grayling, burbot, walleye, and northern pike are the most common fish species that thrive in the region's many lakes and rivers.

Expect to hear the haunting howl of wolves, watch a mother black bear and her cubs grazing the riverbank, cycle through a wild herd of wood bison, or paddle with a pod of belugas. Red fox and snowshoe hare, beaver and muskrat, mink and river otter, marten and moose, maybe even an elusive lynx or wolverine—these are the sorts of wild travelling companions to watch for along the Trail.

> **Pike Passions**
>
> Jamie Bastedo, *Reaching North*[7]
>
> *Without doubt, the pike is a mean, lean hunting machine. The Koyukon natives of northwestern Alaska call the pike k'oolkkoya, "that which darts or is thrown at something." The French come more to the point and call it a grand brochet, "the big skewer." Together these names celebrate the pike's torpedo-shaped body and its ability to fling itself, fast and forcefully, onto its prey. In stark contrast, imagine the bashful butterfly fish of the tropics with its round, well-finned body specialized for making tight graceful maneuvers in and out of the coral beds. Now imagine the portly tuna with its muscular trunk and high dorsal fins designed for prolonged cruising. The pike is a different kind of specialist, a lunge feeder, built instead for short powerful bursts of acceleration. It owes this mastery to a cylindrical body, large, back-set dorsal and anal fins plus a broad and nimble tail fin. But lunge feeders like the pike, and its saltwater cousin the barracuda, are not known for accuracy. Hence that massive mouth amply loaded with recurved teeth. These renowned assets increase a pike's chances of clamping down on prey even if its aim is a bit off.*

HISTORY

The oldest-known evidence of humans in the Northwest Territories, dating back 7,000 years, was discovered in the early 1960s at Acasta River, situated about 130 kilometres southeast of Great Bear Lake. This is the same Acasta River where, 30 years later, the world's oldest-known rocks were discovered.

Charred bone fragments from hearths indicated that these Paleoindians were not taking aim at mammoths, ground sloths, and other Pleistocene megafauna— they had been extinct for 2,000 years—but at barren-ground caribou, black bear, beaver, hare, and eagles—a mix of animals from both sides of the treeline.

The first humans arrived in this region at the tail end of the Hypsithermal period—"the great warmth" at the end of the last ice age, a period when the treeline was well established far north of its present-day position.

The Sub-Boreal period, which began 3,500 years ago, was a period of pronounced cooling that forced the treeline into retreat—in some areas, hundreds of kilometres south of today's forest edge. It was during this cold period that the Paleoindians drifted south and east, providing the cultural rootstock of today's Cree and Ojibway First Nations. Meanwhile, a different people took over some of their former territory. These were the Paleoeskimos, who probably moved down from the Coronation Gulf area and Victoria Island. Their ancestors, the earliest Inuit, probably kayaked to North America about 4,000 years ago, long after the Bering Sea swallowed the land bridge from Asia.

The cooler climate may have forced the Paleoeskimos south, with increased sea ice disrupting the migratory patterns of the seals and whales they depended on. For the next 1,000 years they ranged widely across the Canadian subarctic.

> **"Hey Nah-Nah Hearne Hoh"**
> Jamie Bastedo
> Sung to the tune, "The Night They Drove Old Dixie Down"
>
> *Samuel Hearne is my name and I worked for the Hudson's Bay,*
> *Exploring land was my game, and cracking rumors of the day:*
> *A fabulous copper mine, up on the coast, beyond the last pine,*
> *And a Northwest Passage to find so our ships*
> *Could bring treasures from Cathay.*
>
> chorus
> *Those great rivers that we journeyed down,*
> *And all our paddles were swinging!*
> *Our guides, they never let us down*
> *With all the Chipewyan singing,*
> *They went:*
> *Hey ... nah-nah-nah, hoh-nah*
> *Hey nah, hoh-nah*
> *Hey nah-nah, hoh-nah ...*

The archaeological record shows that around 2,600 years ago the Paleoeskimos headed back to the coast, at about the time when a completely new cultural signature begins. Short, wide-stemmed spearheads and narrow whetstones made from red slate are among the tools that herald the arrival of the Athapaskans, blood relatives of today's Dene and Navajo people.

More than any other season, winter must have placed its stamp on the first peoples of this region. Had they not had the means and materials to make well-insulated clothing and wind-proof shelters, and to consume a high daily intake of food calories, winter would have meant certain death.

With the onset of the fur trade era in the late 1700s, all wild animals in northern

Canada were now fair game for an economic market thousands of kilometres away. For the original peoples of this land, an ancient way of life based on nomadism and subsistence was to be profoundly transformed by a grand commercial venture that served the fashion whims of European high society.

The Hudson's Bay Company dispatched several waves of trader-explorers through the northern sea lanes and along the Arctic coast. Among them was Samuel Hearne who, in 1771, walked from Hudson Bay all the way to the mouth of the Coppermine River in search of a mythical mine. In 1789, Alexander Mackenzie, an explorer with the competing North West Company, journeyed to the mouth of the Mackenzie River in a failed attempt to find a river link to the Pacific. British Navy captain Sir John Franklin, prompted by his era's hankering to push back trading frontiers, made several expeditions to this region in the first half of the nineteenth century. In the face of

Jaya explores ancient ship's boiler, Slave River Delta

tragedy and privation—much of which sprang from his refusal to embrace Native adaptations to the land—he gathered valuable scientific and geographical data until his mysterious disappearance in 1847 while searching for a northwest passage through the Arctic Ocean.

One of the forces pushing the fur trade north was the need to give over-trapped areas a rest and move into virgin territory where prized furbearers such as beaver were still plentiful. At the close of the nineteenth century, furs were still in great demand. New posts continued to spring up, and trading and trapping intensified. The fur trade had introduced deep frays into the region's age-old cultural fabric. It also had changed the face of the land by causing local depletions in furbearers, big game, and fisheries along with a rise in accidental forest fires.

Increased hunting contributed to a distressing decline in barren-ground caribou. By the 1920s, great numbers were being slaughtered for food or sport by hunters armed with high-powered rifles. Some people concluded that caribou were, like the plains bison, in imminent danger of becoming extinct.

Post-World War I improvements in transportation released a north-bound flood of non-Native trappers and traders to the region. New steamers were chugging regularly from Fort Smith to the Mackenzie Delta. The first aircraft crossed the 60th parallel in March 1921—a pair of World War I Junker airplanes. They belonged to the Imperial Oil Company and were headed for a promising oil discovery near Fort Norman (now Tulít'a) on the Mackenzie. By 1925, the railroad had been pushed well into northern Alberta, much to the relief of those who previously had bumped north from Edmonton by stagecoach.

This was boom time north of the 60th parallel, fuelled mostly by the soaring price of furs. In 1920 there were 110 trading stores in the Northwest Territories. By 1927 that number had almost doubled. But the crash came in 1928.

Fur returns for mink and muskrat hit rock bottom. A three-year complete closure on beaver was declared. Many trappers and traders from the south headed home, leaving behind Native people with little means of securing a livelihood. Some had trapped all their lives and now were unable to fully live off the land as their ancestors had. To make matters worse, rabbits, an important item in the Native diet, were at the low end of their cycle, and caribou were scarcer than ever.

The culmination came the same year when the Dene and Inuvialuit were hit hard by an influenza epidemic imported from Europe. By the time the epidemic had run its course, thousands of Native people were dead. The flu epidemic and the much-weakened fur economy hastened the movement of Native people off the land and into permanent settlements.

> **Step Lightly**
>
> Bruce Cockburn, *Canoeing Canada's Northwest Territories*
>
> *When you travel in the North you carry your fate in your hands, and you carry as well the fate of the landscape itself. Here— where a footprint can last a hundred years— you need to step very lightly indeed.*

The Great Depression of the early 1930s cast its shadow northward in the form of deep plunges in the price of furs. By 1933, fur trading was quickly moving into the shadows while mining crept to centre stage. Even as the Depression kept its stranglehold on much of the nation, Eldorado Mines, on the shore of Great Bear Lake, was making regular shipments of uranium and silver concentrate to markets in southern Canada and the United States.

Two years later, geologist Fred Jolliffe discovered the gold that put Yellowknife on the map, triggering a flood of gold-seekers northward. As prospectors fanned across the land in growing numbers, so did human-caused forest fires, some of them lit intentionally to expose the rock below. Many contemporary forests, particularly around Great Slave Lake, took root in the wake of fires from this era.

Widespread fires carried on into the 1940s with no end in sight. True to the pattern of spasmodic northern development, there suddenly arrived a new actor on the scene with matches in hand: the United States military. Troops building the Alaska Highway wreaked havoc upon the forests through careless fire practices. One of the largest fires ever recorded in North America spread from unburnt slash piled recklessly along the Alaska Highway in southern Yukon. By the autumn of 1942, this fire had consumed an area of forest the size of Ireland (80,000 square kilometres), burning as far east as the Mackenzie River, which it reportedly jumped near Fort Simpson.

Toward the end of the 1940s, it appeared that barren-ground caribou were once again on the decline. Like population trends before and since, the exact cause may never be known. There was even talk of possible extinction, as there had been 100 years earlier. New techniques of population monitoring later dispelled these fears by revealing caribou numbers that far exceeded those of previous surveys.

The 1991 discovery of diamonds in the Northwest Territories drew public attention to the potential sensitivity of barren-ground grizzlies, caribou, and other wildlife to fast-spreading mineral development and possible road expansions. By the close of the century, a development boom in the Mackenzie oil and gas fields raised similar questions, which are still being explored today.

For more information on Northwest Territories history, visit the Prince of Wales Northern Heritage Centre's Web site (http://pwnhc.learnnet.nt.ca).

> **Ultimate Respect**
>
> Rosalie Causa, Fort Providence
>
> *Whoever wants white hair must be a strong believer in the Creator.*

RESPECTING THE LAND

The varied landscapes of the Northwest Territories can be at once inviting and imposing, fragile yet rugged, and by turns serene and exciting. However this region strikes you, there are a few things you must keep in mind in order to protect its unique natural character—and to protect yourself. Specific precautions associated with featured sites along the route are detailed throughout the text and flagged with the code ☠ for "hazard." The general guidelines listed below should be adhered to *everywhere*.

There are two vital principles of backcountry etiquette: attention and respect. Always pay attention to what is going on around you: on the water, on the road, in the sky, in the woods, along the shore, around the campfire, among each other. Not only will you have a richer experience, you will travel more safely. And move through this great wild land with an abiding sense of respect for all that you see. As well, it never hurts to maintain a steady attitude of humility and deference to the higher authority that rules the winds and the weather.

Black bear signature in Slave River silt

Bears—Keep Your Distance

The opportunity to see black bears or grizzlies in the wild is one of the many charms of this region, but always remember that they are unpredictable. NEVER underestimate the potential danger of a bear. To avoid "training" bears that humans mean food, NEVER leave food wastes at a campsite or along the trail. Bears that have made this connection—so-called "nuisance bears"—are the most dangerous because they often show little fear. As complaints and fears mount, such bears are often shot by wildlife officials or cabin owners. The more appropriate term is "nuisance humans," the sloppy ones that cause such unfortunate outcomes.

- Do not cook, eat, or leave any food or garbage in or near tents. The odours may attract bears to your door.
- If you spot a bear that has not seen, heard, or smelled you, observe it quietly while moving away. In other words, leave it alone.
- If a bear becomes aware of you and appears curious, shout, clang pots, or fire a bear banger to scare it away.
- Under no circumstances should you approach a bear for a closer look, a better photograph, or—heaven forbid!—to feed it.
- A mother bear with one or more cubs is generally very aggressive if it feels threatened. Give her extra room.
- For further information visit: www.enr.gov.nt.ca and click on the link, "Safety in Grizzly and Black Bear Country."

> **Funny Bear Noises**
> Agnes Villebrun, Fort Smith
> *We used to see bear sometimes. In the fall time, when we used to go and pick berries, we used to find bear holes. Oh yes, and the bear, he used to sleep in there. Already he is sleeping. We know that, because there is a little hole, where you could see. You could see him growling, making funny noises, but we didn't bother him. We were scared ... In springtime, we'd go there to see if that bear is still there — he's gone!*

Bison—Not As Gentle As They Look

Bison are dangerous and unpredictable, and they may charge without warning. Bison can weigh over 900 kilograms (2,000 pounds) and sprint at 50 kilometres per hour, three times faster than you can run.

Bison Own the Road

Bill Bell, *Beyond the Northern Lights, 1952*

We rounded a curve in the trail and found a large bull buffalo confronting us. Billy slammed on the brakes. I took a photograph through the windshield and was ready to press on, assuming that the beast would move off the road to avoid us. But Billy informed me that he had tried that approach on a previous occasion and the buffalo had

Pickup trashed by bison *(Northern News Service)*

charged, hitting the front of the truck, raising it in the air and running its head and shoulders underneath the front suspension. Unbeknownst to Billy—nervously waiting for the beast to stand up and perhaps flip the vehicle on its side—it was dead of a broken neck ...The truck had won the joust.

- Bison are at their most dangerous during the rutting season, which spans from mid-July to September.
- Watch for warning signs of agitation—raised tail, pawing of the ground, head-butting, and general restlessness—and give them as much space as possible.
- Stay in your vehicle or on your bike and do not approach bison by the roadside.
- Keep at least 50 metres away at all times.
- Never come between two bison, particularly a female and her calf.

Bugs—Be Prepared

The northern forest and tundra are well-watered lands offering abundant habitat for mosquitoes and black flies. Although their numbers can vary greatly from one year to the next, you should assume that, from about mid-June to early August, at least some insects will find you while out on the trail.

- Wear clothes that are "light and tight": light since most biting insects are attracted to dark colours such as brown and blue, and tight since black flies especially like to creep down loose collars and up dangling pant legs to find dark cozy places to feed. Pack along special protective clothing such as screened bug hats or jackets just in case the bugs really get thick.
- A good bug repellent is required. DEET, the magic ingredient that insects despise, comes in strengths ranging from 5 to 95 percent. Since this substance can be hard on the skin and eyes (and plastic), experiment with different repellents containing a range of strengths to see which brand works best for you.

Generally, concentrations over 15 percent are overkill.

Fire—Don't Light the Fuse

Runaway campfires are a common cause of forest fires along regularly used hiking trails, canoe routes, and camping areas.

- Douse your fire and surrounding area thoroughly. Stir the ashes. Douse again. If you can't stick your bare hands in the ashes, douse again.
- Keep campfires small. If you have a fondness for larger bonfires, make sure you build it on an open, inflammable surface like a wide beach or bare rock outcrop, with an offshore breeze or, better, no breeze at all.
- Never leave fires unattended.
- Use only deadfall for firewood. Do not cut live trees.
- Always build your fire well away from trees or overhanging branches. Use existing fire pits or rings if available.
- Folding metal fireboxes provide an efficient cooking source and create minimal impacts. Take one if you can.
- If you make a new fire pit or ring, always remove all evidence of fire after use.
- Use stoves when the fire hazard is high.

Water—Beautiful! But Beware of Its Hazards

- Summer water temperatures are very low in big lakes and rivers, which means that a dumping can cause instant numbing. Stay near the shore if possi-

---

Bug Clothes—The Lesser of Two Evils

Ernest Thompson Seton, *The Arctic Prairies, 1911*

Every one, even the seasoned natives, agree that [the mosquitoes] are a terror to man and beast; but, thanks to our fly-proof tents, we sleep immune. During the day I wear my net and gloves, uncomfortably hot, but a blessed relief from the torrent. It is easy to get used to those coverings; it is impossible to get used to the mosquitoes.

Torching the Bugs

Philip Simba, *Fort Providence*

In the old days we lived in tents made of twelve moose-hides with room for three families. We made it smoky at night to keep the mosquitoes out. There were so many mosquitoes that when we moved camp, we had to hold up a burning branch. It was a hard life but a good life.

Fires from Hell

Jamie Bastedo, *Reaching North*

The flow of forest fires reached a crescendo in the late 1920s when much of the region south of Great Slave Lake was set ablaze. In 1929 a fire covering over fifty square kilometres almost engulfed the town of Fort Smith. Fires in Wood Buffalo National Park burned so far and wide that warden D'Arcy Arden seriously considered kicking all trappers, native and white, out of the Park to help prevent more conflagrations. "The whole country is on fire," he wrote adding that, "Fire came like hell!"

ble and avoid travelling through wavy waters that may threaten to swamp your craft.

- If you do get wet accidentally, remember that loss of body heat in wet clothes is 200 times faster than in dry clothes! To avoid hypothermia, get warm inside (hot drinks) and out, and dry as soon as possible. Make this your top priority. It may save your life.

- Most smaller lakes and ponds are swimmable from late June to early August. Always look before you leap. Avoid peaty, tea-coloured waters where submerged hazards are obscured.

- Northern waters are among the cleanest on earth but avoid drinking in the vicinity of mines, urban areas, or sled dog tie-ups.

- Do not drink water where there is abundant sign of beavers since they are potential carriers of a serious intestinal disease called giardia, or "beaver fever."

> ### Deadly Dunking
>
> Anonymous, *Canada's Northwest Territories*
>
> *In September, 1955, Arthur Moffat swamped his canoe in a rapid on the Dubawnt River, 250 miles from Baker Lake. His companions picked up all the packs first, then the swimmers. Although Moffat was conscious when his friends pulled him out of the water, he was in a serious hypothermic condition. He insisted that he was "okay," however, and was placed in a sleeping bag inside his tent. No attempt was made to warm him or give him hot drinks. Sometime later he was found dead.*

- Avoid drinking water near loafing or breeding areas heavily used by waterbirds such as gulls, terns, and ducks.

- It's like a poker game out there and you never know what hand the wind will deal you from moment to moment. If you are paddling, expect sudden changes in wind direction and strength, and be ready to get off the water quickly if necessary.

- On the Slave and Mackenzie rivers, generally the lower the water, the higher the standing waves in areas of pronounced current.

Riverbanks — A Work in Progress

- Much of the water route takes you past riverbanks that could topple down on you or cave in to the water as you walk or camp on top of them. This is especially true of outside curves carved into fine, loose sediments. Avoid these areas both from the water and on land. If you are camped on a high, steep bank, place your cooking area and tent sites well back from the edge. Otherwise, they might not be there when you wake up.

- River water levels can change significantly over the course of just a few hours. This is especially true on the Slave River where upstream rainstorms or large releases from Alberta's W.A.C. Bennett dam can cause a dramatic increase in flow volumes. No matter how attractive a riverside beach may appear, always camp *above* the high water mark, usually indicated by caked mud and/or a distinct line of driftwood.

- ALWAYS tie up your boat, canoe, or kayak at night. If rising waters don't take it away, high winds might.

> **Running with Wood**
> Mike Keizer, Communication Director,
> Wood Buffalo National Park
>
> *In 2001 we had a massive rainstorm in northern Alberta and the river here literally ran with wood. The high water just caved in the banks and everything fell in—mud, trees, whole forests went into the drink. You could almost walk across the river for all the wood that covered it. That was from one storm.*

Remoteness—So Near and Yet So Far

- Remember that a walk or paddle just a kilometre or two off any northern road takes you into a wild country that sees very little human traffic. Assistance in an emergency or accident situation may be a long time coming, especially if you wander far from a path or chosen water route.
- Even if you plan to explore just a small segment of a route for only a few hours, tell someone reliable of your route and expected return time. If you are planning a much longer journey, you should call and register with the RCMP, indicating your start time and place, your route, and where and when you plan to return. If no one knows where to find you, getting lost or injured could have major consequences. Minor mishaps could prove fatal. Do not cause the disruption and expense of unnecessary rescue efforts. Use the RCMP contact information provided in the route descriptions to check in while passing through communities. And don't forget to check out when your trip is over.
- Take some extra food, water, and first aid supplies for any backwoods expedition, no matter how short.

No-Trace Camping—Leave Nothing but Footprints

- There is nothing more disgusting in the wild than to discover a

Myles rolls a low-impact cinnamon roll

hiking trail, lakeshore, riverbank, or campsite littered with cans, plastic bags, and broken bottles. What is carried in must be bagged and carried out or burned.

- Tinfoil, cans, bottles, and "tetrapack" containers do not burn. Always pack them out. Your grandchildren will thank you.
- Human waste should be buried in a small shallow pit (15–20 centimetres deep) at least 35 metres from open water.
- Used toilet paper, feminine hygiene supplies, and disposable diapers should be burned or packed out. If you are opposed to burning or bagging your toilet paper, at least use single-ply and bury it completely. For the pure of heart, three-ply alder leaves applied backside up (the leaf, not you) work great, or try a thick clump of feathermoss. Don't worry, there is no poison ivy north of 60. One of our party preferred to wipe with a smooth piece of driftwood or river-worn stone. Get creative!

Northern Roads—Long, Winding, and Wild
- Roads in the Northwest Territories are generally chip-sealed or all-weather gravel. Because distances are long, make sure you have enough water and food if you are biking and enough gas if driving.
- Expect hazards such as loose gravel, ruts, potholes, and dust. Some sections can become extremely slippery when wet.
- Keep a sharp lookout for wildlife, such as bison, bears, or moose. In all cases, assume they own the road, and stop and wait for them to move. Do not attempt to push through them no matter what you're driving. Vehicles should always be driven with headlights on.
- Sections of the Dempster Highway have notoriously loose, steep banks with no guardrails or fencing. Stay well away from them, especially if traffic or dust is heavy.

RESPECTING THE PEOPLE
A basic understanding of the Northwest Territories' eight Aboriginal groups will help you respect their distinct cultures. The magic of bridging cultures could be a highlight of your northern trip. Dance under the midnight sun at a Métis fiddle jam; learn how to play "hand games" from Tlicho elders; go fishing with a Slavey guide; visit a Gwich'in cultural camp; or walk the Beaufort Sea coast with an Inuvialuit whale hunter.

Tlicho (formerly Dogrib)
The Tlicho people occupy traditional territory that spans from the northern shore of Great Slave Lake to Great Bear Lake. They live mainly in the communities

of Behchokò, Whatì, Gamètì, and Wekweetì. Behchokò, which appears as Rae-Edzo on some maps, is the largest community in the Tlicho region. You will hear Tlicho spoken by young and old alike in any of the four Tlicho communities. The Dogrib name derives from a story about a benevolent ancestor whose body was half man, half dog.

Yellowknives

The original people of the south shore and East Arm of Great Slave Lake were a large and powerful band, active in the early fur trade. Their Chief, Akaitcho, rescued survivors of the first Franklin Expedition in 1823. The people later dispersed among the Chipewyan at Fort Resolution, Lutsel K'e, and Yellowknife. Today the Yellowknives' band headquarters is located in N'dilo, on the outskirts of the city named after them.

Chipewyan

Descendants of barrenlands caribou hunters, the Chipewyan were middlemen in the fur-trade era, trading with the Dene of the west as well as the Cree in the east and with the English who built forts on Hudson Bay. Their famous leader, Matonabbee, led Samuel Hearne to the mouth of the Coppermine River. Many Chipewyan people still live in the Athabasca region of Alberta and the Northwest Territories communities of Fort Smith, Fort Resolution, and Lutsel K'e.

Fort Providence kids ready for take-off

South Slavey

People of this Aboriginal group live mainly in the southern Northwest Territories, on the Hay River Reserve in the South Slave Region and the communities of the upper Mackenzie or Dehcho Region, including Fort Providence, Fort Simpson, Fort Liard, Trout Lake, Nahanni Butte, Kakisa, Jean Marie River, and Wrigley. Many still rely on traditional activities, such as hunting, fishing, and trapping, as a central part of their livelihood. The South Slavey language, or Dene-thah, is spoken widely from the southern Northwest Territories to northeast Alberta and northwest British Columbia.

North Slavey

Speakers of the North Slavey language include the Hare, Mountain, and Sahtu Dene groups concentrated west and north of Great Bear Lake, in the Sahtu Region. Most live in the communities of Délįne, Tulít'a, Fort Good Hope, Colville Lake, and Norman Wells.

> **Happiness Is ... the Land**
> Elise Bonnetrouge,
> Fort Providence
> *I am happy here.*
> *This is my land.*
> *This is where I belong.*

Gwich'in

The traditional territory of the Gwich'in people now living in the Northwest Territories includes the Mackenzie Delta and northwestern mountains. They are related to Gwich'in groups in the Yukon and Alaska, and long ago adopted some of the customs of the Tlingit on the British Columbia coast, with whom they traded. Their Land Claim region includes present-day Tsiigehtchic, Fort McPherson, and Aklavik. Many Gwich'in also live in Inuvik.

Inuvialuit

The people of the western Arctic coast traditionally spoke Inuvialuktun, an Alaskan version of the circumpolar language, Inuktitut. They moved into the Northwest Territories from farther west when their predecessors, the beluga-hunting Mackenzie Inuit, were wiped out by disease. They were mainly whale hunters by tradition, while the people of the Arctic Islands hunted on both land and sea. Today's Inuvialuit live in Inuvik, Tuktoyaktuk, Paulatuk, Aklavik, Sachs Harbour, and Ulukhaktok (formerly Holman Island). Today English has become the common language of the Inuvialuit. Only 10 percent of the roughly 4,000 Inuvialuit now speak Inuvialuktun, but its revival appears hopeful thanks to local education efforts.

Métis

Many Northerners of mixed heritage descend from Cree-French families of the fur-trade era. Like their French-Canadian ancestors, Métis became voyageurs, fur-trade middlemen, post managers, and river pilots. Other northern Métis have Scottish or English ancestors who came north with the Hudson's Bay Company.

The next wave of southern Métis came here in the 1940s and 1950s to settle at Hay River and Fort Smith. Politically, Métis have generally allied with Dene groups to settle Land Claims.

On the Trail

In most Aboriginal cultures in the Northwest Territories, "paying" the land or water is a sign of respect that can add a reverential imprint to each day. This tradition is practiced by pausing for a reflective moment—to give thanks for another day and wish for a safe journey down the trail—then offering a simple gift to nature such as loose tobacco or tea (avoid potential bear attractants). On the Mackenzie River, we started each day with this practice, asking for "calm winds, calm waters, and calm minds" as we sprinkled tobacco into the water.

- If circumstances arise where you feel you must use a backcountry cabin, leave it and the land around it in better condition than you found it. Replace any firewood that you use and add a little extra.

- All historic sites and/or archaeological artifacts of any kind are protected by law. Removing artifacts or altering structures destroys irreplaceable information from the past. Take as many pictures as you like—and a GPS waypoint while you're at it. Some archaeologist or land-use mapper might thank you some day—but leave all human-made items where they lie. For more information on the Northwest Territories Archaeological Sites Regulations, visit the Prince of Wales Northern Heritage Centre Web site (www.pwnhc.ca) and go to the "Legislation and Policies" link.

> **Paying the Water**
> Rosalie Causa, Fort Providence
>
> *I've traveled to where the mountains meet the water and it is so blue and there are islands. I remember what my mother told me and I take a cigarette, warm tea and sugar and throw them into the water so there will be no wind. It's true. It has worked for me.*

- When visiting small communities, go to the band office or visitors centre if you are interested in participating in activities associated with Aboriginal cultures.

- In most cases, casual recreational travel is unrestricted on Aboriginal lands identified in regional Land Claims. Follow the golden rules of no-trace camping and non-interference with Aboriginal use and enjoyment of the land. However, it is a welcome act of courtesy to contact the appropriate Aboriginal group and enquire about special restrictions or sensitive areas, especially when travelling in a large group.

- The communities along the rivers and roads of this part of the Trans Canada

Trail provide a wonderful window on life in Canada's remote North. Build some community time into your schedule. Not only is a relaxed visit a sign of respect for the people who live there, but you may gather some of your best trip memories while with them.

- Aboriginal cultures across the world generally bestow high respect to their elders and the Northwest Territories is no exception. Take advantage of any opportunity to spend time with elders you may meet along the way whose stories and songs can open up this landscape for you in profound and unexpected ways.

TLC for Elders

Elise Gargan, Fort Providence

When I was young I really loved the elders. I used to wash their clothes and heat water for them so they could wash, just as if they were the parents I never had. I believed that for every cup of tea I placed before them I gained one more day on this earth for myself. I enjoyed doing these things for them out of love.

2

WATER ROUTES

3 THE SLAVE RIVER

APPROXIMATE DISTANCE 325 kilometres

HIGHLIGHTS

✸ Fort Smith riverside scenery, rich history, arts, museum, and college
✸ Wood Buffalo National Park's salt plains, bison, and whooping cranes
✸ World-class whitewater kayaking
✸ Abundant moose, black bear, and waterfowl
✸ Historical sites from the paddlewheeler days
✸ Relaxed, week-long (+/-) river paddle with convenient road access at both ends

OVERVIEW

The Slave is a large, lazy river, second in grandeur only to the Mackenzie. It winds north from Alberta's Peace and Athabasca river systems. From the late 1700s to the mid 1900s, the Slave served as a key artery in the "Gateway to the North," linking Canada's resource-rich northwest to the rest of the world. Tangible signs of the river's multi-layered history line its banks in the form of abandoned sawmills, woodcutter camps, outfitter lodges, experimental farms, and trading posts. Long before York boats or paddlewheelers plied the Slave, it was used as a traditional travel route and rich reservoir of fish and wildlife for countless generations of Aboriginal people. The Slave marks the natural boundary between the rolling Canadian Shield to the east and the lowland plains of the Slave River valley to the west. Except for the four sets of magnificent rapids in the 30-kilometre stretch between Fort Fitzgerald and Fort Smith, the Slave is a quiet, flat-water paddle all the way to Fort Resolution. The current varies considerably, depending on the river's width, but is generally about 8 kilometres per hour with an average gradient of 0.11 metres per kilometre (0.6 feet per mile). Wildlife is abundant along this productive corridor of life. Expect to see black bear, moose, and bison. You will be travelling down a major flyway for migratory birds, and the numerous lakes, ponds, and wetlands adjacent to the river provide excellent nesting habitat for a variety of ducks, geese, and other waterbirds.

CAMPING TIPS

Because of its steep, unstable banks and fickle water levels, camping on the Slave River can be challenging unless you know what to look for. The exposed, breezy ends of many mid-stream islands offer good campsites, especially during bug season. Partially vegetated banks incised by creeks or ephemeral streams are relatively stable and provide easier access to flat ground. Open forests of mature spruce or balsam poplar are usually uncrowded by thick shrubs that can make camping difficult elsewhere. There are virtually limitless high dry benches above

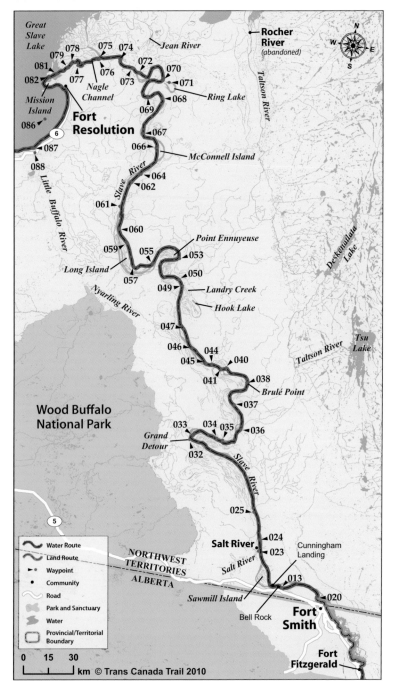

Great Slave Lake

078
079
081
082
Mission Island
086
087
088
Little Buffalo River

075 074 *Jean River*
072
076 073 070
077 *Nagle Channel* 071 *Ring Lake*
068
069
067
066 *McConnell Island*
064
062
061 *Slave River*
060
059 055 *Point Ennuyeuse* 053
Long Island 057 050
049 *Landry Creek*
Hook Lake
047
046 044
045 040
041 038 *Brulé Point*
037
033 034 035 036
Grand Detour 032

• **Rocher River** (abandoned)

Taltson River

Deskenatlata Lake

Tsu Lake

Taltson River

Fort Resolution
6

Nyarling River

Wood Buffalo National Park

Slave River

025

5

024
Salt River • 023 Cunningham Landing
013
NORTHWEST TERRITORIES *Salt River*
ALBERTA 020
Sawmill Island **Fort Smith**
Bell Rock

Fort Fitzgerald

Water Route
Land Route
Waypoint
Community
Road
Park and Sanctuary
Water
Provincial/Territorial Boundary

0   15   30
km © Trans Canada Trail 2010

the river that make for great camping—that is, if you can access them. Many of the best campsites along the river already have a cabin on them and are surrounded by large clearings. If you choose to camp near any of these cabins, leave the site without a trace of your presence.

FORT SMITH
Population 2,600

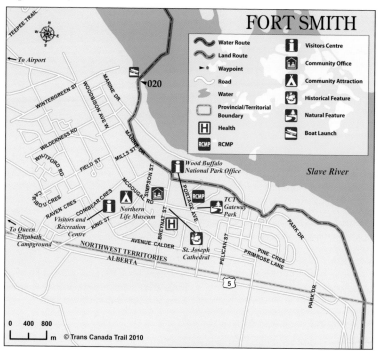

Community

This quiet town sits on Highway 5 along the Alberta border, 333 kilometres southeast of Hay River. Nicknamed the "Garden City of the North," it also straddles a major natural border with the lake-studded Canadian Shield to the east and the limestone karstlands of the boreal plains to the west. The capital of the Northwest Territories until 1967, Fort Smith

Choosing a route above the Slave River Rapids

remains an important administrative centre for the region. It is the main staging and supply centre for Wood Buffalo National Park and is home to the Thebacha Campus of Aurora College. Most tourists come here to see the park and its abundant wildlife, to kayak the world-renowned Slave River Rapids, or to marvel at winter's aurora borealis. The community is also steeped in Native and non-Native

> ### Slave to the River
> Shawn Grono, kayaker
> *The Slave River is a spiritual place. It connects us to the earth in a unique way. To surf its waves and play in its sun-drenched currents makes us realize that we're in a special corner of the world which few get to enjoy. We are ultimately reminded how important it is to keep our rivers clean, free and flowing, unimpeded by human design.*

history and, with creative tourism development, could one day be the "Louisbourg of the North."

Visitor Information

Fort Smith's Visitor Information Centre is located in the community recreation complex. This is a good place to have a shower or access the Internet if the need arises. Open year-round. PO Box 147, 108 King St., Fort Smith, NT, X0E 0P0 (867-872-3065, fax 867-872-4848, visitorinfo@direcway.com, www.fortsmith.ca).

Biking from Fort Fitzgerald to Fort Smith

Things to Do

✳ Northern Life Museum. Free admission. Open 8:30–6 PM Mon–Fri and 1–5 PM Sat and Sun, Jun–Aug. Be sure to visit the outside grounds, including the infamous *Radium King* tugboat, which shipped the uranium ore from Great Bear Lake used to build the world's first atomic bombs. 110 King St., Box 420, Fort Smith, NT, X0E 0P0 (867-872-2859, fax 867-872-5808, nlm@auroranet.nt.ca).

✳ Fort Smith Mission Historic Park, behind St. Joseph's Cathedral. The site of a far-reaching Catholic mission established in 1912. Don't miss the Grotto, a meditative mountain of rocks built by the Oblate Brothers complete with cave and outdoor pews. Open year-round for self-guided tours.

✳ Wood Buffalo National Park Visitor Reception Centre, McDougal Rd. and Portage Ave. Open daily mid-June to Labour Day, Mon–Fri the rest of the year. Box 750, Fort Smith, NT, X0E 0P0 (867-872-7960, 24-hr hotline 867-872-7962, fax 867-872-3910, wbnp.info@pc.gc.ca, www.pc.gc.ca/buffalo).

✳ St. Joseph's Cathedral, Fort Smith's architectural centrepiece, was built in 1959 as the seat of the Northern Diocese of the Roman Catholic Church. Tours available upon request (867-872-2052).

✳ Aurora College at the west end of Connibear St. began as a trade school in the 1960s, and is now a major learning centre for teachers, social workers, and renewable resource specialists (867-872-7000). Offers Summer Arts Festival workshops with hands-on lessons in Aboriginal arts and crafts. Contact The Artists of the South Slave Society, PO Box 1288, Fort Smith, NT, X0E 0P0 (867-872-3123).

Family outing on the the Trans Canada Trail

✳ Riverbank Park. Stroll above the river on a boardwalk running from the north end of Breynat and Wapiti streets or descend the bank to a riverside trail that leads upstream to "The Rocks" lookout above Rapids of the Drowned. Watch for feeding white pelicans. The large grassy area below the park boardwalk was the site of a major landslide in 1968.

✳ Trans Canada Trail, 30-km riverside trail connecting Fort Smith to Fort Fitzerald in Alberta. Accessed via the Riverbank Park or off the east end of Pickerel Cres. Connects with side trails to all the major rapids along the route as well as the Pelican Rapids Golf & Country Club. The TCT Gateway Park at the corner of McDougal Rd. and Portage Ave. offers picnic tables and a relaxing forest setting.

✳ North of 60 Books, known as the "biggest little bookstore in the north," has an impressive northern collection. 66 Portage Ave. Fort Smith, NT, X0E 0P0 (867-872-2606).

Accommodation

✳ Portage Inn, 72 Portage Rd. Large, comfortable rooms with microwaves and stoves (867-872-2276).

✳ Pelican Rapids Inn, 152 McDougal Rd. Across from the Wood Buffalo park visitor centre. Standard hotel rooms and family

---

It's All Here in Fort Smith

Raymond Davies, journalist, 1943

There are two big cities along the 60th parallel. Leningrad, in Russia, population, 2,500,000. Fort Smith, in the Northwest Territories, population 250. Leningrad is the "big city" in Northern Russia. Fort Smith is the "big city" along the upper reaches of the Mackenzie River basin. For all intents and purposes this is the administrative centre of the Territories. All revenue comes here; all disbursements are made from here; the "law" is here.

restaurant (867-872-2789, fax 867-872-4727).

✳ Thebacha Bed & Breakfast. Comfortable guest home with all facilities. 53 Portage Ave. Can arrange backcountry tour packages and/or accommodation at Spotted Eagle Adventure Lodge. Taiga Tour Company, Fort Smith, NT, X0E 0P0 (867-872-2060, fax 867-872-2401, www.taigatour.com, taigatour@ northwestel.net).

✳ Whispering Pines Cottages. Self-contained three-bedroom guest home with washer/drier, kitchen utensils. Nice main house but beware of lumpy beds in backyard cottage. 85 Pine Cres., PO Box 300, Fort Smith, NT, X0E 0P0 (867-872-2628, fax 867-872-2906).

Camping

✳ Queen Elizabeth Territorial Park Campground. Sites $12, open May 1–Sep 15. At the end of Teepee Trail, 4 km west of the town centre on the banks of the Slave River. Showers, bathrooms, firewood, children's playground (867-872-2607, www.campingnwt.ca).

✳ Pine Lake campground, 60 km south of Fort Smith. This is the only road-ac-

---

Slave River Pelicans

The white pelicans of Fort Smith are peculiar birds indeed. The population of about 60 birds is one of the smallest colonies of their kind in the world. They are the world's northernmost white pelicans and the only ones known to nest among rapids—among the most forbidding and isolated sets of rapids in Canada. How they manage to feed in the fast, murky waters remains a mystery.

Divine Birds

Jacques "Van Pelican" Van Pelt, tourism outfitter and naturalist

We all must work together to do what we can to protect these wonderful birds. If we don't, we're going to lose them. They belong to you, me—all of us. They are our pelicans. To me they are among the most impressive manifestations of the divine.

Whitewater Citadel

Ernest Thompson Seton, *The Arctic Prairies*, 1911

The northmost large colony, and the one made famous by Alexander Mackenzie downward, is on the great island that splits the [Mountain] Rapids above Fort Smith. Here, with a raging flood about their rocky citadel, they are safe from all spoilers that travel on the earth; only a few birds of the air need they fear, and these they have strength to repel ... Drifted like snow through the distant woods were the brooding birds, but they arose before we were near and sailed splendidly overhead in a sweeping wide-fronted rank.

cessible campground within Wood Buffalo National Park, open May long weekend to Labour Day weekend. Water, firewood, outhouses, playground, no hook-ups, tent sites $10 per night. Day use area features an aquamarine lake and a beautiful sandy swimming beach (867-872-7960, wbnp.info@pc.gc.ca, www.pc.gc.ca/buffalo).

* Thebacha Campground (Elder's Village), on the bank of the Salt River. Turnoff is 15 km northwest of town on Highway 5. Four cabins, gazebo, large kitchen cabin. Must be booked in advance through Métis Council office, 25 Camsell St., Fort Smith, NT, X0E 0P0 (867-872-2643).

Outfitting/Hardware

* Northern Store on Breynat St. just north of McDougal Rd. (867-872-2568); Fields Stores, 88 Portage Ave. (867-872-3130); Kaeser's Stores, 76-80 Breynat St. (867-872-2345).

Amenities

* Accommodation, restaurant, store, bank, bank machine, visitor information, pharmacy, medical services, police, airport, gasoline, diesel, propane, automotive service.

Tips

* *Thebacha Trails: A Guide to Special Areas Around Fort Smith* by Libby Gunn is an excellent guide to local natural history, hiking opportunities, and outdoor attractions near Fort Smith, including Wood Buffalo National Park. Available at North of 60 Books.

* Recognized as "a legend in his own time," Métis artist, sculptor, and storyteller Sonny Mac-Donald is worth looking up while in town. Exquisite artwork available. Sonny's Place, PO Box 136, Fort Smith, NT, X0E 0P0 (867-872-5935).

Emergency

* Hospital/Clinic (867-872-6200).

* RCMP (867-872-1111).

Fine dining along the Slave River

WOOD BUFFALO NATIONAL PARK

Wood Buffalo is huge. Larger than Switzerland, it is nearly 45,000 square kilometres and is Canada's largest national park. Established in 1922, two-thirds of this wilderness World Heritage Site lies in Alberta and one-third in the Northwest Territories. It includes a vast land of boreal forest dotted with bogs and crisscrossed with the countless channels of the largest freshwater delta on earth, the Peace-Athabasca Delta. Though two roads penetrate the park's eastern and northern sections, much of the park is inaccessible to vehicles.

The park provides habitat to one of the world's largest free-roaming bison herds—over 2,500 animals—and is the only known nesting habitat for the endangered whooping cranes that migrate here each spring. From a low of 15 birds in 1941, the park's population has grown to 214 (as of May 2006), thanks to international conservation efforts. Attempts are being made to establish a new migratory flock. Moose, black bear, lynx, and wolves abound. More than a million ducks, geese, and swans stage in the Peace-Athabasca Delta and the park's many wetlands. Besides the delta, other major features include the Salt Plains and limestone karst topography, which includes hundreds of sinkholes and an invisible network of underground rivers. Many scenic areas lie a short hike from the road, although some, like the Peace-Athabasca Delta, can only be accessed by boat. Mosquitoes and horseflies can be a torment from mid-June to mid-July, so come prepared for battle.

Bedlam at Bell Rock

Raymond Davies, journalist, 1943

The coming of the Americans brought great changes. Where the Fort Smith warehouses and docks handled as many as 10,000 tons of freight in a peak year, they now take nearly five times as much. There is a rush and crush and clouds of dust never have time to settle.

Loaded trucks seem to float through the dust to the river's edge. Cranes pass, their long necks above the dust clouds. Now and then barges pass on land on their way to Bell Rock where they are unloaded and shoved into the water.

The waterfront is bedlam. Dominating everything is a huge, black oil tank brought in sheets from the United States and welded or bolted together here. Nearby, piled high, are skip boxes filled with almost everything from needles and camera film to hydraulic machinery, false teeth and oil drills, for the north. Barges crowd barges to be loaded ...

Hurry, hurry, hurry is the word! Beat the cold! Beat the frost! Beat the wind! Beat the ice! Hurry! One discerns this in the everlasting, 24-hour cacophony of sound played by the gigantic, maddening orchestra of trucks and cranes and "cats," to which the whistles of the steamers and tugs provide a welcome relief.

The park's visitor reception centre offers various orientation videos, exhibits, and hiking maps (but not topographical maps).

There is currently no admission fee for the park.

Time-worn remains of paddlewheeler wharf, Slave River

Park Activities

Several day-use areas provide access to hiking trails. The Salt Plains, off Parson's Lake Road, is a 1-kilometre walk to a vast plain of salt formed by the evaporation of mineral-laden water seeping out of the earth. Near the Salt River, a short trail leads past a red-sided garter snake pit. These are the northernmost reptiles on the continent and can be observed entwined in mating balls during the April–May mating season. For ambitious hikers there is a 16-kilometre trail that loops through a surprising variety of ecosystems, including boreal woods, wetlands, salt meadows, and salt flats. One of the most popular trails is the 30-minute hike to Grosbeak Lake, an impressive salt flat strewn with weirdly-shaped glacial erratics. Crystal clear Pine Lake is a good place for swimming.

Backcountry hiking, geared toward bison watching, is available around Sweetgrass Station. The park office should be contacted well in advance for safety information and backcountry permits. Three outfitters for canoeing and backcountry hiking operate out of Fort Smith (for a list see www.pc.gc.ca/buffalo).

Finding the Providence

Earl Evans, Slave River resident, 2005

They used to build boats at Cunningham Landing because it was one of the only places near Fort Smith where they could go up the bank and get some good timber. The banks were too steep everywhere else. Right at the creek by my cabin there's a depression, and if the water is low enough, you'll see, in the mud, there's a single engine steam boiler from an old boat. I found a board off it and I could still read the word "Providence" on it. A few years later I happened to read in Up Here *magazine about an RCMP boat called the* Providence *that used to be based out of Fort Resolution. It's the right length and shape so I'm sure it's the same boat. Old David King told me that this boat broke down one fall, years ago, so they pulled it into the creek. But when things froze over the ice smashed it all up.*

➤ 🏃 💺 😊 Take in the grand view of the Slave River and, just upstream, the Rapids of the Drowned, before you descend the high riverbank from town to the **Fort Smith boat launch** [WP20]. Nature has largely reclaimed this stretch of shoreline, which was once lined with warehouses, barges, and paddlewheeled steamers. Watch for river otters that may welcome you to the starting point of the water portion of the Northwest Territories' Trans Canada Trail.

Busting Guts Down the Slave

Jim Green, *Summer on the Water*

It's only about 160 kilometers from Fort Smith to Great Slave Lake as the raven flies (as if a raven would ever choose to fly that far in a straight line), but the river meanders through the Slave River Lowlands, chalking up a watercourse of some 328 kilometers. It took us nine hard, head-down, gut-busting, shoulder-wrenching days of punching into a raging headwind to make it. Charles Camsell and friends did the reverse trip, upstream, in nine days in 1914. They must have had the same fierce wind behind them as we had blasting in our faces.

➤ 🔍 Not far downstream on river left is a thin, cigar-shaped island that offers almost three kilometres of sheltered, creek-like paddling along its southern shore.

➤ 🏃 😊 Just when you think you've finally propelled yourself into the boreal wilderness after paddling a couple of hours from Fort Smith, you arrive at **Bell Rock** [WP13], which marks the downstream end of the historic 30-kilometre portage around the Slave River Rapids. The only evidence of this once-bustling transhipment centre is a large grassy area edged by a handful of modest homes. Splintered timbers and twisted metal along the shore are all that is left of the

---

Salt River Hospitality

Olive Fredrickson, *The Silence of the North*, 1923

Where the Salt River came into the Slave we went ashore at a camp where Indians were drying fish. A cluster of smoke-blackened tents stood on the bank; men, women, and children were all over the place; and gaunt sled dogs were tethered to stakes, their wild and eerie howling echoing across the river. Fish by the hundreds, split open, were drying on pole racks. Mostly jackfish or northern pike, and goldeyes, with a few big "coney fish" mixed in. They were inconnu, known as sheefish in many places in the Arctic, weighing an average of eight to twelve pounds [5 kilograms].

When we left the camp the Indians gave us enough fish for our evening meal, for ourselves and our two dogs. We had come to a land of plenty, we agreed, a dream country for a young trapper and his family.

busy piers where count-less watercraft were re-launched on their journey north.

> ✒ Just downstream from Bell Rock on river right is **Cunningham Landing**, the site where, for over one hundred years until the 1950s, all manner of river craft were hauled up the sloping banks for re-

Geared up for a grey day on the Slave

pair and winter storage. A single log home is visible near the site.

> ✒ If the north wind is blowing, you will get your first healthy dose of it as you swing past **Sawmill Island**, named for a large sawmill operation established by the American military in support of its Canol Road construction activities in the 1940s. Though the west channel around the island is easily navigated, the east channel is the traditional and most direct route. A cleared area at the extreme south end of the island is the site of a tent camp used for outdoor education by Fort Smith schools.

> ✒ Settled in the 1870s, the tiny community of **Salt River** [WP23] is one of the oldest Métis settlements in northern Canada. It is the last formal settlement and road link until you reach Fort Res-olution, almost 285 kilometres downstream. There are no facili-ties here (though rental cabins may soon be available) but it's worth a short paddle up the Salt River to experience the tranquil beauty of this traditional riverside settle-ment. Another option is to pull up to the gravelled launch on the

---

These Banks Really Move!

Earl Evans, Slave River resident

All these snyes were at one time part of the river sys-tem. Lots of them have filled in over time and we're driving our four-wheel quads down them where, 20 years ago we used to zip through in our boats. Everything, the whole river, seems to be slowly shift-ing over towards the northeast as the southwest side fills in. These banks are really on the move, always cutting, cutting, cutting. For instance I've lost 55 feet [17 metres] of riverbank at my cabin since 1996. I've got to move my cabin back because now I'm only 21 feet [6 metres] from the edge. If things keep shifting the way they have, I'll only have another three or four years to winch it back into the bush before the river claims it.

south side of the Salt River mouth and walk in (approximately 200 metres).

➤🖾 Directly across from the Salt River boat launch, on the east bank of the Slave, is a small **traditional cemetery** that should be shown the highest respect.

➤🔍 ⛺ The **first island cluster north of Salt River** [WP24] shows several navigable channels along the river's

> **Secret Channels in a Big River**
>
> Julian Thomlinson, canoeist
>
> *The occasional narrow channels skirting the islands totally changed my impressions of the river. They give you a sense of intimacy with the land. You're able to see everything up close—the muskrats and beavers, the ducks and the flowers. Each island is different. Each little channel around them. This river has a lot more faces than I first thought.*

west side. Don't take them unless you're sight-seeing. Most of these have silted in or become clogged by willows over the 20-plus years since the standard maps were created. Camping on the upstream end of the biggest island affords a pleasant view of the river if you are prepared to lug your gear up the bank.

➤🖾 🏠 As you proceed downriver, you will occasionally catch a glimpse of a **traditional trail** that roughly parallels the west bank. Over hundreds of years, this trail has been traversed by moccasined bison hunters, dog-sledding trappers and traders, snowmobiling moose hunters, and, most recently, a bulldozer that cleared the trail in 2005 to allow rugged four-wheel winter access to hunting cabins downstream. It has also been used to herd bison south from the "prairie" lowlands adjacent to the Slave River to an abattoir at Hay Camp (south of Fort Fitzgerald) and beyond, to bison ranches in northern Alberta. This trail is quite evident across the river from a handsome log cabin [WP25]. The cleft in the bank just north of this cabin marks the beginning of another traditional trail that eventually connects with the Taltson River and heads east to the barrenlands.

> **Writing on the Walls**
>
> Grafitti on the Grand Detour cabin and outhouse
>
> *Here again.*
>
> *Came for moose. Got one duck.*
>
> *Opened road to cabin with cat. Two feet of snow.*
>
> *One young buffalo. Very fat. Got two more fat cows today. North burn.*
>
> *Canoeing from Ft. Smith to Ft. Resolution. Left yesterday.*
>
> *Saw a bear swimming across the river. Came up.*
>
> *Clean up your booze and garbage.*
>
> *No moose but got a duckie.*
>
> *Replace wood.*
>
> *Hot!*

The Straight Goods on Meanders

David Harrison, *Physical Geography of the Hay River Area*

Meanders are formed by the river eroding and undercutting the outside bends and depositing sediments on the inside bends. As this continues, the river becomes increasingly winding or meandering. At the mature stage of the river, large loops form with only very narrow necks separating the bends of the river. During the old age stage, these river loops are cut off to form oxbow lakes. Eventually these oxbow lakes become filled with sediment and covered with natural vegetation. Meanders are found in many parts of the world on both large and small rivers, for example the Slave River, the Red River in Manitoba, and the Mississippi River. These river valleys usually have rich alluvial soils because of periodic flooding and resorting of sediments.

3

➤ Enter the **narrow channel on river-left** for a pleasant 8-kilometre shortcut where no wind can find you. The long, skinny island that forms this channel is known locally as **Raspberry Island**—and for good reason.

➤ A rustic log cabin at **Grand Detour** [WP 32] marks an important node of historic and current activity on the land. A traditional trail and portage route connects this site to the Little Buffalo River, west of the Slave, which in turn, provides a major all-season "highway" to Great Slave Lake. The cabin itself, now used as a base camp for hunting moose, bison, and ducks, dates back to the 1950s when this site was used by the federal government to test agricultural forage species for bison. Once parked beside the river, the cabin is now 300 metres from the water, testifying to the Slave's dynamism

First-class camping at Grand Detour

over half a century. Watch for a crude trail cut through the willows that leads to the cabin. It's worth the walk. This spot offers good tent sites, an expansive view of the river, plus the luxury of a picnic table and outhouse. Enjoy the delphinium flowers and raspberries that grace the side of the cabin. A network of trails radiating from this site and its abundant berries and grasses draw many kinds of wildlife. If you camp here, your supper music may be provided by howling wolves. Take extra precautions for bears. A thump in the night could well be a bison.

➤ ◼ ◼ ◼ The loop now forming **Grand Detour** may one day be pinched off by the inexorable forces of siltation and undercutting to form an oxbow lake. In the meantime, it is aptly named, creating a 25-kilometre diversion from the Slave's northward course that steamship captains were sorely familiar with. Many smaller craft and canoes used to bypass this route via a traditional portage that sliced the neck of this feature but which has been rendered inaccessible by retreating cutbanks. The first **island channel** beyond the cabin [WP33] provides a navigable compromise, but stay close to its east shore as the west side is fast filling with silt. In 2001, two canoeists who had camped beside this channel woke to discover that fierce winds and rising waters had stolen their canoe overnight. They somehow managed to hitchhike back to Fort Smith on the next boat south. Their canoe was eventually found cast ashore near the town of Hay River, several hundred kilometres northeast. The moral of this story: either secure your canoe or kayak, or bring lots of cash for a helicopter rescue.

More Writing on the Walls

Grafitti on hunting cabins near Brulé Point

Fort Smith Boys.

Came out to have a look. Beautiful fall.

Lots of swans and ducks.

Halloween. Ptarmigan in. No ducks.

No moose. Lots of tracks. Can't eat tracks.

October 5th to 7th. 1 inch of snow. Saw 2 bears, 3 wolves.

May 18th. 49 ducks. Saw 3 moose. Flood in cabin. 8 inches.

Oct 13th. Lots of ice and wind. 1 bull moose at Hook Lake.

3 year old. Fat!

Saw one moose. Didn't get him.

Still no moose.

Shot bull moose below Hook Lake.

1 bull came into camp and took a look.

Hunting beaver, rats and moose. Got lots.

Brought picnic table today. Nice and sunny.

You still have to pay for the plywood.

Lots of moose tracks in islands.

What islands?

No moose.

Fort Res Boys.

Going home.

Thanks!

➤ The **pocket of tall spruce** that stands out along the north shore [WP34] are so-called "veterans" of a major 1950 forest fire that swept south from Point Ennuyeuse almost to Fort Smith.

➤ Olive Frederickson, author of *Silence of the North*, spent the winter of 1922–23 with her husband and young daughter in a crudely built **trapper's cabin** on the west bank of the Slave somewhere near [WP35]. Her gripping book describes "the hair raising experiences of her first years in the frozen wasteland … an ordeal almost too terrible to be endured."

➤ This unnamed, **navigable creek** [WP36] marks another access point to the traditional "highway to the barrenlands," still used by hunters and trappers today. Every wild river deserves a good ghost story. Long ago, near the mouth of this creek, a trapper by the name of Oulten built a cabin for himself and his family. One particularly hungry winter, the trapper bid his wife and two young sons goodbye and set out on his snowshoes to harvest furs from the forest. He was gone for a very long time—so long that the mother eventually went mad with loneliness and hunger. She ended up killing her 10-month-old baby and chasing her older son onto the cabin roof with a shotgun. When she finally came to her senses, she bundled her remaining son onto a dog sled and went searching for her long lost husband ... You can fill in the rest of the details around the campfire.

➤ A **distinct clearing** [WP38] just before the hairpin turn toward **Brulé Point** offers relatively easy access from the water and flat, dry camping for several tents.

The unsung Slave River, wild, winding, and free

➤ 🎴 🏠 🏔 This **navigable creek** [WP40] is known as **Squirrel Channel** by Fort Smith hunters who have cabins along this productive stretch of river. By veering left as you proceed down this channel, you can take an intimate side trip and return to the Slave 5 kilometres downstream [WP44]. Before deciding to go exploring, be warned that, on the Slave, water levels can vary widely from year to year, even day to day.

➤ ⛺ 🏠 On the back of the door of this small **cabin**, [WP41] reminiscent of Henry Thoreau's spartan home beside Walden Pond, the owner has written, "Built in June 1991. Feel free to use but leave in clean condition." The clearing in front of the cabin offers good tenting. The cabin is invisible from the river, but keep an eye out for the clearing on river-right just as the Slave angles abruptly to the northwest.

> **Hell's Gate**
>
> Earl Evans, Slave River resident
>
> *Hell's Gate, oh that's a bad one. If it gets rough in there, oh man, even in big boats you can get into a lot of trouble, ducking and diving through the waves. All the water in the Slave pours right through there, the narrowest part of the river. There's no place else for it to go. It can get pretty ugly in there if you're not careful.*

➤ 🎴 Just downstream from the tip of a 4-kilometre-long island you may spot on either bank a clean interruption in the riverside forest where dense deciduous growth has filled in a former trail [WP45]. This is the old "**bison trail**," still marked on many maps, down which bison were herded south for slaughter from the "million dollar prairies" west and north of Hook Lake.

➤ 🔍 ☠ Welcome to what local river people call **Hell's Gate** [WP46], where every drop of the Slave's water funnels through one of its narrowest stretches. After drifting down this lazy river for over 130 kilometres, the pronounced waves and wonky currents of this bottleneck may catch you off guard. Even on a windless day this stretch may be crowned with whitecaps. A black bear observed swimming across Hell's Gate seemed to be having a tough time. Stay near shore and watch the surface carefully.

➤ 🎴 A few scraps of errant lumber and plywood dangling over the right bank [WP47] alert you to the presence of an historic **game outfitter's camp** that may date as far back as the 1930s. It's a tough climb up the steep sandy banks— ropes may be needed—but it's worth it. This must have been a spiffy operation, complete with two large cabins, several tent frame pads for guests and staff, horse corrals, and a hay bin all still plainly visible amid the ruins. The open meadows around these structures where pack horses once graz-ed are now choked with high-yield raspberry bushes. Paddlewheelers delivered passengers to this site

Resourceful backwoods shelter (bank machine out of order)

from as far away as Texas to hunt wild bison on productive "prairies" to the east. The cabins and trail they used are still shown on most maps.

➤🏠 Like so many features on northern maps, the large island across from the outfitter's camp has no official name, though Aboriginal or home-grown names often abound once you start talking to the river people. To Earl Evans, who lives on the Slave River, this is **Thanksgiving Island**. Why? Because he regularly gets a moose here during his Thanksgiving hunt.

➤🐻 The Hudson's Bay Company's fleet of steam-powered paddlewheelers, launched in the 1880s, had a voracious appetite for fuelwood, burning upwards of two cords of wood every hour (and sometimes the neighbouring forest due to sparks from their stacks). Local demands for timber grew with the expansion of mission and trading activities, and by the 1930s, with Yellowknife's burgeoning gold mines. A half dozen **sawmills** sprang up along the banks of the Slave to meet

Of Bears and Bearberries

Ernest Thompson Seton, *The Arctic Prairies*, 1911

In the dry woods bear tracks became extremely numerous; the whole country, indeed, was marked with the various signs. Practically every big tree has bear-claw markings on it, and every few yards there is evidence that the diet of the bears just now is chiefly berries of Uva ursi... Quite the most abundant carpet in the forest here is the Uva ursi or bearberry. Its beautiful evergreen leaves and bright red berries cover a quarter of the ground in dry woods and are found in great acre beds. It furnishes a staple of food to all wild things, birds and beasts, including foxes, martens, and coyotes; it is one of the most abundant of the forest products, and not one hundred yards from the fort are solid patches as big as farms.

this demand, one of which can be explored on river-right two kilometres south of **Landry Creek**. Though you may have to hunt around, several structures are clearly visible, including a main cabin (which may soon end up in the river), a large tent platform, ancient sawhorses, an impressive pile of sawdust, and a rare, endangered four-holer outhouse. The site is marked as "cabins" on most maps.

⟋ 🐊 🏠 🛶 🏕 🦌 Landry Creek [WP49] marks the outflow of **Hook Lake**, a classic oxbow lake that once formed a hairpin turn on the Slave River. This clear-running creek is easily navigated, even with a motorboat in high water, and is a popular hunting route to productive moose and

> ### Burning Bison at Hook Lake
> Earl Evans, Slave River resident
>
> *Hook Lake was a really good area for bison with miles and miles of meadows. We call them prairies. They had a little airstrip back in there and a few corrals. They built a few cabins for the game warden and all the workers, guides and hunters. There were usually a few firefighters in there too. You can still see some of the old buildings.*
>
> *I worked at the Hook Lake camp in 1970 when they had an anthrax outbreak. They brought a bunch of young guys in there and we used to bury buffalos. They'd fly us out to the meadows to find a buffalo killed by anthrax. We'd have to dig a great big hole, usually half under the animal, otherwise you couldn't tip it over. They're so darned heavy. We'd push the bison in, then cover it up with a bunch of dry brush and sticks. Then we'd throw some fuel in and light it up. We'd come back the next day, dump some lime all over the place and cover him up with dirt. It was quite a process.*

bison pastures inland. A side trip to Hook Lake offers excellent wildlife viewing opportunities. The clear water of Landry Creek attracts fish-eating birds, including bald eagles, osprey, and an amazing density of belted kingfishers. Lots of ducks and Canada geese also gather here to feed amidst the marsh-lined shallows. Paddle quietly along the shore of lovely Hook Lake or tromp inland

to the grassy meadows, and your chances of seeing a moose or bison are about as good as they get anywhere in Canada. From the late 1960s to the mid 1990s, various outfitter camps and government ran-ches were established on these meadows. Long before that, Christian mission workers came here

Birch frame for treating moose hides

to round up bison and drive them south to provide meat. Follow the trails leading from the shore of Hook Lake or marked on most maps and you will likely run into old cabins, fencing, corrals, and even a crude airstrip. There is a large **plywood cabin** at the mouth of Landry

Fireweed graces a steep cutbank, Point Ennuyeuse

Creek (river-right) which is accessed via an easily spotted trail up a steep grass-lined bank. Although this cabin, built as a government base camp, had been recently trashed by a black bear when we were there in 2005, the clear poplar-lined area around it, picnic table, and outhouse make this an attractive place to camp. Another much older cabin about 100 metres north of this cabin testifies to the long-established use of this site as a traditional node for hunting, trapping, and fishing. If you want a break from paddling and would prefer to walk into the Hook Lake meadows, there is a plainly visible trail that parallels

---

So Much for Supper!

Dr. Suzanne Carrière, ecologist

We'd camped up on a high bank on an outside curve of the river. We were eating supper, watching the fast water cut away at the bank and calculating how much time before the trees would fall in. At first we were in denial. We'd look at those big spruce and say, "They've been standing there for at least 150 years. How could they fall in? Why now?" We'd been up at 2:00 AM to do bird surveys and were very tired. We were thinking lazily, saying, "We're not moving this camp, damn it." Then more trees fell in and we figured, "Well, at least we have time to finish supper." More trees keeled over so I said, "I don't think we'll have time to wash the dishes." Finally, in the space of a few minutes, we went from, "We'll probably be okay for the night" to "Forget supper! Move now!" We ended up moving the whole camp back about fifty feet from the bank.

We spent most of the night listening to trees falling in the river. You could hear this huge sucking sound, then sometimes a splash and a crack. We were back far enough that we didn't worry too much. It wasn't frightening really, until we got up and saw that another 25 feet [8 metres] of shoreline had caved in overnight. A small forest of trees went with it. Luckily they always fell into the river, not on us. It was like a giant bulldozer had passed through. If we hadn't moved, our whole camp would have disappeared. Out in the water. Gone.

Landry Creek for approximately two kilometres, then heads east into bison country. Keep an eye out for a big set of moose antlers locked together along the trail—and do leave them behind for future hikers to enjoy.

Enjoying a touch of backwoods civilization

➤ The "**cabin**" at [WP 50] marked on most maps consists of ruins of a very old frame structure that is collapsing into the river. Likely the site of a small sawmill, there are also some large timbers and long metal rods visible, suggesting a steamer dock or ramp.

➤ Though we didn't verify it, there is supposed to be a trail to a **fire tower**, which is marked on most maps, that begins on river-left at a creek mouth just before you slingshot toward Point Ennuyeuse. It is said to be roughly a 45-minute walk one way. Good luck finding it.

➤ For a change of scale or to get out of the wind, take the river-right channel on the last major bend before **Point Ennuyeuse**. This is a pleasant, sheltered route that abounds with Canada geese, dabbling ducks, and muskrats. If you are following your course with a map-loaded GPS, you may be surprised to discover that you are supposedly paddling over dry land for much of this chan-

---

The Power of Water

Jamie Bastedo, *Shield Country*

Ancestral Great Slave Lake had the same basic profile that it does today, except that it had three arms instead of two. Its present shape gives it the appearance of a swan in flight, the East Arm being the head and neck, and the North Arm being one of its extended wings; 8,700 years ago the other wing was clearly visible. The extreme south shore of Great Slave Lake once came within 10 kilometres of the future Fort Smith townsite. What now is the Slave River valley was filled to the brim with water.

This south arm was a very active environment back then. Sedimentation at the mouth of the Slave River was the main land-building process. Fed by erosion off the newly exposed landscape, the delta edged forward at the remarkable rate of about 20 metres a year. Meanwhile, postglacial rebound contributed to this process, particularly for the first 2,000 years after Glacial Lake McConnell subsided. During this time, the whole valley literally was lifting out of water at a rate of almost centimetres a year. Together, these processes transformed a 180-kilometre-long arm of Great Slave Lake into terra firma in just over 8,000 years.

nel. This is another expression of the Slave River's dynamism where the dual processes of sedimentation on the inside of the bend and shore erosion on the island have conspired to render your maps—electronic or otherwise—rapidly out of date. On this river, both the water and the land are in constant motion.

Nimisha explores remains of a 1930s hunt camp

➤ 🔄 ☠ **Point Ennuyeuse** translates into something like "Annoying Point," perhaps reflecting the consternation of river pilots anxious to reach Great Slave Lake. This is one of the river's tightest hairpin turns; it bends so far back on itself that you must head due south for 5 kilometres before resuming your northward journey. Like the bend at Grand Detour, this will one day be cut off and transformed into an oxbow lake. Judging by the rate of sedimentation on the inside curve and the dramatic undercutting on the outside curve [WP53], that day is not far off. As tempted as you may be to cut this corner, it may cost you more time than you save after running aground on fresh mudbars lurking out of sight just below the surface.

➤ 🔄 After several days of mud and silt, it is indeed a treat to encounter a humble **pile of rocks** lining the shore. Though not geologically astounding (a pedestrian mix of fossiliferous limestone and igneous till typical of Great Slave's East Arm), these rocks are apparently famous from one end of the Slave to the other. They occur in two spots only, on river-right [WP55] in the vicinity of a high knobby point, and again along a grassy shore around the next major curve [WP57]. Either spot is a good place to rest or have lunch. In high water, both are inundated by the Slave River.

➤ 🔲 🔄 The channel along the east side of **Long Island** is the most direct route but can funnel the north

> ### Boy Was It Busy!
>
> Isadore Simon, former resident of Fort Resolution
>
> *That Slave River, it used to be real busy. Oh boy was it busy! You'd get two guys in that magic rhythm, cutting wood with those big crosscut saws, and I tell you, would that sawdust ever fly! In no time they'd have woodpiles stacked along the shore higher than a house. There used to be six or seven big mills up and down that river. Most of them have since fallen into the river.*

wind. The longer route along its west side offers more shelter and a variety of scenic channels. Don't be confused near the north end of Long Island by the appearance of a substantial willow-topped island [WP59] and several smaller ones downstream that don't appear on maps. These recent depositional features are further examples of the Slave River's dynamic personality.

➤ Just downstream of Long Island is a series of skinny islands that offers an attractive and **sheltered channel** on river-right [WP60]. This route takes

---

Making Drymeat

Agnes Villebrun, Fort Smith

There was lots of moose— in September, that's when you see lots of moose—and they were really fat. You can't see their ribs, 'cause they're so fat. To make drymeat, you cut it in thin slices. Then, you look for dry wood. Spruce is no good because when you smoke it, the drymeat tastes only of spruce tree. You're supposed to use poplar wood. That one is good, poplar. We'd make a big smoke fire, and put all our drymeat there and hang it over the smoke. It tastes good that way. When it's really dry, you put it in canvas and step on it with your feet, so the juice comes out from the drymeat. Then sometimes we would put them inside canvas and hit it with an axe and make it soft. Then we'd put some sugar and lard, and roll them in that. Oh, it was really good.

---

you past lush willow and marsh vegetation, giving it a kind of Amazonian feel, and is a popular hangout for Canada geese, several species of dabbling ducks, beavers, muskrats, and bald eagles.

➤ As you emerge from this channel, look left and a little downstream and you will spot an old **fire tower** [WP61] used to watch over the timber-rich forests lining this stretch of the river. This task is now more commonly per-

formed through remote satellite surveillance and a lightning position ana-lyzer, a device used by weather forecasters to track the progress and di-rection of thunderstorms.

➤ If your naviga-tion tools include the 1:250,000 "Klewi River" mapsheet, you will en-counter the **Shit Islands** as you paddle off the top

Lunch stop within sight of Fort Resolution

of it [WP62]. The source of this un-
official name remains a mystery
even to local river people though
various versions of the explanation
abound. As you pass the first of
these islands, you will notice evidence of **recent logging operations** on the right-hand shore. As
recently as 1999, the wood from
this area was skidded across the ice
and trucked, via a winter road on
river-left, to a large sawmill in Fort
Resolution until it shut down. The
narrow channel formed by the
northernmost islands on river-right

Woodcutter camp that supplied thousands of cords
of wood for paddlewheelers

[WP 64] is easily and pleasantly navigated.

> 🖼 Take the west channel around **McConnell Island**, and visit the long-aban-
doned **Cinnamon sawmill**, marked as "cabins" on most maps at [WP66]. This
site may be very difficult to find without a GPS since it is located on river-left
along a narrow channel choked with dense willow and alder shrubs. Fifty years
ago it was impossible to miss this place. Cinnamon sawmill must have been a
bustling operation in its heyday; numerous work buildings and living quarters
are still standing. Due to its age, this is technically an archaeological site, so
please take nothing but pictures.

Delta Dreams

David Harrison, *Physical Geography of the Hay River Area*

*A delta is formed by the deposition of sediments which are carried in the water especially during the
spring run-off. A large, swiftly flowing river is able to carry vast amounts of suspended material, but
when the river water enters a quiet lake, the speed of the water is reduced. As a result, the suspended
sediments begin to be deposited, first the coarse gravels and sands, next the smaller silts and finally
fine clays.*

*As the sediments slowly build up above the water surface, the river channel starts to subdivide to
form secondary channels called distributaries. As each distributary deposits sediment, it too becomes
subdivided to form more new channels. Over time, the delta grows forming a complex of channels and
intertwining lowlands, while slowly extending into the lake. The delta area grows by repeated annual
floodings which not only extend the length of the delta but gradually fills in the lowland between each
of the branches.*

➤🔍 🛶 The locals speak of "**bubbling water**" near the entrance to a channel formed by the island at this bend [WP67]. Though we saw no bubbles, the name may refer to the frothy waves when the northeast wind blows unobstructed along the west side of the island. Windy or not, this channel is easily navigated

Shore lunch near Shit Islands

and the most direct route. There is no shelter and few pullout options for the next 10 kilometres, so don't take chances along this stretch if winds are strong.

➤🔍 The **navigable channel** on river-left [WP68] offers good protection from wind.

➤🔍 🦌 Beginning on river-right [WP69], there is a scenic, sheltered **5-kilo-metre shortcut** that shows you a quieter, more intimate face of the river.

➤🔍 🏔 🛶 🦌 🐾 🏠 The creek flowing out of **Ring Lake** [WP 70] shows much the same pattern as Landry Creek and Hook Lake—a relatively lush,

Well-loved cabin, Ring Lake

clear-water outflow draining an oxbow lake. A side trip up this short creek into Ring Lake offers excellent wildlife-viewing opportunities, including moose, beaver, muskrat, and several kinds of ducks. You may spot a bald eagle or osprey hunting over Ring Lake. The abundance of wildlife makes this a popular hunting and fishing destination for people from Fort Resolution. A **log cabin** on the north side of the lake [WP71] stands on the site of an old trading post; some of the original planks have been reused in the cabin's outbuildings. There are good tent sites in the vicinity if you choose to camp here.

The direct **channel** on river-right [WP72] offers good shelter. Most maps show a network of "**timber trails**" in this area, reflecting its traditional importance for wood-cutting operations based out of Fort Resolution. You may see clearings along the bank indicating their presence.

THIS IS YOUR HOME AWAY FROM HOME TAKE GOOD CARE OF IT

Beginning about 275 kilometres downstream from Fort Smith [WP73], the **Jean River** marks the first major channel cutting through the **Slave River Delta**. This is a traditional hunting and fishing corridor still used regularly by residents of Fort Resolution. Though it offers a sheltered and scenic route to

Leave cabins better than you find them and replace firewood

Great Slave Lake, unless you are planning to hang a right to the lake's East Arm, this would not be a prudent route if you are aiming for Fort Resolution. Possible exposure to high winds, nasty swells, and unpredictable currents characterize the delta's ever-shifting mouth.

An abrupt elbow in the river course creates an area of turbulence and curling waves known as **Big Eddy** [WP 74]. Though potentially hazardous, especially for open canoes, you can avoid most of the commotion by favouring the inside curve. The sprawling wetlands and feathery meander scars on the east side of this bend (visible on large-scale maps) create extensive feeding and nesting habitat for ducks, geese, and shorebirds. The productivity of this area and its proximity to Fort Resolution made it an important "haying" site for the early Catholic missions. Meadow grasses and wetland plants were harvested here to feed horses and oxen in Fort Resolution which, in turn, helped

Shrine-like campsite at the mouth of Nagle Channel

cultivate food crops such as potatoes and turnips for remote outposts down the Mackenzie valley. Some of the original trails are kept open to provide snow-mobile access to winter hunting grounds. Look for distinct breaks in riverside vegetation.

➤ 🔍 🏠 ⛺ 🎣 Of the many delta channels emptying into Great Slave Lake, **Nagle Channel** [WP75] is the preferred small craft route. Hug river-left as you approach the channel and you can't miss it. A four-wheel, all-season trail from town leads to a frame cabin and picnic area at the entrance of this channel. Abundant tent sites and a shrine-like campfire pit make this a fun option for your last night on the mighty Slave River. On your way down the channel, watch for two **traditional log cabins** on river-right about 150 metres down-stream [WP76].

➤ 🚶 🏠 Halfway down the channel, prepare yourself for your first potential contact with contemporary civilization in several days: the **Nagle Channel boat launch** [WP77]. If for some reason you are in trouble or feeling especially lazy, chances are good that you could hitch a ride into Fort Resolution.

➤ Most maps show a potential branch route, **Connu Channel** [WP78], that connects northward to **Steamboat Channel**. *Don't take it*. Like many other water courses in the Slave Delta, this channel is gradually filling in with sediments and is unnavigable except perhaps in the highest floodwaters.

➤ Keep your eyes peeled for the clapboard hull of a stranded boat, barely visible through the dense shrubbery on river-right at [WP79]. It is the *Immaculata*, a small steamship dating back to the 1920s that belonged to the Roman Catholic Mission in Aklavik, on the Mackenzie Delta. Until the early 1960s, this boat was used to collect Aboriginal kids up and down the Mackenzie valley and deliver them to residential schools in Aklavik or Fort Smith. The Roman Catholic Brothers also used it for ferrying fish, supplies, and sled dogs from mission to mission. This site must have once been a dry dock or repair area for mission boats,

Julian inspects abandoned shipyard, Nagle Channel

1920s steamer, the *Immaculata*, pride of the Roman Catholic fleet, Slave Delta

indicated by a rotting barge, several burned-out boat boilers, and a few teetering shacks and outhouses to be found a few metres west of the *Immaculata*. In its prime, this facility would have been much closer to Great Slave Lake, but half a century of delta infilling has left it several kilometres from open water.

If you are navigating with a map-based GPS, turn it on as you near the **mouth of Nagle Channel.** Don't be alarmed if it shows you well out into **Nagle Bay** even though you still have willow-lined terra firma on both sides of you. It's not a malfunction. The channel ends about 500 metres farther downstream [WP81], beyond where it is shown on most maps, another result of a hyperactive river delta.

Cuthbert Grant and Laurent Leroux of the Northwest Company established the Northwest Territories' first trading post at **Grant Point**, on the northeast side of the Slave River Delta in 1786. A few years later the post was moved to **Moose Deer Island** [WP82] to catch the prevailing canoe traffic that spilled out of Steamboat and Nagle channels. This settlement was abandoned when the post was rebuilt on the shore of Great Slave Lake and named Fort Resolution. The building on the island's southeast tip is used as a base for a local summer camp.

On the home stretch before Fort Resolution, Nagle Channel

➤ 🔲 ⬆ ☠ Most maps show a tempting **channel connecting Nagle Bay to Resolution Bay**. Don't be fooled. This channel once severed Mission Island from the mainland. Though still navigable in the 1920s, gradual sediment deposition and, ultimately, the construction of an airstrip by the United States military in the 1940s blocked this shortcut from the delta to town. Unless you thoroughly enjoy portaging, you will have to paddle around Mission Island.

➤ 🏛 The two-storey **log building** that stands alone on **Mission Island** dates back to the late 1800s. The building, accessible by road from Fort Resolution, has served as a school, medical clinic, residence, and warehouse, and remains in remarkable condition.

APPROXIMATE DISTANCE 275 kilometres

HIGHLIGHTS
✳ Fort Resolution fur trade and mission history, Chipewyan hospitality
✳ One- or multi-day guided trips from Fort Resolution on Great Slave Lake
✳ Breathtaking big-lake paddling on Great Slave Lake and Beaver Lake
✳ First-hand contact with Great Slave fishing industry, past and present
✳ Rich bird life, including bald eagles, white pelicans, and waterfowl
✳ Little Buffalo and Buffalo rivers
✳ Scenic beaches of the "Great Slave Riviera"
✳ Hay River trails, restaurants, historical museum, Dene Cultural Institute
✳ Fort Providence Rapids

OVERVIEW
The south shore of Great Slave Lake is full of surprises. Sudden shifts in wind or wave patterns will keep you on high alert as you cross this hugely exposed stretch of water. Weather aside, this shoreline offers largely unsung treats in the form of expansive pebble and sand beaches, secluded coves and river mouths, abundant wildlife, and unique fishing history. Hay River, the Northwest Territories' second largest town, is located roughly halfway between Fort Resolution and Fort Providence. Known as the "Hub of the North," it is a welcoming community with a wide variety of visitor services and accommodation options, from lakeside campgrounds to first-class hotels. The wild shoreline west of Hay River leads you to the start of the Mackenzie River about 55 kilometres away. Just when you think you have left all big-water travelling behind you, the Mackenzie opens into massive Beaver Lake, lined with lush wetlands that have supported traditional fish, furbearer, and waterfowl harvesting activities for centuries. The Mackenzie narrows again at the Fort Providence Rapids, which offers some of the fastest, most enjoyable current on the river.

SMALL CRAFT WARNING!
At 480 kilometres long and over 100 wide, Great Slave Lake is an inland sea that is nothing to sneeze at in any kind of watercraft. The south shore is notoriously shallow, barely giving you enough water to thrust a paddle into until you are several hundred metres off shore. The result is that a strong onshore breeze can create dangerous rolling waves and ocean-type surf capable of swamping even the most skilled paddlers or boaters. As well, the shoreline offers little in the way of shelter from Fort Resolution to the mouth of the Mackenzie, 200 kilometres away. Hay River is the only other community on the south shore and, with 135 kilometres

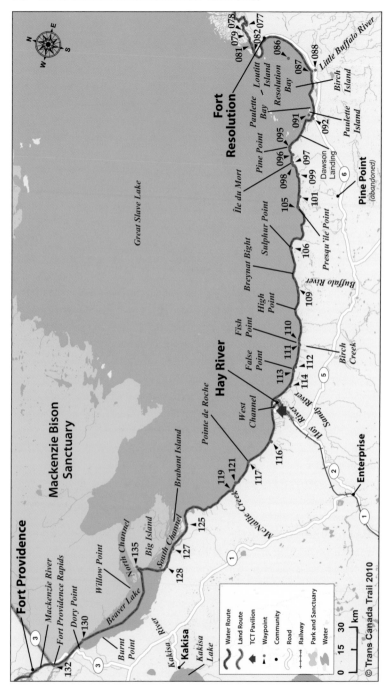

© Trans Canada Trail 2010

separating the two communities, don't even think of making a run for it if the weather looks at all threatening. Allow plenty of time to wait it out. Pack extra food and books. Chances are good you will need them. If you are canoeing, spray skirts are highly recommended for this crossing.

CAMPING TIPS

Camping options between Fort Resolution and Hay River range from broad pebble terraces to sprawling sandy beaches as yet undiscovered by

> ### Fearsome Waves on Great Slave
> Clayton Klein and Verlen Kruger,
> *One Incredible Journey*
>
> *At eleven A.M., we thought the wind was dying down a little, so we snugged our spray skirts up around us and pushed off to make the big traverse. Immediately we were into some pretty big swells, but handling them very well. About two miles out, the wind that we thought was dying down had only been resting up for a bigger blow! The huge swells started to crest on top, sometimes washing across our canoe. It got to be too much. Without any argument we headed back to the south side of Mission Island.*

the Northwest Territories tourism industry. They are marvelous. The most magnificent beaches are found several kilometres east and west of Hay River. Camping is also good on the lee side of most nearshore islands and in the occasional sheltered cove (usually marked on charts and maps). A word of caution: don't be drawn far away from shore to investigate camping options on some enchanting-looking island that beckons from the horizon. Ignore its siren call! The weather can change quickly on Great Slave Lake, making such trips foolhardy on even the cheeriest of days. The shoreline is loaded with driftwood, and dry firewood should be available in adjacent spruce forests even after a heavy rain. Camping is poor along the 20 kilometres of low, wet shoreline from High Point to False Point. Finding high, dry campsites is also challenging west of Pointe de Roche as you advance toward the Mackenzie River. Camping opportunities improve once you reach the South Channel of the Mackenzie. On the north shore of Beaver Lake, camping is virtually impossible due to its wide, unbroken wetland fringe. The south shore is much more amenable to camping, with its pronounced points offering the best sites.

St. Joseph Catholic Church, Fort Resolution

FORT RESOLUTION *(Deninu K'ue, or Moose Island)*
Population 575

Community

Fort Resolution is a small Chipewyan village about 155 kilometres east of Hay River on Highway 6. The oldest community in the Northwest Territories, it was established in 1786 when Cuthbert Grant of the Northwest Company built a trading post on the east side of the Slave River Delta. Strategically located at the junction of traditional water routes, it soon became the main gateway and supply base for the early northern fur trade. The community's

> ### Fort Resolution: A Northern Crossroads
> Bill Bell, *Beyond the Northern Lights, 1952*
>
> *Fort Resolution was established in 1786 as [the region's first] Northwest Company trading post, an organization that eventually merged with the Hudson's Bay Company after many years of fierce competition between the two rival firms. For well over one hundred years the village had been a crossroads for travellers in the North, including such historical figures as Peter Pond, Sir John Franklin, George Back, Warburton Pike, Ernest Thompson Seton and John Hornby.*

traditional Chipewyan name is Deninu K'ue, meaning Moose Island, named after a popular gathering place for moose on the delta's west side. The community moved to its present site in the 1820s. A Roman Catholic Mission was built in

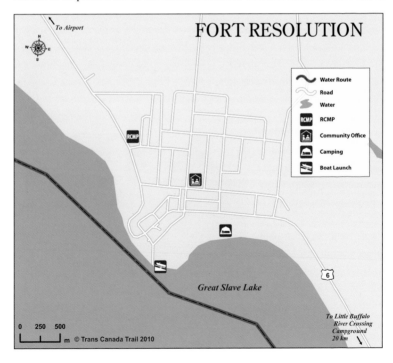

FORT RESOLUTION

To Airport

Water Route
Road
Water
RCMP
Community Office
Camping
Boat Launch

Great Slave Lake

6

To Little Buffalo River Crossing Campground 20 km

0 250 500
m © Trans Canada Trail 2010

1890, and an RCMP detachment arrived in 1913. The Oblates and Grey Nuns built a residential school and tuberculosis hospital in 1938. The rich forest of the Slave River Lowlands supports traditional hunting and trapping activities and, until recently, a local sawmill.

Geoff picks luscious strawberries at Dawson Landing

Visitor Information

✻ Deninu K'ue First Nation office, PO Box 1899, Fort Resolution, NT, X0E 0M0 (867-394-4335, fax 867-394-5122) or Deninoo Community office (867-394-4556, fax 867-394-4515).

Things to Do

✻ St. Joseph Catholic Church, built in 1925. Tour available on request (867-394-3303).

✻ Edjericon Bison Ranch. The Northwest Territories' only government bison ranch (130 animals) was founded just out of town on Portage Rd. It was established in the mid-1990s to quarantine and breed wild, disease-free bison for eventual restoration of herds in the Hook Lake area that were decimated by tuberculosis, brucellosis, and anthrax over the past 30 years.

✻ Mission Island. Take Airport Rd north, then first main left to visit an amazingly well-preserved nineteenth century mission building, the ancient cemetery behind it, and walk the pleasant shoreline trail that rims the "island."

✻ The Arbor. By the lakeshore, an outdoor community meeting place constructed from Slave River timbers. The plaques on its north side commemorate the 100th anniversary of Aboriginal Treaty #8, signed in Fort Resolution in 1900.

Accommodation

✻ J's Bed and Breakfast. Clean, comfortable singles and doubles, homey and hospitable, backcountry and aurora tours, fishing packages available. Box 231, Fort Resolution, NT, X0E 0M0 (867-394-3115, fax 867-394-3116, jbnb@northwestel.net, www.jbnb.ca).

✻ Hunter's B & B. Accommodates 5 guests in 4 rooms, laundry services, cable TV. General Delivery, Fort Resolution, NT, X0E 0M0 (867-394-4451).

Camping

* There is no formal campground in or near town. Short-term camping is possible in lakeside park with permission from Deninu Community office (867-394-4556, fax 867-394-4515).

* Little Buffalo River Crossing Territorial Park, 20 kilometres west of town on the Fort Resolution Highway (No. 6). Twelve non-powered campsites. Also accessible by water via Resolution Bay crossing and a short paddle upstream on Little Buffalo River. Open May 15–Sept 15 (800-661-0788, www.campingnwt.ca).

Outfitting/Hardware

* Northern Store. By the shore on Lakeview Rd. (867-394-4171).

Amenities

* Accommodation, restaurant, store, medical services, police, airport, gasoline, diesel, automotive service.

Tips

* Try the cinnamon rolls at Marg's Kitchen restaurant. Offers basic meals and local chat.

* The Deninu Community Hall sometimes offers traditional "country foods" from the land (867-394-3431).

The Most Beautiful River in the World

Ernest Thompson Seton, *The Arctic Prairies, 1911*

The Little Buffalo is the most beautiful river in the whole world except, perhaps, its affluent, the Nyarling. This statement sounds like exaggeration of mere impulsive utterance. Perhaps it is; but I am writing now after thinking the matter over for two and a half years, during which time I have seen a thousand others, including the upper Thames, the Afton, the Seine, the Arno, the Tiber, the Iser, the Spree, and the Rhine.

A hundred miles [160 kilometres] long is this uncharted stream; fifty feet [15 metres] its breadth of limpid tide; eight feet deep [2.5 metres], crystal clear, calm, slow, deep to the margin. A steamer could ply on its placid, unobstructed flood, a child could navigate it anywhere. The heavenly beauty of the shores, with virgin forest of fresh, green spruces towering a hundred feet [30 metres] on every side, or varied in open places with long rows and thick-set hedges of the gorgeous, wild, red Athabaska rose, made a stream that most woodmen, and naturalists would think without fault or flaw, and with every river beauty in its highest possible degree.

Emergency

✳ Hospital/Clinic (867-394-4511).

✳ RCMP (867-394-4111).

➤ ☠ ⚲ ⌂ 🦌 You will get your first full-on taste of Great Slave Lake's power as you paddle out into **Resolution Bay**, which offers all the shelter of a dinner plate rim. If a strong wind is blowing from the north or west, enjoy a few more hours of Fort Resolution hospitality before pushing off when the wind abates. We were fortunate to cross this 20-kilometre gap under clear, calm skies. In such conditions, you may spot distant **Louttit Island,** floating like a green zeppelin just above the horizon. This is a popular feeding roost for white pelicans. Farther on, **Birch Island**, a sheltered camp for local fishermen, may create a similar mirage. If making a beeline from Fort Resolution to **Little Buffalo River**, first aim for the highest ground visible

Tea time on Resolution Bay

from town. Then, as you get closer to the river, aim for the **fire tower** on the shoulder of the same hill. Paddling at an average speed of 6.6 kilometres per hour, we arrived at the mouth of the river in three hours. If you happen to be travelling by motorboat, beware of a nasty shoal a couple of kilometres offshore near [WP86]. The waters are very turbid here, and you will probably feel it before you see it.

➤ ⌂ ⌂ ⛺ 🏊 🦌 Our arrival at the mouth of the **Little Buffalo River** [WP87] was announced by a rising chorus of birds, including 50 Canada geese, several flocks of mallards and American wigeon, arctic terns, a northern harrier, and a profusion of bald eagles. As you approach the river, look for a vivid colour change in the water, from a milky brown to a deep blue. The clear, productive waters of the Little Buffalo attract a myriad of bird species. Take a few minutes to paddle upstream and enjoy the aquatic garden rimming both sides of the river—yellow pond lilies, Richardson's pondweed, and water smartweed with its spike of pink flowers breaking the surface. A sip of this water reveals a hint of brine, leached from the salt plains upstream. Besides crossing a clearwater boundary, a brief journey up the river takes you across a **latitudinal**

boundary, from 61° to 60°, the famed threshold marking Canada's "Far North." The Little Buffalo River is a traditional travel route between the Fort Smith region and Great Slave Lake and is still used today throughout the year. The river mouth is an important spawning area for several species of fish. Every Father's Day, fishermen from Fort Resolution gather here for the annual "Conny Contest," named after the inconnu that spawn here.

Fisherman's Credos
Signs in Eddy Lafferty's lodge
Early to bed
Early to rise
Fish all day
Make up lies.
Women love me.
Fish fear me.
Born to fish.
Forced to work.

One reason for all the eagles in the area is Eddy Lafferty, nicknamed "Eddy the Eagle," who owns and operates the **Det'an Cho Tourist Camp** a little over a kilometre upstream on the west bank [WP88]. In 1992 he plucked an injured bald eagle from the choppy waters of Great Slave Lake. Eddy hand-fed this bird, a female later named Goldie, for over three months. To this day, Goldie never strays far from Eddy, often accompanied by her extended family, and feeds within sight of the lodge. This cozy, family-friendly camp offers a 10-bed lodge, cabin rentals, a large tipi (adorned with eagles, of course), motorboat and canoe rentals, guided fishing services, a smokehouse, and various winter activities such as dogsledding and cross-country skiing. Meals can be provided by pre-arrangement. The lodge is accessible via a short gravel road from the Fort Resolution Highway (No. 6) (867-394-4411).

Eddy Lafferty points to "Goldie," the eagle he rescued from Great Slave Lake

Just south of the Fort Resolution Highway (No. 6) bridge is the **Little Buffalo River Crossing Territorial Park** on the east side of the Little Buffalo River. This park provides 12 non-powered campsites and is reported to be an excellent spot to reel in some nice pickerel or northern pike. Open May 15 to September 15. Contact Northwest Territories Tourism for more information (800-661-0788).

➤ 🏕 🏠 🔍 🐾 🏃 **Paulette Island**
[WP91] is one of the last major islands offering convenient shelter
or camping before you swing
around **Pine Point** to face 90 kilometres of island-less shore to Hay
River. A dagger-like point on the
north side of Paulette Island creates a protected cove, which may
provide suitable tent sites. If
windy, check out the south side of

Stashed fishing gear along the Great Slave shore

the island to explore a wider selection of camping options. **Paulette Bay** is an
important staging area for geese and tundra swans during the spring migration.
The red caboose and white-washed shacks parked on the mainland south of
Paulette Island [WP92] make up a **fish camp** regularly used by Hay River fishermen. A short gravel road connects this site to Highway 6.

➤ 🏕 🦫 🛁 Protected bays are few and far between along the south shore of
Great Slave Lake. Windy or not, **Dawson Landing**, on the southeast side of
Dawson Bay, is definitely worth a visit. This former fish-processing plant from
the 1950s offers excellent shelter, first-class tenting sites on huge grassy meadows, and a vivid glimpse of a once-thriving fishing industry. Remains of the
original plant include a huge
cement foundation, collapsing frame walls, an old log
cabin, a stalwart outhouse
that refuses to fall, and a
scattering of fish buckets and
nets. Sawdust piles remain,
formerly shipped in to insu-
late huge chunks of lake ice
to protect the fish harvest.
A more recently constructed
bunkhouse cum mess hall
and a few overturned dories
suggest that this site is
still used by local fishermen.
Gooseberries and raspberries
grow over the ruins, and a

> ### Pulling fish
>
> Bill Bell, *Northern Lights*, 1952
>
> *Our nets caught mostly whitefish, quite a few conies
> (inconnu), too many jackfish (pike) and ling (burbot), some
> pickerel and suckers and, very occasionally, a nice lake
> trout. Ling were unwelcome catches because they would roll
> around in the net and wrap many yards of it, preventing
> other fish from being caught in that section. When taking
> them out of the net, they would drape themselves around
> your arm like a big eel. Pike were even more unwelcome
> catches because, with their mouthful of sharp teeth, they
> could ruin large segments of net [and] your benumbed fin-
> gers as you fumbled to get the fish out. Conies were the
> largest fish caught, some so heavy that it was a difficult task
> to throw them from the canoe onto the dock.*

west-facing cobble beach presents a glorious sunset view.

➤ 🛶 🏊 🎒 🦌 Welcome to **Pine Point** [WP95], the northernmost mainland along the south shore of Great Slave Lake, and one of the first of many points on the way to Hay River, roughly 10 kilometres away. As you paddle around this point, take in the view of the last offshore islands you will see until the mouth of the Mackenzie River.

> **Big Sky Country**
>
> Myles Woodman, canoeist
>
> *The points are conveniently spaced apart in case the wind comes up. There are lots of good camping options. Plenty of firewood. The big sky is amazing. It's really a beautiful paddle. I love this shore.*

Bald eagles use these points as fishing and nesting sites, and you will likely flush one or two from every point you pass.

➤ 🔺 About four kilometres beyond Pine Point there is a nice **beach** [WP96] with a wide, flat, campable area behind it.

➤ ⛺ 🎒 🦌 **Île du Mort** [WP97] is not an island at all but a sharp point which, when approached from the east, looks like a fallen giant. Plan to stretch your legs here on the attractive limestone beach. A large navigation beacon affords a rare aerial view of Great Slave's vastness if you are prepared to negotiate its narrow metal ladder. A sturdy wooden helicopter pad offers a good tent site, but if you hear a helicopter closing in, you will quickly learn who has priority. The origin of this point's name — "Island of Death" — is unclear but local stories suggest that tribal tensions over fishing rights may have resulted in bloodshed at this site.

White pelicans soar over Île du Mort

➤ 🦌 About 1 kilometre southwest of Île du Mort is a tiny unmapped island that's prime real estate for about 50 **white pelicans** [WP98]. Though the nearest nest site is on the Slave River at the Fort Smith rapids, adult pelicans traditionally feed along Great Slave's south shore as far west as Fort Providence. Keep an eye out for their swirling aerial ballets.

➤ 🏠 🐫 🚶 A cloud of wheeling gulls may alert you to the presence of another **fish camp** [WP99]. White pelicans also love the smell of fish and are often observed wherever large numbers of gulls congregate. You may already have seen several floating flags marking commercial fishnets. It is at camps like this where the harvest is processed for market. Great Slave fishermen are a busy lot, but if you are hungry for an expertly filleted whitefish or two, they will gladly take your money. The old "**Waterline Road**" from the abandoned Pine Point lead-zinc mine connects this camp to Highway 6. This is the last direct contact with a major road until Hay River, 115 kilometres to the west.

Checking for whitecaps beyond Sulphur Point

➤ 🐫 Watch for another **white pelican** feeding roost on a small island just off-shore [WP101]. In mid-August, we observed 60 birds loafing on this site.

➤ 🔍 🐫 🦌 🏠 Once you reach **Presqu'ile Point** [WP105], if the winds are calm you may be tempted to chart a beeline to Sulphur Point 10 kilometres away. Don't. The wind on Great Slave can rise rapidly, with dangerous waves following soon after. Aim instead for the unnamed point midway between them, where you'll likely be rewarded with more pelican and eagle sightings, then veer east-northeast to Sulphur Point. You will likely see more net flags in these two large bays, which are extensively used by commercial fishermen.

➤ ⛺ 🐫 🛶 🐢 Great Slave's south shore offers many treasures, such as **Sulphur Cove** [WP106]. Though spelled oddly, this area is named for the sulfur springs that leak into this cove—you can smell it in the air. There are actually two "coves." The western one offers the most shelter and the

A night to remember at Sulphur Cove

Julian muses over abandoned fish camp, Sulphur Cove

best camping on a smooth gravel beach piled high with driftwood. Part of each cove is rimmed with rich marshland that attracts ducks, and the sheltered coves also draw in pelicans and bald eagles. If you find a tall, curving pile of driftwood on the beach, don't burn it—it's a hunter's duck blind. On the western side of the western cove is an abandoned fish camp, consisting of two well-preserved cabins dating back to the 1950s. There is a **navigation beacon** on **Sulphur Point**.

➤ Sulphur Point marks the beginning of what our canoe party dubbed the "**Great Slave Riviera**." Extending 20 kilometres west to **High Point**, this stretch of shoreline offers lovely pebble beaches suitable for camping, loafing, or lunching. A few small islets just east of **Breynat Bight** also looked promising. Where the beaches are not as flat as you might like, they can be easily made so with a driftwood rake.

➤ The mouth of the **Buffalo River** [WP109] is stunningly beautiful. A

Drowned Rats on Great Slave

Mabel Bourne, Hay River resident and newlywed, 1999

My first boat ride on Great Slave Lake, Billy took me in a skiff for a picnic. We took some wieners and pop and stuff. Coming back the wind flared up. The waves are pretty high and I'm scared stiff. He said, "We'll go further out and I'll come back in at an angle." I said, "No, no, no, because the waves will be higher over there. I'm going to jump off and walk in." He said, "You crazy fool, you'll drown." You know, I jumped off the boat. I did. Thank God I hit a sandbar and I walked ashore on the beach ... He saw I was walking on sand, so he jumped out too and pulled the boat behind him. We hit the bush and tied up the boat. The bush was really congested with all kinds of undergrowth. The mosquitoes were terrible. We were wet. Bulldog flies were after us. We walked on the road and as soon as we heard a vehicle we'd dive into the bush and hide. We looked like drowned rats. Bill was embarrassed and didn't want anyone to know what a dumb thing happened.

small sand-rimmed island at the outflow provides an excellent spot to rest or camp. There is an active fishing cabin on river-left and an older cabin on the other side that may have been impounded by a black bear. As you approach the river mouth, watch for a distinct change in the water colour. The milk-tea shade of the lake gives way to the river's strawberry-brown silts, derived from a distinctive reddish sandstone. You may also detect the strong scent of sulfur from upstream springs. Originating in **Buffalo Lake**, 60 kilometres to the south, the Buffalo River (sometimes called the "Big Buffalo") has been a traditional route for Hay River Dene

> ### Bear Lodge
> Andrea Bettger, Hay River resident
>
> *It was fun paddling all the way down the Buffalo River then seeing this old cabin with a bear sitting on the front steps. It seemed to be ruling over its own private fishing lodge. It casually watched us as we paddled by. While eating lunch on the island at the mouth of the river, we saw it swim across, maybe drawn by the fish smells from the other cabin. The bear climbed out of the water near us but we scared it back in and watched it drift with the current over to the opposite shore.*

people for hundreds of years. They often wintered at Buffalo Lake, hunting and trapping there, then came down the river in the spring with a rich harvest of furs to trade.

If you are seeking only a weekend taste of this part of the Trans Canada Trail, a trip down the **Buffalo River** then west along the lakeshore to Hay River is a good choice. The 20-kilometre stretch of river from Highway 5 to Great Slave can be comfortably done in about five hours. Seven kilometres north of the road, on river-left, you will encounter the **Mellor Rapids**, created by a reddish sandstone ledge. The main current flows through a gradual shoot on river-right with a few easily negotiated standing waves. However, because of great variability in water levels, scouting from the left bank above the rapids is highly recommended. Some upstream ferrying may be needed to line yourself up for a safe descent. Alternately, you can access a short portage on the west side. As for camping, there are plenty of adequate campsites from the bridge down to the fork in the river created by a large island about 5

Celebrating calm waters along Great Slave's south shore

kilometres from the lake. Beyond this, the banks become wetter and brushier—not suitable for camping—but you will find prime beach camping at the mouth. For the last few kilometres, the river presents you with a fun set of Class 1 rapids. As you paddle down the river, note the yellow-stained, sulfur-rich rivulets flowing in from both banks. If you don't have your own gear or need a ride to the bridge, contact Doug Swallow of Canoe North in Hay River at 867-874-6402.

Mike and Andrea welcome us to Buffalo River

➤ 🏠 **High Point** marks the beginning of a swampy 20-kilometre-long stretch of shoreline that offers virtually no camping options or firewood. We called this Great Slave's "Black Lagoon." Things quickly look up once you pass **False Point**, where some amazing beaches begin.

➤ 😃 One of the toughest challenges of our trip was trying to walk to a spooky, long-abandoned fishing camp on **Fish Point** [WP110]. Though it lies only a few metres from shore, the tangled overgrowth and storm-tossed logs make hiking treacherous. Although the main cabin looks like a giant jumped on it, clean kitchen implements still hang on the wall and there is a tidy plastic cover over the bed—as if the owners just went to town for groceries.

The Queen of all Steamers

Griffith Taylor, Geography professor, 1944

The Hudson's Bay Company has about a dozen steamers on the Mackenzie River and its tributaries, of which the SS Distributor *is the largest. This boat makes two or three round trips to the Arctic Ocean, depending on the character of the season ... The total fare for passage, cabin, and meals for this five week journey was $330.50; which seems reasonable in view of the tremendous distance all our food was brought. The boat was crowded but comfortable, with a nice ship's library; and the food was excellent, there being no [wartime] rationing north of latitude 60° N.*

Glenbow Archives NA-3394-65

➤ 🏕 🚶 🦌 **Birch Creek** [WP 111] is described by local paddlers as a "slow but pretty day trip" if you are considering a short water-based tour through the Hay River hinterland. Its clear water and marsh-rimmed banks attract many ducks, muskrat, and beavers. You might even spot a bear or moose during your lazy paddle to the big lake. There is a cabin on river-left near the creek mouth. There is no camping between Birch

West Coast Rival

Geoff Ray, canoeist, after a short round of beach golf

These beaches are amazing! Why didn't anybody tell me about this place. This shoreline could rival anything along the west coast.

Creek and False Point, 10 kilometres to the west, so if you must camp in the cleared area around the cabin, please treat it with the greatest respect. Like the Buffalo River, Birch Creek is accessible from a bridge on Highway 5. The earlier in the season the better, as low water levels and/or beaver dams may impede your progress later on. For logistical help, contact Doug Swallow of Canoe North in Hay River at 867-874-6402.

➤ 🏕 🚢 🧰 As eager as you might be to paddle in to Hay River for that warm bath or ice cream cone, the sprawling 10-kilometre sand beach between **False Point** [WP112] and town may slow you down. It's gorgeous. Remember though, that the wind can come up quickly. The flattest, most sheltered tent sites are amidst the tall white spruce and stabilized sand dunes that line the beach.

Picnic on a pebble beach, Great Slave Riviera

➤ About 1 kilometre west of False Point, keep your eyes peeled for a thrilling bit of history: the mammoth spokes from a great paddle-wheel steamship that plied the Mackenzie and Slave rivers between 1920 and the mid-1950s [WP113]. It was here that the ship became stuck in the mud for the last time.

➤ The **Sandy River** [WP114] flows through the heart of the K'atloodeeche First Nation, the only Northwest Territories reserve, established in 1973. Good fishing and a wide, smooth beach make the river mouth an attractive place to stop before paddling the last seven kilometres to Hay River. In high spring waters, this river offers a potentially scenic side trip past some of the biggest white spruce trees in the region. A primitive road to town begins on the river mouth's west bank and parallels the lakeshore. This site, a traditional fish camp for thousands of years, is now regularly used for camping and outdoor education activities by the Hay River Reserve school.

HAY RIVER
Population 3,835

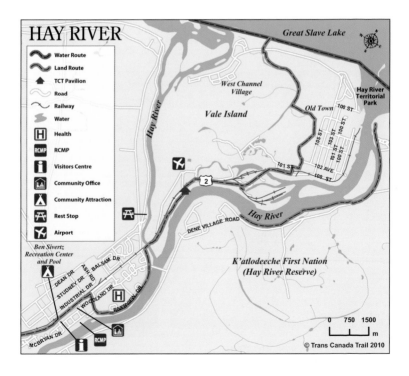

Community

Located 200 air kilometres southwest of Yellowknife and 134 kilometres from the Alberta border via the Mackenzie Highway, Hay River is the biggest community in the South Slave region. Though recent archaeological discoveries suggest centuries-long occupation of the Hay River mouth by a variety of Aboriginal people, the community itself is a late bloomer on the northern map. It wasn't until 1868 that a Hudson's Bay Company trading post and Roman Catholic mission were established on the east bank of the river. Within 10 years, both had closed their doors but a Slavey community, led by revered chief Founder Chiatlo, eventually took root. In 1892 he invited the Anglican Mission to what is now the Old Village area in the Hay River Dene Reserve. The community gradually expanded and by 1939, the northern trade route through Hay River had supplanted the traditional one down the Slave River. Completion of an all-weather road from the south in 1948 and the opening of Pine Point lead-zinc mine in 1951 accelerated the town's growth and commercial prominence. Commercial fishing boomed in the 1950s and early 1960s, at its peak boasting nine major buyers and processing plants, most of them located on the West Channel of Vale Island. Regulatory changes eventually soured the economic climate for this industry that now con-

---

Hay River: Hub of the North

Vicky LaTour, *A Brief History of the Port Town of Hay River*

If there was one event in the last 60 years which really hastened change in the NWT it was the onset of World War II. Hay River particularly became a focus of such change, largely because of its geographical position on the banks of the river and the sandy, southwest shore of Great Slave Lake. The community lies some 130 km (80 miles) from the Alberta border, and less than 100 km (55 miles) from the start of the Mackenzie River at the western end of the lake. It was a good jumping-off place for flights down the Mackenzie Valley; it had a good harbour—and it lay pretty much in the path of the winter tractor road which had been pushed through in 1939 from Grimshaw in the Peace River country of Alberta in order to get supplies into Yellowknife where gold mining was fast putting that community on the national map.

Hay River to the Mackenzie, final leg across Great Slave Lake

tinues on a much smaller scale. Locals report that there is still good fishing along this channel.

Hay River remains a busy transportation hub with supply barges regularly setting out for remote communities and hydrocarbon facilities down the Mackenzie Valley. You will hear people speak of two distinct areas, "Old Town" at the north end of Vale Island and the newer uptown section rimmed by the highway. Much of the for-

St. Peter's Anglican church, 1893, Old Village, Hay River Reserve

mer is a deltaic structure averaging three metres or less above the water and is therefore highly flood-prone during the surge of spring breakup. A whopper of a flood in 1963 covered much of Vale Island, but residents and businesses continue to call this special part of town home.

Visitor Information

✳ Visitor Information Centre is at Mackenzie Highway and McBryan Dr., open 9 AM–9 PM daily from May 15–Sept 15 (867-874-3180).

✳ Town of Hay River, 73 Woodland Dr., Hay River, NT, X0E 1G1 (year-round

---

Totally, Royally Spoiled

Hay River resident, Joy Stewart, gives a kid's-eye view of Hay River's fishing industry in its glory days.

That's where my love for fishermen and the fisheries came in. I was probably three or four. I remember the big companies—the Menzies', the Carter's, and the Trefiak's. I had my fish boots. They were little gumboots, not cool, not rolled down, gumboots, poker straight up. I think my dad was fairly smart. Most of these men didn't have their families with them. How bad could a fish inspector be when behind him toddled this little three or four year old? I ended up knowing all the fishermen by name. I was right there when they were filleting. I remember the huge production that would come through those doors. There was the smell of fresh fish and ice and cold, the smell of the cook camps and the cookies coming out of the oven and being totally, royally spoiled as a little girl going into those camps and treated so respectfully. I'm sure a lot of them were dads and I reminded them of home …

I remember the fishery as being very big. You can't look at Hay River and see that now. I think that's a real shame. There were very big companies. The fish would just pour in, and a lot of men. Big, big crews. That's one of my first memories in Hay River. That would have been about 1952.

867-874-6522, summer hotline 867-874-3180, fax 867-874-3237, www.hayriver.com).

Things to Do

* Visit the Trans Canada Trail Pavilion, located on the Hay River Trail halfway between Old Town on Vale Island and uptown. It is on the east side of the Mackenzie Highway, opposite the entrance to the Hay River Airport. One of 86-red roofed Trail pavilions across the country, it acknowledges the contributions of local donors and supporters. The Hay River Trail begins on the shore of Great Slave Lake and is a primarily flat 9-kilometre route suitable for cycling and hiking.

* The broad, sandy beach on Vale Island is lovely, and you can fish in the surf.

* Several kilometres of trails wind along the town side of the river (Kiwanis Trail) and across Vale Island. Easy access behind the school grounds or Visitor Centre.

* Vale Island Snye, a landlocked ancient channel of the Hay River about 4 kilometres long, offers a peaceful paddle out of the wind with abundant wildlife and birds. Located close to the Hay River Campground. Access from canoe dock at north end of snye a few metres off Mackenzie Highway or portage in via trail from 105 St.

* West Channel Village, on the west shore of Vale Island at the mouth of the Hay River, was founded during the town's fishing heyday and is now the commercial fishing headquarters for Great Slave Lake. Watch for "Fish for Sale" signs for some of the freshest, cleanest fish on earth.

* Hay River Heritage Centre. Recently opened historical museum housed in the former Hudson's Bay Com-

> **South Shore Charm**
>
> Diana Ehman, former Mayor of Hay River
>
> *Coming from British Columbia, it took me a while to appreciate the charm of the Hay River landscape and surrounding lakeshore. It's not like the mountains where every view quickly changes as you move along. The beauty here is more subtle. What really gets me is the vastness. The tranquility and the primeval vastness.*

Riverside grave marking sacred ground, Hay River Reserve

pany store. Eclectic collection of Native and non-Native artifacts from south of Great Slave, artistic performances, and displays. Contact Hay River Museum Society for schedule and programs, 39 Lakeshore Dr., NT, X0E 0R9 (867-874-3539).

✳ The Dene Cultural Institute, on the Reserve side of the river, offers tours of the Hay River Native Reserve including the Old Village and its historic churches, Hudson's Bay buildings, and traditional cemetery (by appointment only). Several insightful displays on Dene culture. Open 1 PM–5 PM Mon–Fri, May–Sept. Admission free (867-874-8480, www.deneculture.org).

✳ Fisherman's Wharf. Colourful outdoor market open every Sat, 10 AM–2 PM, May–Sept. South end of 100 Ave. on Vale Island.

✳ Vale Island shipyard. Visit dry-docked tugboats and massive boat lift. Phone Northern Transportation Company Limited to arrange tour (867-874-5100).

✳ Mackenzie Place apartment building. 17-storey oddball in the

Basking on a subarctic beach, Hay River Territorial Park

middle of downtown provides amazing views of West Channel Village, the vast boreal forest, and Great Slave Lake. Ask about access at Visitor's Centre (867-874-3180).

Accommodation

✳ Harbour House Bed & Breakfast on Vale Island. Comfortable rooms, right next to beach. Common kitchen, living area, and washrooms. Likely the best value in town. 101-31 Capital Dr., NT, X0E 1G2 (867-874-2233, greenway@ssimi-cro.com). If full, try The Anchorage, which is nearby and under same management.

✳ Ptarmigan Inn Hotel. 42 basic rooms with private bath, pub, dining lounge, restaurant. 101 Gagnier St., NT, X0E 1G1 (867-874-6781).

✳ Caribou Motor Inn. 29 rooms with kitchenettes, some with whirlpool or steambath. Restaurant and lounge next door (867-874-6706).

✳ Migrator Motel. 24 rooms, suites, and kitchenettes, 912 Mackenzie Highway, Hay River, NT, X0E 0R8 (867-874-6792).

✳ Cedar Rest Motel. 29 units with 12 kitchenettes, waterbeds, laundry, TV, store, propane. Box 540, Hay River, NT, X0E 0R3 (867-874-3732).

* Homesteaders Inn. Mile 5 Mackenzie Highway (867-874-4479).

Camping

* Hay River Territorial Park. Lovely beach park located on Vale Island at the mouth of the Hay River; 35 powered camp-

Retired tugboat, Vale Island

sites connected to the beach by trails. Full services including showers, kitchen shelters, firewood, playground, volleyball nets, and boat launch. Open May 15– Sept 15 (867-874-3772, www.campingnwt.ca).

* Paradise Garden & Campground, 24 kilometres south of town just off Highway 2. Delightful open setting on a sweeping bend of the Hay River. Tent and RV sites, locally grown organic produce sold in summer. Kitchen facility (867-875-4430, Paradisegarden@northwestel.net, www.paradisegarden.piczo.com).

Outfitting/Hardware

* Canoe North. Canoe and kayak rental/sales, managed by Doug Swallow. Can arrange out-trip drop-offs or pickups to destinations near (e.g., Vale Island beach) and far (e.g., Fort Simpson). Can also outfit your entire trip from canoes to satellite phones and arrange equipment return to Hay River. Ask about half- and full-day side trips on the Hay River. 47 Studney Dr., Hay River, NT, X0E 0R6 (867-874-6337, fax 867-874-3866, www.canoenorth.ca).

* Wright's Home Hardware, 70 Industrial Dr., (867-874-6722).

Amenities

* Accommodation, restaurants, store, bank, bank machine, visitor information, pharmacy, medical services, police, airport, gasoline, diesel, propane, automotive service.

Fisherman and guide, Shawn Buckley (kneeling), and friends

Tips

✳ Shoreline Café, downtown on Courtorielle St., offers specialty coffees, lattes, smoothies, Italian sodas, and light wholesome meals (867-874-3760). Try Joey's Sweets 'N Things downtown on Courtorielle St. (867-874-3300).

✳ Woodshed Garden Café at 16 Studney Dr., specialty beverages, gourmet desserts, Internet access (867-874-4581).

✳ Other local eating favourites, from least to most fancy, include the Hay River Bakery (867-874-2322), Board Room Restaurant (867-874-2111), and Back Eddy Lounge (867-874-6680).

✳ Contact local fisherman and raconteur Shawn Buckley about a Great Slave Lake tour or commercial fishing trip in his 42-foot boat (867-874-3617).

✳ The Northwest Territories Centennial Library offers free Internet access.

Emergency

✳ Hospital/Clinic (867-874-7100)

✳ RCMP (867-874-6555)

➤ 🔍 ☠ 🏕 ⛰ The first good stretch of beach you pass beyond **West Channel** is known variously as "New Beach" or "Nude Beach" (you can do your own research). You will reach the end of Hay River's famous sand beaches at **Six Mile Creek** [WP116]. They quickly dwindle westward, as do driftwood and dry,

Checking for campsites beyond Six Mile Creek

sheltered campsites. Wide, virtually impenetrable marshes dominate the shoreline from here to the Mackenzie River. These wetlands are, however, attractive to ducks, geese, and shorebirds. The water gets shallower along here and you may find you have to go farther from shore to get a decent sweep with your paddle. Beware of large breakers in even the lightest north winds. The water gradually clears as you head west, and you will likely see bald eagles, ospreys, arctic terns, Caspian terns, common mergansers, and common loons—all fish-eaters that prefer to feed in transparent waters. Six Mile Creek is a popular destination for Hay River fishermen in early summer when the pickerel and whitefish are running.

➤ 🏠 🏚 😊 🛶 Along a stretch of lakeshore starved for shelter and dry land, **Pointe de Roche** [WP117] comes as a welcome relief, and you can't possibly miss it. A navigation beacon stands tall above the point. Smooth pebble beaches, lots of driftwood, abundant raspberry bushes, large gla-

Spokes from the SS *Distributor's* giant paddle-wheel

cially ground erratics, and dry grassy clearings near the base of the beacon make this an attractive place for a lunch stop or campsite. You certainly won't be the first. Numerous fire rings speak of a long history of use. Several cabins and tent frames on either side of the point are used as a base for hunting and fishing in and around nearby cattail marshes that attract ducks, Sandhill cranes, and white pelicans. In very light winds, we paddled directly from Hay River to Pointe de Roche in four hours.

➤ 🏠 🏚 The small **island cluster** [WP121] marks your last chance to camp for the next 30 kilometres until you reach the mouth of the Mackenzie. These islands offer more pebble beach tent sites and good shelter. There is a traditional camp used by local fishermen and hunters at the west end of the largest island, marked by a bicycle wheel antenna propped on a pole.

> **Travels on Beaver Lake**
>
> Marie T. Gargan, Fort Providence
>
> *My husband and I have travelled far [from Fort Providence] to Kakisa and to Beaver Lake. The women used to walk along the shore while the men went by boat. They would always arrive long before we did. Some women used to pack babies on their backs. I don't think you could do that now!*

➤ 🏔 🎒 🛶 Watch for the marshy mouth of **McNallie Creek** at [WP119], an important habitat for ducks and several species of spawning fish, particularly pike and pickerel. Although this creek is not navigable from the Highway 1 bridge, if your rubber-tire travels take you along that route, stop at the **McNallie Creek Picnic Area** to enjoy views of a 17-metre waterfall and dramatic creekside cliffs.

➤ 🏠 🌊 🛶 The welcome pull of current signals that you have entered the mouth of the mighty Mackenzie, Canada's longest river. Just 80 kilometres to Fort Providence and about 1,740 kilometres until you spill out into the Arctic Ocean! Upon entering the river, our average speed jumped from 5.5 to 8 kilometres per hour. Camping options do not improve until you enter the river's **South Channel**, after which the wetlands give way to occasional gravel beaches and promising riverside clearings among the spruce. You may spot some of the last western vanguards of **white pelicans**,

Footprint of an intense forest fire, South Channel

which occasionally feed on the upper Mackenzie River. Throughout the month of May, the mouth of this river acts as a giant funnel for thousands of ducks, geese, and swans migrating to their Arctic breeding grounds.

The first telltale sign of a major **forest fire** is evident at [WP125]. Behind this distinct gap in the riverside forest is a massive burn scar that stretches far south and west. These scars become more pronounced as you paddle the next few kilometres along the South Channel's southern bank. Take a moment to get out and explore one of these sites. The charred remains and lush regrowth tell an age-old story of destruction and regeneration.

There is a first-class fishing lodge on **Brabant Island** on the north side of this channel that should only be visited in an emergency. If you would like to make this a stop along your journey, contact the owners, Ellen and John Pollard of Hay River, well in advance, at 867-874-2600. For more information, visit their Web site at www.brabantlodge.com.

> ### Struggles on Big Island
> Margaret Sabourin Sr., Fort Providence
>
> *When I was a child I lived in a house on the shore of Big Island. Once when we were out hunting in the bush, our house burnt down and we lost all our possessions. When my father went trapping that autumn he had to use deadfalls, as all his traps were lost in the fire. We rebuilt our home using the same logs again, only with the outside peeled off. The roof was flat and covered with moss and mud. We used old flour bags for windows.*
>
> *In spring we caught and dried fish and stacked it in our house for the winter. In summer we went hunting. No one ever complained about the mosquitoes. We had nothing to protect us from them. We didn't even have a decent blanket. When it rained, we sheltered under the branches. We seldom used a tent in the bush.*

➤ 🛏 🏠 ⛴ There is a prime picnic spot on river-left at [WP127] with several sturdy tables, a relatively bug-free clearing, a beautiful swimming beach, and an outhouse. As tempting as it may be to camp here, this site is regularly visited and maintained by Brabant Lodge, the guests of which have preferential use.

➤ 🔍 💧 The narrow channel south of the **island cluster** at [WP128] is a scenic, sheltered option before negotiating the expanse of Beaver Lake. This route is shallow and becomes increasingly weedy over the summer. It is a very popular hangout for ducks.

➤ 🛏 🔍 ☠ Beaver Lake may come as a bit of a surprise if you have become attached to the idea that you are now paddling a river. Beaver

> **When the River Rules the Road**
>
> Indian and Northern Affairs'
>
> *Backgrounder: Dehcho Bridge*
>
> *The [Fort Providence] crossing is closed for an average of 4 weeks during spring break-up. Service is also interrupted with little notice for 1 to 3 weeks in the fall and early winter, due to low water levels and ice jams and while the ice forms sufficiently to cut the ferry channel. During these periods of isolation, there is no road connection between the region and southern Canada. Any passenger traffic must be by air. Freight traffic to the region is also interrupted. Some freight is trucked to the river, transferred onto slings and shuttled by helicopter across the river where it is loaded onto other trucks and transported onward by road.*

Merv Hardie ferry

Lake is vast, reaching a width of 10 kilometres. It can throw as many tricks at you as Great Slave. Northerly winds may inspire you to cross the South Channel and seek shelter in the lee of **Big Island** and Beaver Lake's north shore. If you choose this course, be forewarned: there is absolutely no camping along the north shore. If you thought the marshes lining Great Slave's southwest shore were endless, wait until you see the north side of Beaver Lake! Make sure you have enough daylight to at least get back into the river where dry riverbanks resume. Also, beware of strong currents flowing out of the **North**

Bull bison grunts us out of our tents near Willow Point

Channel which, when combined with any significant wind, can create wonky, dangerous waves.

> Though little is visible on the ground, there was once quite a collection of buildings on the western end of **Big Island** [WP135]. This is the site of the first Roman Catholic Mission in the region, which was moved to present-day Fort Providence in 1861.

> **Willow Point** marks the southernmost boundary of the **Mackenzie Bison Sanctuary**.

Hay River mayor, Diana Ehman, foiled by marshlands lining Beaver Lake's north shore

This wildlife reserve covers 10,000 square kilometres and contains the world's largest wild wood bison herd of about 2,000 animals. Established in 1963, it represents the first successful transplant of healthy wood bison into their historic range. If you paddle this route you might spot a small herd grazing in the wet sedge meadows lining the north shore of Beaver Lake.

> The mouth of the **Kakisa River** is a traditional fishing area for the people of **Kakisa**, particularly for pickerel, pike, and whitefish. A short paddle upstream brings you to higher, drier ground suitable for camping—a good place to watch for the river mouth's abundant ducks, beavers, and muskrat.

> The south shore of **Beaver Lake** is by far the wisest camping choice. Though there are still long stretches of marshy shoreline, there are lots of excellent camping options from the mouth of the **Kakisa River** westwards, especially at **Burnt Point** and **Dory Point**, the latter of which is a modest territorial park offering picnic tables, a kitchen shelter, and outhouses. The **winter ice road crossing** at [WP130] is another easy-to-find option.

An intense case of speed intoxication on the Fort Providence Rapids

➤🏠 Four kilometres downstream from Dory Point is the Merv Hardie **ferry crossing**, which operates from late May, except between midnight and 6 AM, and closes for the season when the upstream ice bridge takes over. The crossing is closed for several weeks during spring breakup and fall freeze-up, when neither system is up and running. The proposed multi-million-dollar Dehcho Bridge across the river may soon end this era of our northern frontier.

➤🔍 ☠️ 🚣 However far you have paddled to this point, the **Fort Providence Rapids** [WP132] come as a welcome reward for surviving Beaver Lake. As you

Eagle's-eye view of Fort Providence, looking upriver (GNWT)

approach the **Providence Narrows**, watch out for shallow water with numerous boulders and gravel ledges. Beyond this, the rapids themselves are quite deep, posing no obstacles to your fast and free flow into town. At the beginning of the rapids, our average speed jumped from 8.5 kilometres per hour to 12.5 kilo-

metres per hour. At their narrowest, we maxed out at a breathtaking 21.4 kilometres per hour as the bobbing channel buoys streaked past us like Sea-Doos charging upstream. Keep control of your boat and your eyes on the water. The main hazard of these rapids is speed intoxication.

Still life canoe by Diana Ehman

➤🚶 Within the town of **Fort Providence**, the best access points to off-load or load your boat are a set of cement stairs behind the **Snowshoe Inn**, which come directly down to the river—a steep but direct option—or the community boat launch at the **Mission Dock** just downstream from the big white church.

APPROXIMATE DISTANCE 300 kilometres

HIGHLIGHTS

* Fort Providence Mission's history, unique handicrafts, riverside trail
* Waterfowl on Mills Lake
* Historic military base remains at Axe Point
* Traditional community of Jean Marie River
* Current boosts at Head-of-the-line and Green Island

Relics found beneath Our Lady of Providence Church

* Historic sawmill and trading post at Spence River
* Fishing, swimming, and whitewater fun on the Rabbitskin River
* Confluence with the great Liard River just above Fort Simpson

OVERVIEW

The Mackenzie is the Northwest Territories' most accessible river. Visitors lacking the time to travel its entire length can choose to visit or omit any of the nine communities along the route. Fort Providence is the most popular put-in point. Though the current is relatively slow for this portion of the river, the trip from Providence to Simpson makes for an easy week-long paddle with ample time for relaxing, fishing, or exploring tributaries along the way.

CAMPING TIPS

A low, sandy island just before you enter Mills Lake [WP172] makes for a good campsite, especially if you are waiting out strong winds. Camping is poor along the marshy shores of Mills Lake but improves from about Axe Point [WP177] onwards. Some of the best campsites are found at the mouths of the many creeks and rivers that flow into the Mackenzie from either bank. Excellent campsites like Brownings Landing will quickly erase any wind or weather troubles you may encounter.

Riverside Trail, Fort Providence

© Trans Canada Trail 2010

FORT PROVIDENCE *(Zhahti Kue, South Slavey for "mission house place")*
Population 840

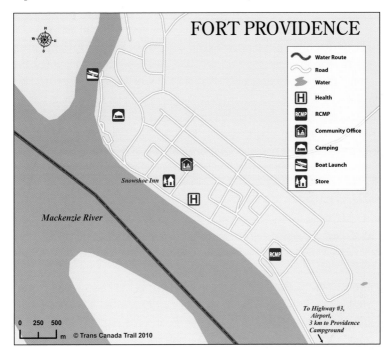

5

Community

Whether paddling, biking, or driving into Fort Providence, you will likely be struck by the tall white spire of the grand old Catholic church and the farm-like openness of the adjoining mission fields. Soon after the Oblates arrived here in 1861 and built a Roman Catholic Mission, this flat, fertile land was carpeted with potatoes and grain crops that fed other missions up and down the Mackenzie Valley. The Hudson's Bay boys followed close on their heels, establishing a post in 1867, the same year that the RCMP and Grey Nuns set up shop. Slavey Dene were drawn to the area, and their youngsters were soon reciting French in the Northwest Territories' first school, established by the Grey Nuns. The missionaries

Canoe regatta, Fort Providence

were a prominent force in Fort Providence for 90 years until 1958, when education and other public services came under government jurisdiction.

In the late 1950s, construction of the Mackenzie Highway and a ferry crossing just upstream from Fort Providence established the town as one of the Northwest Territories major transportation hubs. This economy is supported today by steady hotel business, road maintenance activities, traditional crafts, and forest-fire fighting. Trapping, hunting, and fishing are still very much part of the fabric of life here.

Visitor Information

✳ Some literature and Web sites indicate a visitor centre beside the river, but it has since been closed. Contact the Hamlet office for information (867-699-3441).

Things to Do

✳ A walk along the riverbank trail is a must to take in the Mackenzie River's ever-changing personality and the unique pastoral setting of the town.

✳ Several kilometres of pleasant hiking trails (or ski trails) branch off just north of the community campground picnic tables.

✳ If you haven't yet seen a wood bison, your chances will improve with your arrival in Fort Providence, the bison capital of the Northwest Territories. You may see small herds of them grazing on the lush grasses of the mission fields while mothers pushing baby strollers amble by nonchalantly. Give the bison ample space.

✳ Our Lady of Providence Church, built in the 1920s, is an arresting sight both inside and out. The spire cross is a popular roost for ravens, while cliff swallows decorate the church's topmost eaves with their nests. Contact the rectory office for a tour (867-699-4361).

✳ The large rock plunked in the middle of the Mission fields commemorates a visit by Queen Elizabeth in 1978. The prominent cross marks the centennial of the arrival of Oblates in 1858 and the Grey Nuns nine years later. Another riverside plaque pays homage to

Community barbecue celebrating the Trans Canada Trail, Fort Providence

Alexander Mackenzie's famous float-by in 1789, which opened up the Mackenzie Valley to fur trading.

✳ There are two interesting cemeteries, both of which are worth a respectful visit. The formal one, on the east end of the mission fields, is a memorial site dedicated to the memory of local Dene and Métis elders and to the children who attended the mission residential school. The other, a community cemetery, lies just north of the community campground behind a line of poplars and resonates with local history.

✳ Dene Fur Clouds is a unique northern business that has transformed a traditional local craft into stylish yet functional clothing of international repute. The main draw is sheared beaver fur that is knitted into remarkably warm and colourful accessories, clothing, and blankets. Visit the small gift shop stocked with other fine craftwork, and ask to see how this amazing fabric is created in the adjoining workshop. It is located behind the Band Office marked by a one-word sign, *Ek'o*, the Slavey word for "watch out!" (867-699-4922, denefur@ssimicro.com, www.ek-o.net).

> **Mashed Potatoes over Mills Lake**
>
> Lyn Hancock, *The Mighty Mackenzie*
>
> *North and west of Fort Providence the river widens into Mills Lake, a giant bulge 11 miles wide and anywhere from 15–30 miles long [24–48 kilometres]. Here the boatman is subjected to sudden storms and squalls. As soon as the fluffy mounds of mashed-potato type clouds darken to create angry anvil shapes streaked later by lightning and emitting ominous thunderclaps, then one must seek comfort from the onslaught of sluicing rain ashore.*

Accommodation

✳ Big River Motel and Service Centre, 3 kilometres from Fort Providence on the river's north side just downstream from the ferry crossing, near the intersection of Highway 3 and town access road. Basic rooms adjoining one of the north's busiest service stations, café, and small store (867-699-4301).

✳ Snowshoe Inn, on Riverside Dr. in the town centre across from Aurora Market. Clean, modern rooms; café, gift shop, dining room, and lounge (867-699-3511, snowshoe@ssimicro.com).

Paddler's pie made from wild gooseberries and cranberries

Camping

✳ Fort Providence Territorial Park, 2 kilo-metres west, along the access road to Fort Providence. Twenty-one non-pow-ered campsites on the bank of the Mackenzie River. Well-maintained and equipped, playground, kitchen shelters. Great sunset viewing, bird watching, and fishing. Downside: 3 kilometres from town, not visible from the river, and direct river access virtually impossible due to steep banks. Open May 15–Sept 15 (867-874-6702, www.campingnwt.ca).

✳ Fort Providence Community Camp-ground, located on large field near the Catholic church and public dock. Picnic tables and outhouses. Popular local pic-nic area and visitors are welcome to camp at no cost.

> ### Warplanes Stashed in the Hills
>
> *Ask local river people about Axe Point, and you may hear the story about how the Amer-icans may have stashed two P47 Thunder-bolt fighter-bombers somewhere along the old winter road to Norman Wells. Then again, it may have been a couple of Vought F4U Corsairs—nobody's sure about any of this. Whatever they were, the warplanes are said to sit, with folded wings, in a hollowed-out cave along the base of the Horn Plateau escarpment. According to George Bell, who once lived in a log cabin downstream, "They're still out there somewhere. Wouldn't they be a catch for someone!"*

Outfitting/Hardware

✳ Aurora Market, across the street from Snowshoe Inn (867-699-4321).

✳ Aurora Sport Fishing (867-699-4321).

✳ Northern Store, just west of Snowshoe Inn (867-699-4331).

✳ Local fishing and hunting guides available. Contact Hamlet office if interested (867-699-3441).

Amenities

✳ Accommodation, restaurant, sto-re, bank machine, medical serv-ices, police, airport, gasoline, diesel, pro-pane, automotive serv-ice.

Tips

✳ The gift shop across from the Snowshoe Inn has a unique se-lection of high-quality northern crafts made by Northwest

Nature reclaims cabin at White Man's Point

Territories artists, including moosehair tufting, quillwork, fancy fur pieces, slippers, and paintings.

* Mackenzie Daze Celebration is an annual midsummer festival featuring cultural events and live music, as well as jet-boat and canoe races. Contact Hamlet office to confirm dates (867-699-3441).

* Fort Providence is well known for its healthy blackfly popula-tion for much of the summer.

Collapsed Quonset hut at Axe Point, a World War II military base camp

The distinctive six-sided gazebos around town are popular bug-free shelters where neighbours and friends gather.

5

Emergency
* Hospital/Clinic (867-699-4311).
* RCMP (867-699-1111).

> 🛌 🏠 💺 🚏 🏪 About 24 kilometres down-stream from Fort Providence is the entrance to one of the potentially scariest stretches of the Mackenzie system: **Mills Lake**, renowned for its monster waves and fickle personality. Because of its marshy shoreline and lack of islands, camping is poor around virtually all of Mills Lake. The last chance for good camping is a low sandy island known locally as **Dog Island** [WP172], where the **Big Snye** pours back into the Mackenzie. This is also a good lunch spot, offering expan-sive views of the lake. About 2 kilometres downstream from Dog Island, on the north side of the Mackenzie, a cluster of simple cabins and tent platforms marks the outflow of the **Horn River,** a popular hunting destination and tradi-tional travel route for Fort Providence residents.

> 🔍 🦌 Once you decide to brave the 20-kilometre crossing of **Mills Lake**, stay within easy dashing distance of the south shore in case the wind suddenly picks up. If you aren't too preoccupied with the weather and the waves, keep an eye out for scattered rafts of surf scoters, white-winged scoters, common

> **Redknife Ring**
> Lucy Simon, Jean Marie River
>
> *There's been so much dancing and celebrating at the Redknife River over the years that you can see a distinct ring worn right into the ground.*

mergansers, and Canada geese, particularly during spring and fall migration. This marshy lake is of such significance to waterfowl that it is part of a major conservation area known as *Edéhzhie*, the South Slavey word for "source waters."

> As tempting as **Big Point** [WP 173] may look for drier camping, don't bother crossing unless you're travelling well into July or August, when water levels tend to be lower, exposing more dry shoreline. Generally you should stay south until you re-enter the river.

Alexander Mackenzie as (Possibly) Seen By the Locals

Stephen Kakfwi, former Premier of the NWT

Alexander Mackenzie came to our land. He described us in his Journal as a "meagre, ill-made people with scabby legs." My people probably wondered at this strange, pale man in his ridiculous clothes, asking about some great waters he was searching for. He recorded his views on the people, but we'll never know exactly how my people saw him. I know they'd never understand why their river is named after such an insignificant fellow.

> The first major stretch of sandy shoreline on river-left signals your arrival at **Axe Point** [WP177]. Formerly a small Dene village, in World War II this site became a major staging area and distribution point for the U.S. military while constructing the **Canol Pipeline** (see Norman Wells pg 157). A winter road crossed the Mackenzie at this point, then skirted the **Horn Plateau** visible to the north, and ultimately led to the Norman Wells oil fields. In summer this was a trans shipment point (much like Fort Smith's Bell Rock) for loading pipe sections, crated jeeps, and supplies onto barges also headed for the Wells. Our willow-whacking stroll along the shore revealed tangible signs of the hubbub that once occurred here—a conical headlamp from a Canol truck, a powerhouse engine block, steel cables, a bermed loading ramp, the crumbling remains of the tug boat, *Sikanni Chief*, and a jumble of caved-in **Quonset huts** [WP176]. This military base camp was abandoned just hours after the war ended, with plates, coffee cups, and sugar bowls left where they lay on the mess hall tables. Large clearings, an overgrown airstrip, and numerous road-cuts (more easily visible from the air) testify to the large footprint of the Axe Point camp,

White Man's Point, a window on long-ago life on the river

which is marked as the "Mills Lake Community" on older maps. A more recent clearing just downstream, complete with picnic tables and outhouse, offers a pleasant grassy campsite if you want to explore this site in depth.

➤ 🄰 🄱 🄲 There is good camping 20 kilometres beyond Axe Point on a beautiful sandy beach where the **Bouvier River** [WP178] meets the Mackenzie's south bank, or along the sheltered banks behind the rivermouth. For a change of scenic scale, try a short, easy paddle up the Bouvier, which is generally wide, sandy, and offers few obstructions. The river's French name attests to the rich Métis heritage of this region.

> **Small Town, Big Trees**
>
> Eric Sanguez, Jean Marie River
>
> *People passing through town are so astonished by the size of trees stockpiled at our mill that they assume they must have been shipped up from somewhere like British Columbia. Not so. These logs all come from within four or five kilometres of Jean Marie River.*

➤ 🄳 Five very old but well-preserved log cabins are tucked just out of sight on river-right at **White Man's Point** [WP180], or Eghá Naida in Slavey. Dating as far back as the 1930s, the cabins are laid out in an orderly fashion, suggesting a small settlement of European traders, the nationality of which is unknown. Some cabins display carefully hewn logs with dovetail joints while others were built more simply with stacked logs chinked with thick ropes. It's worth the brief lurch through a rose-choked meadow (wear long pants!) to visit this glimpse into long-ago life on the river.

➤ 🄴 Four hundred metres downstream from White Man's Point are the **gravesites** [WP181] of two adults and one child. The traditional picket fence around these sites marks sacred ground.

➤ 🄵 🄶 The mouth of the **Redknife River** [WP337] is a traditional gathering place for hunting, fishing, seasonal celebrations, special cultural events, and spirit-cleansing ceremonies. During certain medicine ceremonies, metal objects were not allowed in camp and were deposited on the north bank of the river.

Tug boat at Jean Marie River

Because of the cultural importance of this site, river travellers are discouraged from camping here but may pay a respectful visit. This site remains a favourite meeting place for families from Jean Marie River and Fort Providence.

➤ ▨ ▨ ▨ ▨ Scenic **Brownings Landing** [WP182] is named after Jack and Eva Browning, a couple of American homesteaders who came north in the 1920s and established a sawmill and farm on this site. Supplying firewood and potatoes to the steamers, and milled timber to Mackenzie River communities, they ran a self-sufficient business here for almost 40 years. Most of the original buildings have been razed. The remaining cabins, shop, and smoke-house are used by families from Jean Marie River. This site's high, flat plateau and easy shore access inspired the

Giant capstan winch to haul out boats and barges, Brownings Landing

Northwest Company to establish the Trout River Fort (aka Fort Livingston) here in 1796, the first trading post in the Mackenzie Valley. Before that, the sprawling sand beach at Brownings Landing has no doubt served as an attractive campsite as long as humans have travelled this river.

➤ ▨ ▨ Though it isn't marked on most maps, **Head-of-the-line** [WP183] is, for paddlers, one of the most important thresholds on the Mackenzie. For those headed north, it marks the first decent current to catapult you down the river. We celebrated the crossing with a floating lunch while passively drifting at a rate of 7 kilometres per hour. After Head-of-the-line, our average paddling speed soared from 8 to 15 kilometres per

> **A Great Gift**
>
> From a poster of Dene laws in Jean Marie River's community centre
>
> *The Creator has given you a great gift— Mother Earth. Take care of her and she will always give you food and shelter. Don't worry. Just go about your work and make the best of everything. Don't judge people. Find something good in everyone.*

hour until close to Jean Marie River. For those headed south—like voyageurs in fur-laden birchbark canoes—it meant the end of all lining and portaging from here to the rapids at Fort Smith. Ya-hoo!

JEAN MARIE RIVER *(Tthek'ehdeli, South Slavey for "water flowing over clay")*
Population 70

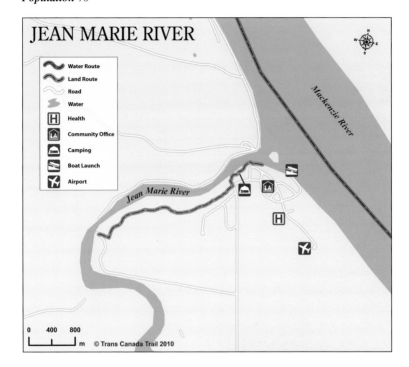

Community

Near the mouth of the Jean Marie River, a local man constructed a log warehouse in 1915 that he used as a trading post for many years. A traditional, independent community sprang up around the post, led for 43 years by Chief Louis Norwegian. The Hudson's Bay Company opened a store here in the mid-1960s, followed soon after by a cooperatively-owned and -operated sawmill. Though the store is long gone, the sawmill continues to thrive, providing wood for fuel and local construction. At peak capacity the new mill unit can trim enough logs

Living the good life near Jean Marie River

in one day to build two average-sized log homes. Jean Marie River is internationally known for the quality and originality of its traditional Slavey crafts, especially porcupine-quill and moosehair-tufted items. Many residents continue a traditional hunting, fishing, and trapping lifestyle. Amazingly well serviced for its size, Jean Marie River was connected to the Mackenzie Highway in 1996 via a 27 kilometre all-season road. The local airstrip is used for charter and private access only.

Visitor Information

Contact the Jean Marie River First Nation band office in the Henry Ekali Memorial Hall, General Delivery, Jean Marie River, NT, X0E 0N0 (867-809-2000, fax 867-809-2002, jmrband @ssimicro.com or chief@jmrfirstnation.com).

> **Sweet Sidestreams**
> Lyn Hancock, *The Mighty Mackenzie*
>
> *Idling along intimate sidestreams is one of the chief delights in store for the Mackenzie boatman. Away from the main river, waters are clearer and the fish more abundant. In fact, pike or jackfish are so numerous that they jostle in competition to get caught on your hook. Here kayaks and canoes have an advantage over motor-driven boats because they can easily leave the well-marked main channel to explore the shoreline and sidestreams.*

Things to Do

✳ Hiking trail, known locally as "Stan's Trail," along the Jean Marie River.

✳ Pickerel Falls at the end of this trail is really a large set of rapids offering good fishing.

✳ The little white tugboat called *Jean Marie River* used to haul milled lumber as far away as Norman Wells.

✳ Moosehair and porcupine-quill handicrafts.

✳ Old log schoolhouse built in 1952.

Accommodation

✳ Lucy's B & B houses up to five people in a clean, comfortable trailer unit that includes a fully-equipped kitchen. Superb breakfasts are provided in the Simon's home adjacent to the trailer. Supper can also be provided if arrangements are made in advance. General Delivery, Jean Marie River, NT, X0E 0N0 (867-809-2031, fax 867-809-2002).

Old meets new in Jean Marie River

Camping

＊ The best riverside access points for this community are the grassy shoreline just downstream from the white dry-docked tugboat, and around the corner, where an earthen ramp meets the mouth of Jean Marie Creek. Though a bit farther from the tiny town centre, the latter access is more reliable in high water and provides flatter, drier sites for pitching tents. There is no formal campground but with permission you can use washrooms and showers in the band office.

Outfitting/Hardware

＊ None.

> **Riverside Necklace**
>
> Lyn Hancock, *The Mighty Mackenzie*
>
> *Fort Simpson is on an island at the confluence of the Liard and Mackenzie Rivers at Mile 207. It's a thriving settlement with neat rows of log cabins and pastel painted wooden bungalows strung like a necklace along steep banks. The oldest settlement still occupied along the river, Fort Simpson was once the hub for fur trading activities of the Hudson's Bay Company. It is still an excellent fur-producing area.*

Amenities

＊ Accommodation, visitor information, medical services, police, airstrip.

Tips

＊ There is no store in Jean Marie River so bring enough food for your stay here if you plan to cook your own meals.

＊ Talk to folks in the band office to locate the best sources for moosehair tufting and other local arts and crafts.

＊ Though there is no library in town, the Louis Norwegian School has an excellent collection of photographic and historical material about the community.

Emergency

＊ Jean Marie nursing clinic (867-809-2900).

＊ Fort Simpson hospital (867-695-3232).

＊ Fort Simpson RCMP (867-695-1111).

➤ 🏕 🏠 The settlements of Jean Marie River and Fort Simpson are intimately connected by the Mackenzie River, tra-

Battered paddle from the 1989 Mackenzie River Race discovered along eroding bank

ditional trails, and shared bloodlines. The eastern trailhead for the **winter mail route** [WP186] between communities lies on river-left at a sharp elbow in the river's course, four kilometres downstream from Jean Marie River. Called *Edihtl'eh Etenih*, or "Paper Trail" in Slavey, this route

Carrie plays in Rabbitskin River rapids

was extensively used by RCMP delivering mail, priests on church business, fur traders, and local families visiting back and forth. Trappers and hunters continue to use this 40-kilometre trail to tap rich wildlife resources inland.

Jack Browning, of Brownings Landing fame, operated another sawmill and small trading post at **Spence River** [WP187]. The original post building and bunkhouse, a stable, and a shed stand on top of a steep bank south of the Spence River mouth. This is the very bank where Browning died when his bulldozer spilled over the edge one cold winter day in 1963. There is good camping in the poplar-rimmed flats at the hill's base or up top where there are few bugs and the view improves. There is even an outhouse behind Jack's place which, if you're lucky, is stocked with dry sphagnum moss. Check out the high riverside trail complete with handrails and a bench. Remnants of a horse-drawn timber sleigh and large loading beams near the shore point to the hubbub of activity that took place on this tranquil site. The old metal sign stamped "BM" stands for Browning's Mill. The impressive stands of even-aged poplar trees along this stretch of the river likely sprang up in the wake of Browning's extensive logging operations.

Ron lives out his pickerel dreams on the Rabbitskin River

About 30 kilometres downstream from Jean Marie, the Mackenzie River makes a distinct left-hand turn. Before dashing off toward Fort Simpson, take some time to enjoy the **Rabbitskin River** [WP188], a warm, semi-clear tributary that offers intimate scenery, good swimming, pick-erel fishing, and whitewater canoeing. A series of Class 1 rapids begins 1.5 kilometres upstream. With few obstructions and long, clean eddy lines, these rapids are perfect for playing. There is a basic campsite just below the first set of rapids in the poplar forest on river-right. South of the Rabbitskin River mouth, two private cabins sit on opposite ends of a large cleared terrace used by Fort Simpson's Norwegian family for over 100 years. Immediately north of the mouth is another, higher terrace offering great views of both rivers.

➤🕱 ⚞ 🔍 Buckle up. The current accelerates dramatically between Rabbit-skin River and Fort Simpson. Though the official source of the name **Strong Point** [WP190] is unknown, we would like to think it honours the powerful pull of the river along this exhilarating stretch. Between Strong Point and Mar-tin Island, near the mouth of the **Liard River**, our average paddling speed was 16 kilometres per hour. Enjoy the ride but stay vigilant because your boat may be rocked by strange boils and unstable water.

➤🍃 🔍 The names of features from here to Fort Simpson offer an interesting study in northern toponymy. **Green Island** [WP191] is, well, green. **Hanson Island** and **Martin Island** are named after map-makers who created the first detailed charts of the Mackenzie during the summers of 1945 and 1946. **Berens Land-ing** and **Naylors Landing** owe their names to Mackenzie riverboat captains who piloted Hudson's Bay Company paddlewheelers. There are no buildings at either landing, but you can make a detour south of Hanson Is-land. As for **Ghost Island**, the source of its name has been lost in the mists of time.

➤🏠 A few kilometres upstream from Fort Simpson, the forest on both sides of the river is cut by a wide linear swath. This marks the path of the **Enbridge pipeline** [WP192], the Northwest Territories' first major pipeline, which pumps oil from Norman Wells to a distribution centre in Zama, Alberta. This controversial project was completed just seven years after Justice Thomas Berger rec-

> **"My nation will stop the pipeline"**
>
> Fort Good Hope Chief Frank T'Seleie gives an impassioned speech against the proposed pipeline, August 5, 1975, during the Berger Inquiry.
>
> *You are the 20th-century General Custer. You are coming with your troops to slaughter us and steal land that is rightfully ours… It is for this un-born child, Mr. Berger, that my nation will stop the pipeline… It is so that this unborn child can know the freedom of this land that I am willing to lay down my life. We, the Dene people will decide what happens on our land. Mr. Berger, there will be no pipeline.*

ommended a 10 year moratorium on such developments due to significant opposition and a general lack of preparedness.

➤ 🕱 🚣 🦌 If you thought the Mackenzie was murky, wait until you cross the
mouth of the **Liard River** on your way into Fort Simpson. This dynamic,
mountain-fed river can be choked not only with silt but with armadas of trees
that will follow you down the Mackenzie from here on. There can be hazardous
turbulence where the two big rivers meet. During June and July, your welcoming party may consist of hundreds of **bank swallows** that breed along the steep
north banks of **Simpson Island**.

APPROXIMATE DISTANCE 250 kilometres

HIGHLIGHTS
* Wrigley ferry crossing
* Postcard views of the Nahanni and Camsell ranges
* North Nahanni River
* Camsell Bend where the Mackenzie abruptly veers north
* Traditional settlement of Willowlake River
* Unusual rapids and rocks at Old Fort Island
* Scenic community of Wrigley

OVERVIEW
If you enjoy mountain views while on the water, you'll love this stretch of the Mackenzie, with impressive ranges often flanking you on both sides of the river. As with much of the Mackenzie, you'll have the best luck fishing with a rod and reel in the clear or semi-turbid rivers and streams emptying into the Mackenzie. Expect to catch arctic grayling,

Mingling with the locals at the Wrigley ferry crossing

pickerel, whitefish, inconnu, northern pike, or lake trout. Wrigley is literally at the end of the road as far as summer driving goes, making it a convenient end point for budget-minded travellers who want to sample some of the best Mackenzie River scenery, then shuttle back south.

CAMPING TIPS
In low water conditions, the Mackenzie has been described as "one long campsite," offering relatively level benches of sand, clay, or river-ground rocks along each bank. In higher water, the abundant sandbars and islands usually offer good campsites, though travellers in power boats may have trouble approaching them. Some hot spots for camping along this part of the route include large sand terraces near Spruce Creek, a scenic clearing beside the mouth of the Willowlake River, and bald limestone outcrops on the upstream end of Old Fort Island.

Docked in Fort Simpson, the *Eckaloo* maintains navigation buoys along the Mackenzie

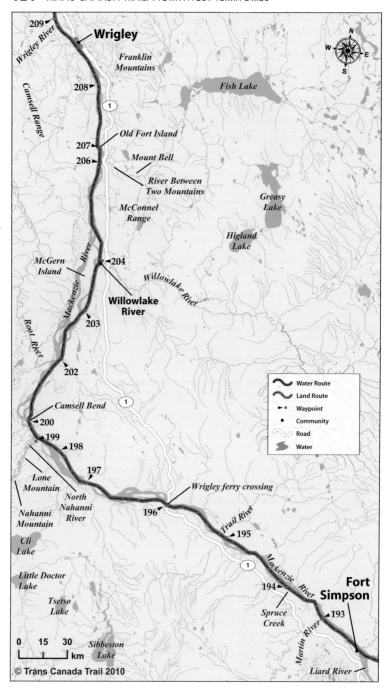

FORT SIMPSON *(Liidlii Kue, South Slavey for "place where the rivers come together")*
Population 1,240

Community

Welcome to the oldest continuously occupied community on the Mackenzie, located on Simpson Island at the mouth of the Liard River. Fort Simpson was established as the Northwest Company's Fort of the Forks by James Porter in 1804. The Anglican Mission arrived in 1858, followed by the Catholic Mission in 1894. Abundant furs, rich agricultural soils, and a strategic transport location have kept Fort Simpson on the map ever since. Fort Simpson is the Dehcho's gateway to the Nahanni-Ram country, a pristine panorama of white water, alpine tundra, and jagged peaks. In town, a trail links historic sites and natural vistas. Highlights include the Papal Grounds and Fort Simpson Heritage Park. The Nahanni National Park Reserve Office provides information on short- and long-term trips into the Park. First class hotels, inns, and B & Bs offer a variety of accommodation options, and high-quality traditional crafts are widely available. Fort Simpson's rich soils and relatively temperate climate have earned it the nickname "Garden of the Mackenzie." A casual summer stroll around town will show that local gardeners have taken this name to heart.

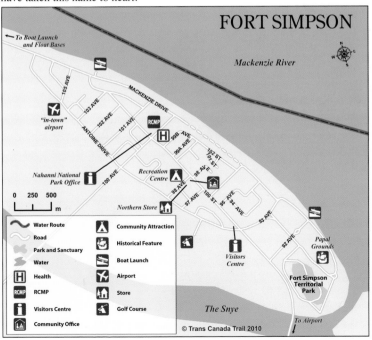

FORT SIMPSON

To Boat Launch and Float Bases

Mackenzie River

105 AVE
103 AVE
102 AVE
101 AVE
MACKENZIE DRIVE
ANTOINE DRIVE
100 AVE
"in-town" airport
RCMP
98B AVE
99A AVE
102 ST
101 ST
98 AVE
98 AVE
97 AVE
100 ST
95 AVE
94 AVE
93 AVE
92 AVE
Nahanni National Park Office
Recreation Centre
Northern Store
Visitors Centre
Papal Grounds
Fort Simpson Territorial Park
The Snye
To Airport

0   250   500   m

~ Water Route		⛺ Community Attraction	
Road		Historical Feature	
Park and Sanctuary		Boat Launch	
Water		Airport	
H Health		Store	
RCMP RCMP		Golf Course	
i Visitors Centre			
Community Office			

© Trans Canada Trail 2010

Visitor Information

Fort Simpson's excellent Visitor Information Centre is the first building on the left as you enter town from the highway. It includes a small museum displaying the history of the area and its people and offering a variety of movies about the region. Open May 1 – Sept 30. Hours of operation are July, 10 AM–8 PM and

Elegant outdoor dining at the mouth of the Spence River

Aug, 10 AM–7 PM. Visitor Information Centre, Village of Fort Simpson, PO Box 438, Fort Simpson, NT, X0E 0N0 (867-695-3182, fax 867-695-2511, www.fortsimpson.com). The odd obelisk across from the visitor centre was built to commemorate the construction of the highway that connected Fort Simpson to southern Canada.

Things to Do

✳ Numerous outlets for local handicrafts, from birchbark baskets and moosehide slippers to landscape photography and diamond willow canes.
See www.fortsimpson.com/business for a complete list.

✳ The Nahanni National Park Reserve headquarters has displays on the history, culture, and geography of the region. If you are planning to visit the Park, please register (867-695-3151, www.pc.gc.ca/eng/pn-np/nt/nahanni/visit/visit 6/d.aspx.

✳ Prospector Albert Faille's cabin.

✳ Seven Spruce Golf Course, one of the most northern in Canada. Nine holes, clubhouse, pro shop with clubs for rent. Longest hole is 475 yards, par 5.

✳ Papal grounds, which commemorate the visit of Pope John Paul II in 1987.

✳ Walking trail around Simpson Island.

Accommodation

✳ Janor's Guest House. Clean and homey B & B described as Fort Simpson's best-kept secret. Canoes and mountain bikes available, free laundry services (867-695-2077, fax 867-695-3945, janorservices@gmail.com, www.janor.ca).

✳ Bannockland. Lovely B & B located above the Liard River, PO Box 656, Fort Simpson, NT, X0E 0N0 (867-695-3337, fax 867-695-2555, bannock@cancom.net).

✳ Nahanni Inn. 40-plus rooms, airport shuttle, PO Box 248, Fort Simpson, NT,

X0E 0N0 (867-695-2201, fax 867-695-3000, nahanin@cancom.net).

✳ Maroda Motel. Fifteen rooms, eight complete with kitchenette, PO Box 250, Fort Simpson, NT, X0E 0N0 (867-695-2602, fax 867-695-3000).

✳ See www.fortsimpson.com/accomodation for complete listings.

Camping

✳ Fort Simpson Campground. Open May 15–Sept 15. Offers 32 sites beside the Papal grounds and within walking distance of town. Drinking water, kitchen shelter, showers, firewood, playground, and RV pump-out station. PO Box 240, Fort Simpson, NT, X0E 0N0 (867-695-7232, fax 867-695-2381, raquel_michaud@gov.nt.ca, pre-book at www.campingnwt.ca).

Jack Browning's abandoned sawmill, Spence River

Outfitting/Hardware

✳ Dehcho Hardware (867-695-2320).

✳ Northern Store (867-695-2391, fax 867-695-2544).

✳ TJ Grocery (867-695-2530).

Amenities

✳ Accommodation, restaurants, store, bank, bank machine, visitor information, pharmacy, medical services, police, airport, gasoline, diesel, propane, automotive service.

Tips

✳ Ask about guided walking tours at the Fort Simpson visitor centre.

✳ The Open Sky Arts Festival held every summer celebrates Dehcho area artists and musicians. Includes traditional feasts and drum dances, canoe races, live music, visual arts, traditional craft exhibitions, and carnival. Contact the visitor centre to confirm dates.

Dream-catcher fashioned by Lucy Simon, Jean Marie River

✳ If you are in a canoe or kayak, the best access points for Fort Simpson are the campground, the west end of the Papal Grounds, or the government dock by Albert Faille's cabin.

Watching the river flow

* The local favourites for dining are the Subarctic Wok ("The Sub") across from the visitor centre, and the Nahanni Inn.
* The visitor centre film "Nahanni" shows the dauntless prospector, Albert Faille, pounding upriver in a late-model outboard while nonchalantly sipping coffee. A hoot!

Emergency

* Hospital/Clinic (867-695-3232).
* RCMP (867-695-1111).

➤ A tidy private cabin on river-left a dozen kilometres downstream from Fort Simpson marks the **Martin River** [WP193]. A short paddle up this tributary leads to a long stretch of pretty but not playable rapids—too many rocks.

➤ A sprawling **sandy point** [WP194] just downstream from **Spruce Creek** on river-left is the first of several attractive campsites along this stretch of shoreline.

➤ An assortment of private **cabins** [WP195] perched on a high bank on river-right just before the **Trail River** is the legacy of several generations of use by the Tetso family of Fort Simpson, including John Tetso, author of the 1970 classic, *Trapping is My Life*. A machinery graveyard on the east end of the property displays an interesting stratigraphy of vintage lawn mowers,

Bankside vegetation hammered by stampeding ice and spring floods

snowmobiles, and outboards. From here you may catch your first glimpse of the mountains with **Nahanni Mountain** being the most prominent.

Eureka! Camsell Bend!

➤ 🛶 🏠 🪑 If you are hankering for some company, the **Wrigley ferry crossing** [WP196] provides a good opportunity to chat with locals traveling to and from Wrigley. The **Johnny Berens ferry** is named for a Métis paddlewheeler captain. Basic camping is possible on the gravel flats with the added luxury of an on-board flush toilet if you talk to the ferry workers nicely. The exact crossing location can vary widely depending on water levels and the age of the map you are using.

➤ 📇 About 25 kilometres downstream from the ferry crossing, the character of the Mackenzie changes dramatically [WP197]. It swells to almost 4 kilometres in width—beware of winds!—and swings to the northwest. From here you get your first postcard view of the **Nahanni Range**. You will be flanked by impressive mountains for many kilometres to come.

> **Social Life on the Mackenzie**
> Lyn Hancock, *The Mighty Mackenzie*
> *For a wilderness river the Mackenzie can be surprisingly social. Hardly a day passes that you don't stop midstream or land your boat beside another on shore, then in the manner of boating people the world over, exchange notes on the weather, fishing, swimming, or report on the progress of other boaters.*

➤ 🛶 ☠ The Mackenzie River is a work in progress as testified by countless landslides, undercut banks, and shifting mudflats. The sinuous pile of muck paralleling river-right is called a **slide front** [WP198], created when a huge chunk of shoreline slides into the river. Just as we landed our canoes, a helicopter set down beside us and out jumped a couple of gov-

Encouraging horn blasts from a barge train

ernment geologists, agog over this fascinating feature. If it's washed away by the time you get here, keep your eyes peeled for others downstream. There is an ancient trapper's cabin just behind the slide. If you choose to visit it, pick stable ground to climb or you could end up under another slide front.

⌐ ☠ ⚠ The lure of the mountains is irresistible by the time you reach the **North Nahanni River** [WP199], the lesser-known cousin of the

> ### Grinding up the North Nahanni
>
> Lyn Hancock, *The Mighty Mackenzie*
>
> *Excited at the prospect of more majestic landscapes we decide to camp up the North Nahanni River at the base of the highest peak. However the river is now on a rampage. Its delta is strewn with debris, the banks stripped 14 feet [4 metres] above the normal high water mark, and bankside trees ripped up and dangling down at all angles. The water is the consistency and colour of cream of wheat …After a mile of battling the strongest currents we have yet encountered, dodging stumps of black spruce lodged in mud banks and logs hurtling downstream, we finally ascertain where the deepest channel lies. But not for long. With the river in flood, our navigation maps are useless and within minutes we are grounded.*

South Nahanni River, which courses through Nahanni National Park. As tempting as the summit of **Lone Mountain**, 6 kilometres upstream, may seem as a hiking destination, this rambunctious river is non-negotiable in anything but a jetboat. It is possible to paddle up the first narrow channel until it meets the main flow where, in low water, you can lunch or camp while enjoying some great mountain views and the wild rush of water. Return to the Mackenzie the same way, but be on the alert for rafts of semi-submerged logs that barrel down this river like torpedoes.

⌐ ⚑ ⛺ 🔍 Five kilometres below the mouth of the North Nahanni, the Mackenzie makes a distinct northward jog at **Camsell Bend** [WP200]. Here the river slams into the mighty **Camsell Range**, which tops out at over 4,000 feet [1,200 metres]. Near the end of the last ice age, a huge block of stagnant ice was bunged into this bottleneck, creating an ice dam that forced water from the

Rita Betsedea and Victor Boots examine historic photos of Willowlake River

Liard, Peace, and Athabasca rivers to detour into Great Slave Lake, then northward to Great Bear Lake. From there, water drained back into the Mackenzie via the Great Bear River. Fortunately, that detour is long gone. However, below Camsell Bend, the river slows and widens markedly, with banks 3 to 5 kilometres apart. Take the right channel for the best current and views.

The **Root River** is an important traditional access route to productive waterfowl, moose, and beaver habitat skirting the base of the **Camsell Range**. It is fed from the south by Carlson Lake and **Carlson Creek**. Just downstream from the Root is yet another Carlson Creek entering the Mackenzie from the east. Who was this Carlson character anyway? At the mouth of the latter creek, a trapper named Ed Carlson built a **cabin** [WP202] over 90 years ago, which remains in amazingly good shape. An old scow capstan stands in a small clearing near the cabin. Carlson lives on in the memory of local elders who knew him simply as *Mayuhulay*—the toothless one. Another claim to fame was his incredible ability to cover great distances on foot or snowshoe. This is a pretty creek that is said to be full of pickerel.

> ### Ed Carlson, the Flat-footed Wanna-be Trooper
>
> Lyn Hancock, *The Mighty Mackenzie*[95]
>
> *When World War One was two years underway, Mr. Carlson walked all the way [from his cabin] to Fort Smith to enlist—a distance of 450 miles [725 kilometres]. When he got there he was rejected on ironical medical grounds— he had flat feet. Undaunted, he turned around and walked all the way back, totaling 900 miles [1,450 kilometres] on those same flat feet.*

Take the deeper, faster right channel as you pass **McGern Island** [WP203], named after Harry McGern, a prominent trading post manager in Wrigley. Watch for the **Wrigley Road**, which rises up the shoulder of the **McConnell Range**.

Willowlake River [WP204] is an amazing little community composed of families from Wrigley who have opted for a traditional life on the land—in spite of the occasional TV satellite dish. Established in the 1930s, this settlement

Grave of George Boots, one of four brothers who founded Willowlake River community

has varied in population from 3 to 40, with lots of dogs. (When we visited, there were more than three times as many dogs as people). Campers are welcome, as is help with the chores. If you are offered a tour, ask to see the ancient "Autoboggan" and chain saw, which the founding Boots brothers used to cut a land line all the way to Inuvik in the 1950s.

Rita Betsedea displays her fine beadwork, Willowlake River

➤ 🏔 If you are feeling especially intrepid, the **Willowlake River** is easily navigated for 50 kilometres upstream until you hit the **Gun Rapids**. In a grand, year-long cycle, Slavey people from the region traditionally used this river to trap furs all the way over to **Mills Lake** via **Bulmer Lake** and the **Horn River**, then journey back downstream to Fort Simpson to sell them. A "strange creature" is said to occasionally cause trouble to boisterous visitors at the mouth of the Willowlake River, so do mind your manners.

> **Beware of Monsters Downstream**
>
> Alexander Mackenzie reflects on the
>
> "Falsity of Native Information," July 5, 1789
>
> *The Information they gave us respecting the River, seems to me so very fabulous that I will be particular in inserting it in my account. Suffice it to say that they would wish to make us believe that we would be several winters getting to the Sea, and that we should be old men by the time we would return. That we would have to encounter many Monsters (which can only exist in their Imaginations). Besides that there are 2 impracticable Falls or Rapids in the River, the first 30 days march from us.*

➤ 🏠 🏔 🏕 By the time you reach **River Between Two Mountains** [WP206], alpine vistas will flank you on both sides of the river for the next 300 kilometres. North of the cleft through which the river passes is **Mount Bell**, which rises to 1,850 feet [564 metres]. One kilometre downstream from the river mouth is a wide grassy clearing and three old cabins, the traditional camp of the late Jimmy Yendi. This site is occasionally used as a culture camp for Wrigley school kids and offers benches, tables, and an outhouse. Please leave all traps and other bush technology where you find it.

Trapper Robert Hardisty with lynx and marten pelts

> ☠ ⌂ ⚑ ⛵ A distinct narrowing in the Mackenzie leads you inevitably to **Old Fort Island** [WP207], created by an unusual limestone outcrop. The island is named for the first of several sites of Fort Wrigley, originally called **Little Rapids Post** by the Hudson's Bay Company. As you approach, you may hear the thunder of not-so-little rapids rushing past the island or, if the water is high enough, slicing right through it. If so, proceed with caution. Don't let the lazy Mackenzie fool you—these rapids could easily flip your boat. You'll find excellent camping options here in the form of flat, open bedrock on the upstream end or a broad sandy beach along the western shore.

Courtesy Robert Hardisty

The late George Boots, a locally revered elder, and his young wife Rosie

> ⛵ 🏕 As you approach Wrigley, look west for evidence of a massive **forest fire** [WP208] that stormed northward in 2005 all the way from Camsell Bend: charred trees, tangled snags, vigorous shrub growth, and abundant fireweed. The smoke was so thick in Wrigley that all the town's elders and children with asthma were evacuated. From here you get a sweeping view of the **Camsell Range** to your left and the **Franklin Mountains** to your right.

6

Life on the River

Ed Lafferty, Wrigley

I used to work with Jack Browning, cutting wood for the paddlewheelers up and down the river. 250 cords here, 85 cords there. I got tired of throwing wood around all summer so I quit. There used to be hundreds of people moving from camp to camp along the river and in the bush. I did a lot of things in my life. I don't worry very much. I took my sons out on the land and showed them how to set traps and hunt and now they can take care of themselves. I don't worry about them either.

APPROXIMATE DISTANCE 350 kilometres

HIGHLIGHTS

✻ Magnificent Roche-qui-trempe-à-l'eau and its unique thermal spring

✻ Entrance into Sahtu lands

✻ Crystal clear Saline River

✻ Smoking hills of Tulít'a

✻ Community of Tulít'a

✻ Sacred Bear Rock

✻ First oil drilling site at Bluefish Creek

A Phenomenal Hike
Gary Yendo, Wrigley
It's a phenomenal hike to
Cap Mountain. Caribou,
moose, blueberries, and
there's a nice cabin we
visit right beside a moun-
tain creek. It's really
beautiful.

OVERVIEW

This is a relatively wild and diverse section of the Mackenzie, including one of the longest stretches between communities. The route is punctuated with sweeping bends that open up to beckoning mountain vistas, high terraces, and dramatic cutbanks that rise over 200 feet above the water. Evidence of several gigantic forest fires follow you for many kilometres down the river. Many layers of history converge along this route, including the telltale footprint of Wrigley's former home, a phantom community of Sahtu gatekeepers, and some of the most sacred sites in the Dene realm. Natural wonders include stunning fossils, thermal springs, burning coal seams, massive landslides, and raptors galore. Go for it!

CAMPING TIPS

Clean, wide gravel benches at the outflow of clear-running creeks and

Impromptu party for the Trans Canada Trail on board the SS *Norweta*

rivers are among the many excellent campsites along this route. Abundant sandbars and flats on both sides of the river offer plenty of options when it's time to call it a day.

WRIGLEY *(Thtedzeh Koe, South Slavey for "clay place")*
Population 168

Community

Wrigley's nickname is "town on the move" for good reason. When the Northwest

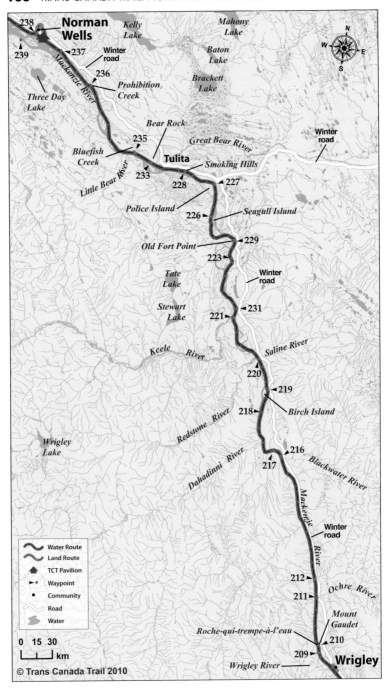

Trading Company's Fort Alexander trading post closed in 1821, the Slavey Dene of this region settled at Old Fort Island, 32 kilometres upstream of the present site. A Hudson's Bay Company trading post was established on the island in 1870. Between 1900 and 1905, over 100 Slavey died of famine and tuberculosis introduced by the traders. Most of the survivors moved to a second site called Fort

Jamie records a CBC dispatch beside a thundering set of rapids, Old Fort Island

Wrigley, a few kilometres downstream from the present site on river-left—now called "Old Town." A power plant, school, and teacher's residence were built on this site in the late 1950s. Repeated flooding and poor living conditions motivated people to move to the present site of Wrigley, which had the advantage of a well-maintained wartime airstrip constructed by the U.S. military for the Canol Project. The Hudson's Bay Company store, warehouse, school, teacher's residence, and even the church were moved by barge down the Mackenzie River to the new site in 1965, joining the 15 new houses that had been built that year. A traditional

7

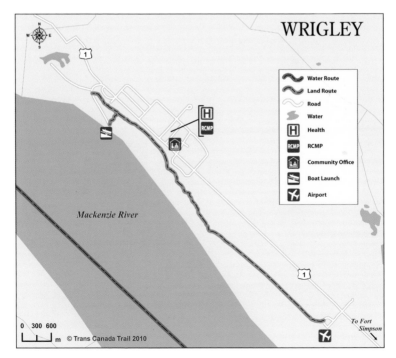

WRIGLEY

Water Route
Land Route
Road
Water
Health
RCMP
Community Office
Boat Launch
Airport

Mackenzie River

0 300 600
m © Trans Canada Trail 2010

To Fort Simpson

hunting, trapping, and fishing lifestyle continues in Wrigley. Road maintenance, construction, arts and crafts, and tourism round out the rest of the local economy.

Natural art by Wrigley chief and fashion designer, D'Arcy Moses

Visitor Info

❋ Pehdzeh Ki First Nation band office General Delivery, Wrigley, NT, X0E 1E0 (867-581-3321, 867-581-3581, fax 867-581-3229, www.wrigleynwt.com).

❋ Wrigley Hotel (www.wrigleyhotel.com/wrigley-northwest-territories.htm).

Things to Do

❋ Hitch a ride a few kilometres down the road and hike to Smith Creek Falls swimming hole.

❋ Take a guided backcountry mountain hike, bike adventure, or jet boat tour of special sites along the river with local tourism operators Morris Moses of M & M River Taxi (867-582-3416) or Gary Yendo of Wrigley's Wonders (867-581-3678, www.wrigleyhotel.com /wrigley-northwest-territories-outfitters.htm).

❋ Visit local chief and internationally-renowned fashion designer and artist D'Arcy Moses.

❋ Local handicrafts include moosehair-tufted artwork, handmade moccasins, embroidered jackets, and beaded jewellery.

> **The Mackenzie Becomes Your Life**
>
> Carrie McGown, river guide
>
> *Why do I love the Mackenzie? It's a river that's big enough to become a part of your everyday life. Stay out here long enough and it becomes your life. It becomes the norm. It invites you to be a part of it. It gives you time and space to think. It makes you accept that every day doesn't have to be "great" to enjoy the overall experience.*

Accommodation

❋ The trailer-based Petanea Hotel offers basic rooms, a restaurant, and laundry facilities, and operates on an irregular basis largely depending on the availability of staff. For information on current status, contact the owner c/o Petanea Development Corporation, General Delivery,

Smith Creek Falls swimming hole

Wrigely, NT, X0E 1E0 (867-581-3121, fax 867-581-3113, innsnorth@ Arcticco-op.com, www.wrigleyhotel.com).

Landslide triggered by river erosion and thawing permafrost (NRCAN)

Camping
✳ Halfway between the river and town is a basic campsite with outhouses and picnic tables.
✳ There is another campground two kilometres south of town near Airport Lake that is more suited for visitors in vehicles or RVs. Known as the Pehdzi Day Use Area, it offers firewood, outhouses, and firepits. Non-powered. A bit overgrown but quiet. Swimming in nearby Airport Lake.

Outfitting/Hardware
✳ Petanea Co-op Store (867-581-3121).

Tips
✳ The precise boat pull-up site varies from year to year depending on water levels and the severity of spring ice excavations along the riverbank. Watch for where local boats are pulled up.
✳ Take a day hike up Cap Mountain with a local guide.

Emergency
✳ Nursing station (867-581-3441).
✳ RCMP in Fort Simpson (867-695-1111).

> ---

Liquid Heart of the Sahtu

Rakekée Gok'é: Places we take care of

The Mackenzie River, from Blackwater River in the south, to Thunder River in the north, has been a very important route for Sahtu Dene and Métis … As a traditional use area, the Mackenzie continues to provide critical domestic fisheries, moose and waterfowl hunting areas, and travel access to many other locations. It is associated with numerous legends, including stories of Yamoria. Called Dehcho or "Big River," the river is a symbolic focal point of Sahtu Dene and Métis culture and history.

➤ 🛶 🏠 Like many northern communities, Wrigley took many years to settle into its final resting place. What locals refer to as "**Old Town**" [WP209] is the third in a series of sites, which was abandoned in the 1960s due to periodic flooding and unreliable barge access. The church, community hall,

Lewis Beck fiddles a fond farewell as we hit the liquid trail, Wrigley

and several homes were skidded southeast across the ice to the present townsite. Fire has since taken all but a few fallen-in cabins, wash tubs, and tent frames from more recent camps.

➤ 🏕 🏖 🧗 🦌 Several limestone benches on the opposite bank from the Old Town site may be suitable for camping or a lunch break. Downstream, these outcrops tilt up abruptly into magnificent limestone slabs that rise hundreds of feet straight out of the river, hence the name **Roche-qui-trempe-à-l'eau** [WP210] (locally translated as "Mountain with toes dipped in the water"). An unusual **thermal spring**, reminiscent of Yellowstone National Park, has created a large lion-shaped mound that gurgles warm sulfurous water into the Mackenzie. Watch for **peregrine falcons** roosting on or soaring above the cliffs around you. This riverside wall of rock tops out at 1,750 feet [533 metres] on the summit of Mount Gaudet which, there and back, makes for an exhilarating half-day hike.

Still life, St. Anthonys Roman Catholic Church, Tulit'a

➤ 🏕 🏖 From Mount Gaudet to the mouth of the Blackwater River, a distance of about 80 kilometres, the Mackenzie runs cleanly north-northwest at a fairly swift rate. Flowing into the Mackenzie from the east, the **Ochre River** [WP211] is named for its bright red waters. A flat gravel bench at its mouth offers a good base for camping, snoozing, or casting in a fishing line.

Paddling the Keele

Black Feather—The Wilderness Adventure Company

The Keele River trip is a unique opportunity for any paddler to experience one of the acclaimed mountain-style rivers of the Northwest Territories. Most of these exceptional wilderness rivers require advanced whitewater skills but anyone can paddle the Keele with expert guides ...The river is broad and flows swiftly but there are no portages. You'll enjoy countless miles of swifts, rapids with standing waves, several canyons and lots of manoeuvering through gravel bars. The river cuts through several beautiful mountain ranges. This is alpine scenery on a grand scale with peaks over 2,250 metres. We can hike into the mountains and enjoy the outlooks high above the river. Natural salt licks on the shore attract large game.

7

➤🏔️ 🛶 About 7 kilometres downstream from the Ochre River, look for a **bridge** crossing an unnamed creek on river-right [WP212]. (The hitch-hiking is poor in the summer as this is part of the winter road to Tulít'a.) The **huge burn** from the mid-1990s that you saw near Wrigley clearly shows

Beadwork rendition of Tulít'a and Bear Rock, Yakelaya family

itself again on river-left. This fire continued northward all the way to the Keele River. Note the three-tiered bench-like effect on this bank that speaks to the gradual shrinkage of **post-glacial Mackenzie River**. That must have been one big river back then!

➤🛶 🛶 The big burn you have been sideswiping for many kilometres appears to have jumped across the Mackenzie near the pronounced elbow north of the **Blackwater River**. In spite of its name, the relatively clear waters of this river are said to support a healthy population of **arctic grayling** if fishing is on your mind. Older maps show a cluster of cabins on the west bank of the Mackenzie about a kilometre downstream from the Blackwater. This was a small settlement dominated by the Neyelle family, nicknamed the "Sahtu gatekeepers," because this camp marked the traditional border crossing between the South Slavey and Sahtu realms. The forest fire obliterated all evidence of this settlement except for the lone grave [WP216] of respected elder Jacques Neyelle, which is surrounded by a miraculous semicircle of tall, untouched spruce.

➤🛶 A distinctive landmark welcoming you to the southern boundary of Sahtu lands

> **Forest fires trigger landslides near Old Fort Point**
>
> Natural Resources Canada, *Permafrost, landslides and slope stability*
>
> *In the Mackenzie area the frequency of forest fires is significantly increased during droughts. If ground conditions are very dry, the entire organic mat can be burnt, exposing icy sediments, leading to an active layer detachment failure, and possibly mobilizing the slope in a rapid debris flow. Even under present climatic conditions a definite link between fire and landslides can be made. Following the large forest fires of 1994 and 1995 in the vicinity of [Tulít'a], numerous flows developed along the banks of the Mackenzie River and its tributaries. Thus, if fire frequency increases in the future, the frequency of skin flows can be expected to increase.*

are the dramatic **cutbanks** that rise over 200 feet (61 metres) above the water along the north side of a **sharp bend** [WP217]. This elbow is one of the few abrupt turns in the Mackenzie's course. After heading westward for 6 kilometres, the river resumes its northerly course at a markedly faster clip.

Yellow lady's slipper orchid, *Cypripedium calceolus,* Bear Rock

➤ ◸ Watch for a massive **land-slide** [WP218] that transported a wide swath of forest from the top of a high bank to almost river height. And you wondered why the Mackenzie was so silty!

➤ ◸ ⛰ ◸ ◸ The recent forest fire that jumped the river and enveloped **Birch Island** was so hot that it scorched the living branches clear off most of the trees, a rare sight in the northern boreal forest. Near the north end of the island on river-right is an unnamed creek [WP219] containing water that is Caribbean-clear and supports **arctic grayling**—for those who enjoy fresh fish. In low water, the **gravel benches** on both sides of the creek mouth offer sites for level camping or loafing. Another **winter road bridge** is visible upstream, the main traffic of which includes bears and moose.

➤ ◸ ◸ ◸ ◸ ◸ Clear water, a wide gravel bar, dry grassy benches, and rumours of good trout fishing make the **Saline River** (locally pronounced sah-LEEN) [WP220] a natural camping or lunch stop. This was the former site of a 1930s **oil exploration camp**, complete with cemetery, all evidence of which has

been swept away by forest fires. A pleasant hike less than 1 kilometre upstream brings you to a lengthy **bridge** attached to a peculiar coarse dirt trail—the base of the Tulít'a winter road. Hike up the hill north of the bridge for an expansive view of the Saline Valley, the Mackenzie,

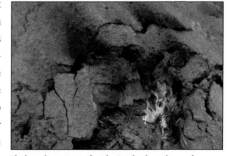

Blackened vents scar fragile riverbank at the smokes

and, to the northeast, **Mt. Clark**. Look for a cutline a bit beyond the bridge. This marks the **Enbridge pipeline** that runs under the riverbed, carrying Norman Wells oil to Zama, Alberta. **Salt flats** another 2.5 kilometres upstream are said to attract wildlife and give the river its slightly briny taste—and its name.

1995 forest fire that almost destroyed Tulit'a (Jim LeFleur)

➤ The **Redstone River** empties into the Mackenzie immediately across from the Saline. A trading post was built near the confluence of the Redstone and the Mackenzie in the early 1800s. Though you may spot some cabins here, the original buildings are long gone.

➤ The **Keele River** [WP221] is held in high esteem by northern paddlers. For a mountain whitewater river it is relatively easy to run, and offers stunning alpine scenery and abundant natural delights. The sprawling forest fire footprint you have followed since Wrigley, finally peters out south of the Keele River. About 60 kilometres up the Keele is **Red Dog Mountain**, one of the most sacred places in the Sahtu realm.

➤ Two kilometres north of the Keele River is a **small, low island** [WP231] that deserves special respect. According to Tulít'a lore, a **giant rat** (i.e., muskrat) lives in the waters surrounding the island. This potentially troublesome creature will allow safe passage only to those who slip by, without a word, on river-left. Watch for unusual eddies in the water as you silently pass the island. The giant rat may be near.

➤ Stay in the right channel as you approach **four large islands** [WP223] above **Old Fort Point**. If winds

> **The Story of Bear Rock**
> Carrie McGown, Mackenzie
> River guide
> *Across the crystal clear waters of the Great Bear River, Bear Rock towers 450 metres (1,488 feet) above. The Dene have a legend about the rock. A giant [Yamoria], after suffering a long cold winter, killed three huge beavers and stretched their pelts on Bear Rock, as a sign that famine would never again come to the land. These "pelts" can be seen today as three red patches high on the rock face.*

permit, stay well away from shore to avoid hitting shallows. This is a dynamic stretch of river, indicated by extensive deposition on inside curves and landslides on outside curves. These islands are designated as **Special Harvesting Areas** under the Sahtu Land Claim, what some in Tulít'a call "our cattle range." To minimize disturbance to moose, waterfowl, and other wildlife, camping on these islands is discouraged.

➤ 🐾 🦫 **Old Fort Point** [WP229] is the site of the second incarnation of Fort Norman, first established in 1810 near the mouth of the Great Bear River, then moved to this point in 1844. The fort was moved a third time in 1851, back to the site where Tulít'a sits today, making it one of the longest continuously occupied settlements north of 60. Although archaeologists have found little from the original fort—two stone chimney piles, a porcelain pipe stem, a strip of copper, and some chinking clay—the old cabin you may see on the point harks back to several generations of continuous use by Tulít'a's Yakelaya clan. A **major landslide** on river-right was a direct result of permafrost collapse following major forest fires in the mid-1990s. A warmer climate could mean that the Mackenzie's banks will collapse even faster.

Tulít'a Coal Development

Bob Weber, *Vancouver Sun*

A proposed Mackenzie Valley natural gas pipeline…is creating massive new plans for industrial development in the Arctic. [A Vancouver-based company] has unveiled plans to strip-mine extensive coal reserves along the Mackenzie River and begin building $2 billion worth of coal gasification plants to tie into the pipeline…[It has] bought about 1,100 square kilometres of leases in three areas of the Northwest Territories estimated to contain 2.1 billion tonnes of coal. Two of these are near Tulít'a…The coal could be barged to market along the Mackenzie River. But gasification—turning the coal through heat and pressure into synthetic natural gas—is [the company's] priority.

➤ 🦫 Exposed along the steep riverbank west of **Seagull Island** [WP226] is a thick outcrop of unusual white sediments. This indicates the presence of a massive **coal deposit** that may soon change the wilderness character of this part of the Mackenzie Valley. A Vancouver coal mining company has plans to begin widespread strip-mining and gasification of this deposit, which lies under hundreds of square kilometres on both sides of the river.

➤ 🛶 🐾 🦫 🏚 After rounding the major bend by **Police Island** [WP227] you will get a compelling view of sacred **Bear Rock**, 25 kilometres downstream. Unusual eddies in this bend lead some locals to believe that this is another hangout of the giant rat you appeased near the Keele River. Police Island is the site of an early RCMP outpost.

Tugboat *Jock McNiven* moored at Tulít'a wharf

⟩ 🏴 ⬭ 🏊 🍖 The same coal that has recently caught the eye of southern mining companies has kept Tulít'a's **Smoking Hills** [WP228] burning for countless centuries. About 8 kilometres upstream from Tulít'a, keep a close eye on the steep northern riverbank for black strata poking out of the sand; unusual blonde, red or orange limestone—some impregnated with large, well-preserved **plant fossils**; an acrid, oily smell in the air; or, of course, wisps of blue smoke leaking from the sand.

These are all sure clues that you are near what locals call "The Smokes," a deep bed of lignite coal mysteriously burning just below the surface. Alexander Mackenzie left us the first written record of this phenomenon in 1789. The precise location and number of vents vary from year to year, depending on spring ice conditions and bank subsidence. We found four discrete vent systems over a span of 800 metres. Not only could they cause serious burns or collapse underfoot, they are highly sacred to the people of Tulit'a. Watch for **bank swallows** twittering through the smoke as they dash to and from their riverside colonies.

> ### Mackenzie Visits the Smoking Hills in 1789
> Alexander Mackenzie, *Voyages from Montreal*
>
> *The whole bank was on fire for a very considerable distance. It proved to be a coal mine. The beach was covered with coal, the mineral with which the natives render their quills black.*
>
> ### A Special Place
> Cathy Menacho, Tulít'a
>
> *My father always used to tell us that the Smokes are a very sacred place. We'd stop there by all the coloured rocks and pay the water, maybe with a little tobacco or something. He'd tell us to always treat that whole area with respect. Everybody should. It's a special place.*

7

TULIT'A *(North Slavey for "where the waters meet")*
Population 489

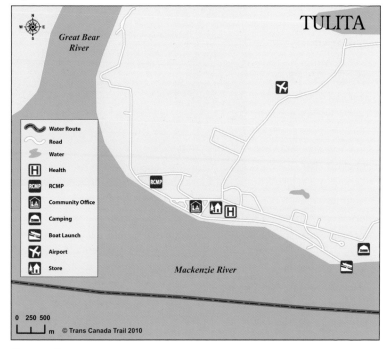

Community

This picturesque Sahtu Dene community is perched above the confluence of the Great Bear and Mackenzie rivers. The Northwest Company established the region's first post in 1805 on the Mackenzie opposite the Redstone River. This post was later moved three times, finally settling on the present site by 1810. The explorer John Franklin used this post site as a starting point for some of his grand expeditions. The Hudson's Bay Company took over the post in 1851. Some of the Bay's distinctive white and red buildings still sit prominently above the river. The Roman Catholic Oblates founded a mission in 1859. The Anglicans moved in the next year and built a squared-log church that has gained fame as the oldest standing church in the Northwest Territories. During the Second World War, the settlement grew as a transportation link to the uranium finds at Great Bear Lake. Hunting, fishing, and trapping remain central to the local economy with oil exploration and tourism recently gaining mo-

> **Tulít'a Welcome**
> Scott Carle, Tulít'a[107]
>
> *Enjoy the people. Enjoy the community. I've lived here for just two months but it only takes an hour to figure the place out and even less to feel welcome.*

mentum. Originally known as Fort Norman, the name was changed to Tulít'a on January 1, 1996, a few months after a monster forest fire almost wiped this community off the map.

Bunchberry, Cornus canadensis (rt.) and Twinflower, Linnaea borealis

Visitor Info

✻ Tulít'a Band Council (867-588-3341).

✻ Tulít'a Yamoria Community Secretariat (867-588-3116).

Things to Do

✻ Visit the edge of town to view the aftermath of the 1995 forest fire that miraculously spared the community.

✻ Anglican log church built in 1860.

✻ Hire a local guide to take you fishing on the Great Bear River or climbing up Bear Rock. Inquire at the band office.

✻ Visit the abandoned Hudson's Bay buildings and enjoy one of Tulít'a's best views of the river.

Accommodation

✻ Two Rivers Hotel. Smart new complex with eight rooms, some including full kitchens, laundry access on request. Box 117, Tulít'a, NT, X0E 0K0 (867-588-3320, fax 867-588-3749).

✻ Blueberry B & B. Homey, spacious trailer with full kitchen and living room, three bedrooms. (867-588-3924, fax 867-588-3211).

Camping

✻ Half a kilometre upstream from the distinctive Hudson's Bay buildings is a broad boat launch and camping area. No facilities.

Amenities

✻ Accommodation, restaurant, store, bank, bank ma-

Sheltered from a looming cloudburst

chine, medical services, police, airport, gasoline.

Remains of 1920 oil strike, Bluefish Creek

Tips

✳ The main water access point
for Tulít'a is immediately
downstream from the red-and-
white Hudson's Bay buildings.

Emergency

✳ Nursing station (867-588-
4251).

✳ RCMP (867-588-1111).

➤⚓ **Below Tulít'a**, the river
generally flows in a northwesterly direction between steep clay banks exceeding 12 metres (40 feet) in height. The 80-kilometre stretch to Norman Wells
includes many islands and the river swells to over 5 kilometres wide with a
consequent reduction in current. By the time you reach Tulít'a, the pronounced
muddying effect of the Liard River is somewhat dissipated. And here, for several kilometres below the town on river-right, the Great Bear River brings a
flood of colder, clearer water from Canada's largest body of water almost 150
kilometres away, granite-lined Great Bear Lake.

➤ ◻ ⛺ ⚓ 🏔 🔥 The most important thing to take with you if you want to
climb **Bear Rock** [WP233] is a highly respectful frame of mind, for this is perhaps the most sacred landmark in the Dene realm. The best way to go up is
from the southwest side, starting from the pebble beach near the navigation
beacons—where there is good camping—and making a wide clockwise climb
to a high shoulder that leads to the summit. Then, descend the wide chute on
the other side, keeping the three reddish "**beaver pelts**" on your right. However
you go, the climb is steep and tangled by fire-felled trees, but it's worth it. We
took 2.5 hours to go up and 1.5 to descend. Take time to smell the many flowers, including **arnica**, **fleabane**, and resplendent **yellow lady's slipper**. Watch
for **golden eagles**, **Townsend's solitaire**, and **peregrine falcons**. Some kind
of biodegradable offering should be made at the bottom and top of the mountain. Because of their cultural significance, the lakes near the summit are off-
limits without special permission from the band office in Tulít'a.

➤ 🀫 🀫 Six kilometres downstream from Bear Rock, you can visit the site of a 1920 wellhead that helped kick off the Norman Wells oil boom. Oil seepages along this stretch of the river gave rise to the Slavey name for the area, "*Le gohlini*," meaning "where the oil is." Alexander Mackenzie noticed oil seepages near here when he travelled the river in the late 1700s. Local Dene led geologists to sites like this in the early 1900s, resulting in the drilling of several exploratory wells and, ultimately, in the construction of a refinery at Norman Wells. It is near the sloping eastern bank of **Bluefish Creek** [WP235], about 20 metres in from an old outhouse visible from the Mackenzie. There you will find the **original drill hole** surrounded by a red railing as well as cast-off drilling machinery lying about. This spot was the proverbial launch pad for big industry's first foray into the Northwest Territories. Bluefish Creek is named for the **arctic grayling** that spawn each spring in its clear waters.

➤ 🀫 🀫 🀫 A mini delta formed by **Prohibition Creek** [WP236] offers a flat, sprawling bench for camping, good shelter from prevailing north-west winds, and superb views of the **Carcajou Range** (French for wolverine) to the west. Most of the creeks along this part of the Mackenzie got their colourful names— Helava Creek, Prohibition Creek, Nota Creek, Jungle Ridge Creek—from U.S. military engineers building the Canol road and pipeline project in the 1940s.

➤ 🀫 🀫 The same 1995 fire that almost took out Tulít'a might have consumed Norman Wells (imagine the oil refinery going up!) were it not for the massive **fire break** [WP237] hastily bulldozed through the spruce woods, now evident as a wide gash of shrubs. From here you get your first view of the six **artificial islands** created in the mid-1980s as stable drilling platforms from which to tap the area's abundant oil reserves.

➤ 🀫 As you approach Norman Wells, watch for the red metal roof of the shelter at **McKinnon Park** [WP238], a Territorial campground that offers clean tent sites, picnic tables, and basic facilities. Watch carefully for the park boat launch—otherwise the healthy current could sweep you right past.

8 MACKENZIE RIVER: NORMAN WELLS TO TSIIGEHTCHIC

APPROXIMATE DISTANCE

525 kilometres

HIGHLIGHTS

❊ Great hiking and history around
   Norman Wells
❊ Carcajou Ridge
❊ Sans Sault Rapids
❊ The Ramparts
❊ Fort Good Hope
❊ Our Lady of Good Hope
   Church
❊ Little Chicago
❊ Arctic Circle crossing
❊ Gwich'in National Historic Site
❊ Lower Ramparts
❊ Norman Wells Historic Centre

Twinflower, *Linnaea borealis*, the only species to which taxonomist Carl Linnaeus ascribed his own name

OVERVIEW

Welcome to what many would agree is the wildest, most scenic and exciting portion of the Mackenzie River. Highlights of this stretch include cannonball-like concretions and ammonite fossils spilling out of the riverbank; a limestone cliff called Carcajou Ridge that towers over the water; a stirring memorial for a drowned paddler; a deep but easily-navigated canyon; an ancient church so ornate that it has been declared a National Historic Site; the crossing of the Arctic Circle; a Stoneage spearhead quarry; and a Gwich'in travel corridor packed with traditional camps and stories. This is the longest of the ten route sections described in this guide. Paddlers should allow eight to twelve days for this journey, depending on the degree to which you want to explore this fascinating area and the type of weather you encounter.

8

Fishing Lake, Norman Wells, with Mount Hamar in background

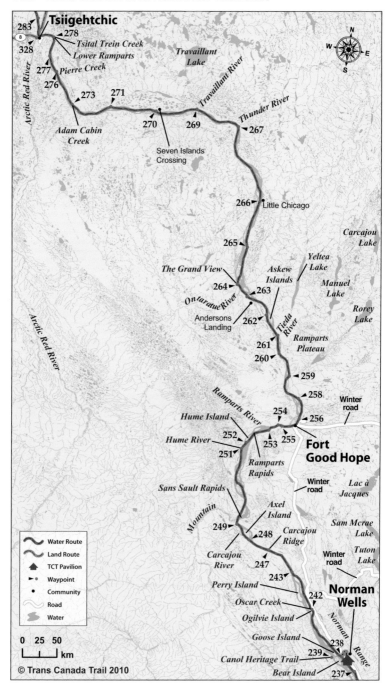

Tsiigehtchic

283
328
278
Tsital Trein Creek
Lower Ramparts
Pierre Creek
277
276
273
271
Adam Cabin Creek
270
Seven Islands Crossing
269
267
Travaillant Lake
Travaillant River
Thunder River
Arctic Red River

266 Little Chicago
265

Carcajou Lake

The Grand View
264
263
Askew Islands
Yeltea Lake
Manuel Lake
Rorey Lake

Ontaratue River
Andersons Landing
262
Tieda River
261
260
Ramparts Plateau

259
258
Winter road

Ramparts River

254
256
255

Hume Island
252
253
Fort Good Hope

Hume River
251
Ramparts Rapids

Arctic Red River

8

Winter road
Lac à Jacques

Sans Sault Rapids
Axel Island
Mountain
249
248
Carcajou Ridge
247
Carcajou River

Winter road
Sam Mcrae Lake
Tuton Lake

Perry Island
243
242
Oscar Creek
Ogilvie Island
Goose Island
238
Canol Heritage Trail
239
Bear Island
237

Norman Wells
Norman Range

Legend
Water Route
Land Route
TCT Pavilion
Waypoint
Community
Road
Water

0 25 50
km

© Trans Canada Trail 2010

CAMPING TIPS

Chances are that by the time you are this far down the river, the natural ebb in water levels will reveal lots of riverside gravel benches or sand flats to camp on.

NORMAN WELLS *(Tlegohti, North Slavey for "where there is oil")*
Population 797

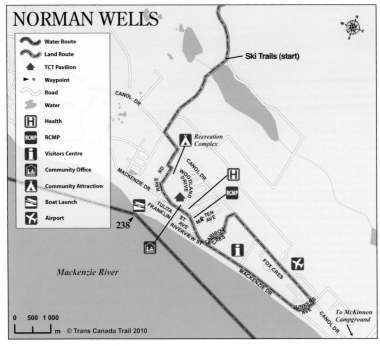

Community

While other communities along the Mackenzie originated primarily as fur trading posts, Norman Wells owes its existence to the discovery of oil. The first hint of the region's petroleum potential was recorded by Alexander Mackenzie who, in 1789, was led to oil seepages by the local Sahtu Dene and described "pieces of petroleum which bear a resemblance to yellow wax." Norman Wells is the Sahtu's transportation hub and largest community. Many years passed before the region's first exploratory wells were drilled in 1919. By the 1930s, Norman Wells oil was feeding the mining industry at Great Bear Lake. During WWII the U.S. military built a pipeline to carry Mackenzie Valley crude to Whitehorse, described as "the greatest construction project since the Panama Canal." The Canol pipeline was abandoned soon after, but the corridor remains a magnet for hikers seeking northern adventure. Though basically an industrial and administrative centre, the rugged hinterland around Norman Wells is spectacular, offering great opportunities for wildlife viewing, hunting, fishing, and backcountry camping.

Visitor Information

✳ Norman Wells Historical Centre, PO Box 56, Norman Wells, NT, X0E 0V0 (867-587-2415, fax 867-587-2469).
✳ Community Web site (www.norman-wells.com).

Things to Do

✳ Canol Heritage Trail offers not only spectacular wilderness scenery but also a window on an unusual episode of northern history.
✳ Norman Wells Historical Centre includes a gift shop, well stocked with local handicrafts and books, plus historical displays and videos related to local geology, the Canol Pipeline, and construction of artificial islands in the Mackenzie.
✳ Trail along Mackenzie Drive, officially designated as part of the Trans Canada Trail, offers a gazebo with picnic tables and firepit.
✳ The Norman Wells Trans Canada Trail pavilion was the first to be built in the Northwest Territories. Opened in September 2000, the red-topped structure is located across from the "Northern Store" parking lot, near the rest area and Town map. Community fundraisers, supporters, and volunteers are recognized for their contributions to the Trans Canada Trail.
✳ Pleasant park across from "Town Square" (Northern Store, etc.) with huge driftwood logs lining funky bridge, short trail, secluded picnic areas.
✳ Ptarmigan Ridge Golf Course, right downtown near Heritage Centre. Legion Hall doubles as clubhouse with golf clubs for rent and beer on tap. Play all four holes!
✳ Take Quarry Road 10 kilometres north of town to Jackfish Lake Road, hang a right at the dump, and enjoy a scenic,

> **The 355-Kilometre Canol — One of the World's Most Coveted Hiking Trails**
>
> Tim Hawkings, *Hiker's Guide to the Canol Heritage Trail*
>
> *Magnificent scenery, abundant plants, northern animals and birds, and historical artifacts make the Canol Trail one of the most spectacular and interesting hikes in Canada. It is also one of the most challenging hikes in Canada. It is remote and long and there are no services on the Trail. Only strong, experienced hikers should attempt the Canol Trail, for once you are on the Trail, you are on your own.*

Radiance after a storm on the Dehcho

20-minute drive to Jackfish Lake. Good fishing and swimming.

* The "split church" that welcomes both Baptist and Roman Catholic congregations.

* Ask about Rope Trail, Ridge Trail, and hikes to Fossil Canyon and Mount Hamar at the Visitors Centre.

Wilfred McDonald (right) shares stories with Geoff by his riverside cabin

Accommodation

* Heritage Hotel. Snazzy, upscale with excellent restaurant and spa facilities, 27 MacKenzie Drive, Box 279, Norman Wells, NT, X0E 0V0 (867-587-5000, fax 867-587-5001, info@heritagehotelnwt.com, www.heritagehotelnwt.com).

* Mackenzie Valley Hotel & Restaurant, PO Box 219, Norman Wells, NT, X0E 0V0 (867-587-2511, fax 867-587-3035, info@mackenzievalleyhotel.com, www.mackenzievalleyhotel.com).

* Rayuka Inn, PO Box 308, Norman Wells, NT, X0E 0V0 (867-587-2354, fax 867-587-2861, rayuka@theedgenw.ca).

* Yamouri Inn, PO Box 268, Norman Wells, NT, X0E 0V0 (867-587-2744, fax 867-587-2262, yamouri_inn@sympatico.ca).

Camping

* McKinnon Territorial Park on the banks of the Mackenzie just upstream from the town centre. Tent sites, picnic tables, water, and firewood. Open from May 15 to Sept 15 (867-587-3514, fax 867-587-2204).

* Jackfish Lake Campground off Quarry Road offers six developed sites, kitchen shelter, firewood, outhouses, a playground, and easy access to Jackfish Lake.

* "Whiskey Flats" at the foot of the second major pier offers very basic camping and outhouses but is

Jamie ponders a carpet of fireweed in a huge burn north of Norman Wells

noted for occasional loud parties.

Outfitting/Hardware

✳ Northern Store (867-587-2345, fax 867-587-2865).

Amenities

✳ Accommodation, restaurant, store, bank, bank machine, visitor information, pharmacy,

Concretions spill out of the riverbank near Carcajou Ridge

medical services, police, airport, gasoline, diesel, propane, automotive service.

Tips

✳ Most Canol Trail hikers descend from the mountains to the river and start or end with a float-plane ride to Canol Lake. This is usually a serious multi-day hike, though fly-in day tours of selected camps are available. Inquire at the Visitor Centre. See http://canoltrail.tripod.com/ harris.htm for some very practical tips on how best to "do" the Canol. Also, see *A Walk on the Canol Road* by S.R. Gage.

✳ Best water access for central part of town is the second major pier jutting into the river.

✳ Ready for a massage? Try Yasuyo Furusato Massage Therapy (867-587-2120).

✳ Be advised that drinking water may be contaminated immediately downstream from the oil development in Norman Wells.

Emergency

✳ Hospital/Clinic (867-587-2250).
✳ RCMP (867-587-1111).

> 🏔️ You can access the trailhead to

> **Mooseskin Boats on the Mountain**
>
> Rakekée Gok'é: Places we take care of
>
> *The Mountain River or Faǽfa Nilîne, is an important traditional trail used by Mountain Dene from Fort Good Hope ... In the old days, mooseskin boats were built to float down the river in spring. Many stories recount the trials and tribulations of mooseskin boat travellers attempting to navigate the many dangerous canyons on the river. At the head of the canyons, the boats would stop to let the women and children out to walk over on the portage trail. Only the men would lead the boats through. Today it continues to be an important moose hunting area, and is known as the shortest route to the highest mountains, and sheep hunting areas. Popular with whitewater canoeists, the river has tremendous tourism potential.*

---

the **Canol Heritage Trail** [WP239] by navigating between **Bear Island** and **Goose Island** and looking for an assortment of tanks and a wharf on river-left.

The Canol Trail's awesome alpine and canyon scenery, abundant wildlife, and tangible links with an amazing chapter in northern history make this a popular destination for long-distance hikers from all over the world.

North of Norman Wells you will be treated to some of the Mackenzie's best mountain scenery, with the jagged limestone cliffs of the **Norman Range** on your right and the lofty **Carcajou Range** on your left. On river-right, a seemingly endless carpet of fireweed created by major forest fires in 2003 adds to this beauty. Go north of **Ogilvie Island** for the best views and strongest current. This channel will also lead you to the impeccable **cabin** [WP242] of **Wilfred McDonald** who welcomes visitors and is overflowing with river stories. About 600 metres downstream from his cabin is **Oscar Creek**, which runs clear and cool, conditions favoured by **arctic grayling**. The creek was named after Oscar Granath, a self-sufficient Swedish trapper known in the 1920s for successfully growing bushel-loads of potatoes.

> **Rock-slinging Giant**
> Rakekée Gok'é: Places we take care of
> *The Ramparts rapids were created when [the giant] Wichididelle threw rocks at a giant beaver. There's also a place where he laid down for a nap—his head and footprints can still be seen today. The small waterfall is where he had a pee. There's a fish camp with cliffs close by where he took a bear. His boat is located above the rapids. Spruce Island is said to be his overturned boat. He said in the legends that he would return one day for it.*

You may see what looks like fossilized dinosaur testicles spilling out of the high, loose banks below **Perry Island** [WP243]. These, rusty-coloured cannonball-like objects are actually concretions formed in ancient sediments through an electro chemical process that causes particles to glom together in a spherical shape. Look also for smooth white or iridescent rocks typical of **ammonite fossils**, some of which are over 30 centimetres in diameter. The river narrows here, greatly boosting the current for the first time since Norman Wells. The alluring precipice ahead of you is **Carcajou Ridge**.

Anyone who thinks the Mackenzie Valley is flat should climb **Carcajou Ridge** [WP247]. It is a stupendous wall of limestone that rises over 500 feet (152 metres) above the river. A visible seismic line soon after the sharp bend in the river provides one option for a "quick scramble" to the top. A higher, more dramatic climb can be done from a pronounced bald spot further downstream. Allow at least a couple of hours for a round-trip climb. Camping is fine at the foot of the ridge when water levels are low. At its west end, cliffs rise sharply from the water with small beaches below, where you can tuck in to behold their glory as **peregrine falcons** and **cliff swallows** wheel overhead.

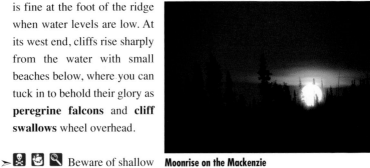

Moonrise on the Mackenzie

➤ 🕱 😊 🔍 Beware of shallow water skirting **Axel Island** [WP248], named after Axel Rosen, a Swedish woodcutter who built his cabin here and supplied fuel for the ever-hungry paddlewheelers in the 1920s and 30s. Though you may encounter more shallows near the mouth of the **Carcajou River**, don't even think of veering toward river-right because that course could take you down the potentially fatal throat of the **Sans Sault Rapids**.

➤ 🕱 😊 🔍 🛈 Just downstream from the **Mountain River** are the **Sans Sault Rapids**, considered by river pilots as the most difficult and dangerous section of the river to navigate. They are formed by a rocky limestone ledge that extends far into midstream from the curved east bank. In high water, four-foot waves bound from the boulder-strewn riverbed. In low water, waves exceeding eight feet have been recorded at these rapids. Regardless of water levels, **KEEP LEFT!** These rapids have claimed the lives of several paddlers, including 20-year-old Hugh Donald Lockhart, who drowned here on August 10, 1961, after choosing a course

> **Tributes to a Drowned Paddler**
>
> *Entries from the logbook at the Donald Lockhart memorial, Sans Sault Rapids*
>
> *He lived through all the singing years, craftsman, musician, naturalist and scholar. (written under Donald's picture, likely by his parents)*
>
> *What a beautiful site to overlook forever.*
>
> *Deep peace of the running waves to you,*
> *Sun and moon shine their light on you.*
>
> *We're taking off home to Fort Good Hope.*
> *Let my friends be safe, and enjoy life to the fullest.*
>
> *To all those who travel the waters of this magical place: go with balance and safety; confidence tempered by humility.*
> *Enjoy wildlife and pleasant unexpected surprises; and find a sense of place.*

on river-right. A **tipi-shaped memorial** [WP249] made from shining aluminum was constructed by his parents to lure future paddlers left and offer emergency shelter if needed. An inscription on its side includes the words, "May this memorial give shelter to those who travel the Mackenzie River…" Stored within the tipi are a metal box of miscellaneous offerings and a logbook recording over 40 years of entries from fellow travellers. Please handle these items with the care and respect they deserve. Just downstream from this monument you will cross the mouth of the **Mountain River**, a popular route for adventurous whitewater paddlers.

> ### The Ramparts—A Glorious Afterthought
>
> Lyn Hancock, *The Mighty Mackenzie*
>
> *For seven spectacular miles [11 kilometres] the Mackenzie narrows to a canyon only a quarter mile wide [0.4 kilometre]. Smooth clay-coloured walls rise sheer to more than 200 feet [61 metres] in height. At the top fantastic pinnacles are like the turrets of a fort or the crenellations of a castle. In an old Hareskin legend the Ramparts is an afterthought. God, having created the wonderful country of the whiteman, had a lot of useless clay left over. Having no use for it he threw it away in disgust and said, "This'll do for the Indians." If that is correct then they got the better bargain.*

➤ 🛆 🏠 One kilometre downstream from the mouth of the **Hume River** is a cluster of **cabins** [WP251] on river-left belonging to Charlie Barnaby of Fort Good Hope. These private trapping and hunting cabins are occasionally used for tourists and workshops. Treat the site with great respect if you choose to camp here. "I would've offered you caribou," Charlie said, when he heard we'd visited his empty camp.

➤ 🖤 🛆 🚣 Camping on the wide flats surrounding **Hume Island** [WP252] offers a pleasant, bug-free option when the water is low. Due west of this island is a huge wetland complex straddling the meandering **Ramparts River**. Many generations of Fort Good Hope families have used this area for hunting, trapping, fishing, and cultural activities. Most of the local elders were born and raised here. Known as *Tsodehnîline-Tuyát'ah*, the community, in partnership with Environment Canada, is

Entering the grand Upper Ramparts, upstream of Fort Good Hope

exploring options for long-term protection of this biologically and culturally rich area.

➤ ☠ 💬 🔍 After Hume Island, make sure that you veer to river-right to avoid the **Ramparts Rapids,** which can be extremely dangerous in low water. The

Our Lady of Good Hope Church, a National Historic Site

surest, safest course is to hug the southeast shore, watching out for erratic but passable turbulence near the mouth of the canyon [WP253]. The upshot: **STAY RIGHT!**

➤ 💬 🏊 🏕 🐾 The magnificent **Ramparts**, or *Fee Yee* as this area is known in Slavey, is the only canyon-like feature on the Mackenzie. Along this dramatic 12-kilometre stretch of river, fossil-studded limestone walls rise 80 metres out of the water like castle battlements. The Ramparts is a traditionally important fishery for Fort Good Hope. In the distant past, it served as a defense against raiding parties, includ-

Dene Pride

Fort Good Hope Chief Frank
T'Seleie, August 5, 1975

Five hundred years from now, someone with skin my colour and moccasins on his feet will climb up the Ramparts and rest and look over the river and feel that he too has a place in the universe and he will thank the same spirit that I thank that his ancestors have looked after his land well and he will be proud to be a Dene.

ing Inuit from the coast. Numerous archaeological artifacts found on the clifftops and adjoining valleys attest to this area's timeless cultural value. **Peregrine falcons** nest here as do several colonies of **cliff swallows**—which you may see picked out of the air by a falcon. Watch for occasional trails along the way that will take you to the top for a unique view of the river. Halfway through the Ramparts, a short hike up a pronounced **side canyon** on

Ancient sod-roofed cabins near Grand View

river-left [WP254] leads you to a landscape reminiscent of the canyonlands of the southwestern United States.

➤ 🔲 🔀 Just after your first sight of Fort Good Hope, look high up on the right bank for a small **statue of the Virgin Mary**. She is said to have appeared here in a vision to the newly-baptized Dene in the late nineteenth century. Soon after, watch for lovely, veil-like **Willow Point Falls** [WP255] tumbling over the Ramparts. There is a small, clear pool beneath the falls where you can cool off after a hot day of paddling.

FORT GOOD HOPE *(Radeyilikoe, North Slavey for "rapids")*
Population 540
Community

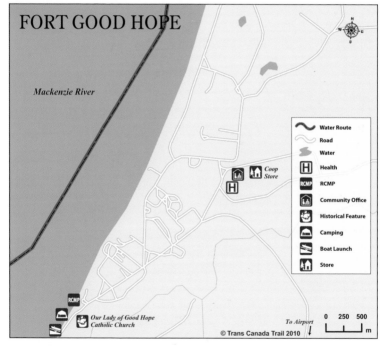

The first Fort Good Hope was the most northerly trading post of the North West Company when it was established in 1804 on the left bank of the Mackenzie near Thunder River. In 1826 the fort was moved 160 kilometres upstream to Manitou Island where it operated until rammed by ice during the spring flood of 1839. That same year the third Fort Good Hope sprang up, high and dry, at its current location. Uncontrolled hunting around the post led to mass starvation in 1844; as a result, the community began a program of food conservation. By 1859, when Father Grollier opened the first Roman Catholic Mission, the numbers of local game had rebounded. He was followed by Father Émile Petitôt, who built and decorated the opulent Our Lady of Good Hope Church over a 20-year period, from 1865 to 1885. Well known as a politically active community, Fort Good Hope was thrust into the national spotlight in 1975 with its vocal opposition to the construction of a Mackenzie Valley Pipeline. Today oil-and-gas-related employment contribute to its economy while traditional land-based activities carry on.

Local river travellers en route from Inuvik to Fort Good Hope

Visitor Information

✳ K'asho Got'ine band office. (867-598-2231, 867-598-2232, fax 867-598-2024).

Things to Do

✳ Our Lady of Good Hope was designated as a National Historic Site in 1977 as an example of a mission church in the Gothic Revival Style. For a tour, contact the local parish Sisters in the yellow house across the street (867-598-2361).

Nagwichoonjik National Historic Site

Gwich'in Social and Cultural Institute

The Mackenzie River (Nagwichoonjik, the "big country river") has been of great importance since the earliest days of history. As far back as Gwichya Gwich'in can remember, their traditional lifestyle has been shaped by their close connection to the land and the river…The history of life on the land and along the river is remembered through names that are given to a great number of places … The meaning of these names is often explained through stories that describe a place's origin, its special qualities, or an important event that occurred there. Out of this multitude of stories and names emerges the world view of the Gwichya Gwich'in and the great importance of the Mackenzie River for their history and culture. The river is a principal repository of the stories that suffuse with meaning the history of the landscape as the Gwichya Gwich'in know it.

✴ Hike up Old Baldy north of town, which sits on the end of an esker 5 kilometres long.

✴ Hike the 20-kilometre route along the top of the Ramparts from town to the mouth of the Tsintu River (also known as Bluefish Creek), a traditional gathering place in spring. Pre-arrange for a boat to pick you up or do it in the opposite direction back to town.

✴ Hire a boat and guide to take you up Fossil Creek behind Manitou Island (river-left) to Fossil Lake to hunt for fossils. Eleven thousand years ago, the Mackenzie River plunged over a huge fall into this lake. The dry cliff and plunge pool below are all that remain.

> **Unplugging on the River**
> Robert Miller, kayaker
>
> *The Mackenzie is so big, so wild, so desolate, uninhabited. I come out here for the solitude, to totally unplug. It's a complete break from everything. Phones. News. Email. Our busy lives. I need that.*

Accommodation

✴ Fah Sene B & B. Separate home with clean, basic accommodation, breakfast provisions, and full kitchen (867-598-2240).

✴ Tee Jay B & B, (867-598-2252).

✴ Ramparts Hotel, 6 rooms for 10 guests, restaurant, overlooks the Mackenzie. Operation uncertain so call to confirm status (867-598-2500).

Camping

✴ Possible on flat area across from church with permission of parish sisters (867-598-2361) or in town's central park area with permission from band office (867-598-2231).

Outfitting/Hardware

✴ Northern Store (867-598-2291).

Amenities

✴ Accommodation, store, bank machine, medical services, police, airport, gasoline.

Tips

✴ Wood Block music festival held every other year brings in regional musicians and dancers. Ask at band office.

River-worn jewels

* Local guides or tourism operators: Charlie Tobac (867-598-2533); Charlie Barnaby (867-598-2542); Wilfred Jackson (867-598-2804); Laurence Tseleie (867-598-2113); Alexi Chinna (867-598-2131).

Emergency
* Nursing clinic (867-598-2211).
* RCMP (867-598-1111).

Wendy sizes up a grizzly bedding area near Thunder River

➤ 🏠 💬 🦙 About 4 kilometres downstream from Fort Good Hope on river-right is the mouth of the **Hare Indian River** [WP256] (also known as the Rabbitskin), which is a popular, road-accessible destination for swimming, picnicking, and fishing (jackfish, inconnu, and arctic grayling). This is part of an important traditional trail system still used for hunting, trapping, fishing, and inter-community visits with the people of Colville Lake, 140 kilometres to the east, and Tulít'a, 206 kilometres to the south.

> **Grizzly Country**
> Alestine Andre, Tsiigehtchic[117]
> *I was hired to help with a botany survey by some pipeline people. We were flying a chopper towards the Thunder River and were about to land when we saw a big blonde grizzly bear. Needless to say, we didn't put down.*

➤ 🏠 💬 One of many backcountry **cabins** [WP258] used by Fort Good Hope residents sits below a communication tower about 15 kilometres downstream from town. The relatively high density of cabins around Fort Good Hope, a community known for its dedication to traditional lifestyles, is reminiscent of an early Oblate brother's observation that "there were 17 miles [27 kilometres] of campfires visible along the shore."

➤ 🏠 💬 The mouth of the **Loon River** [WP259] is the gateway to an extensive traditional trail system that, 15 kilometres inland, intersects at Loon Lake (one of 89

Brenda and Wendy weave willow baskets while waiting out the wind

The Arctic Circle—a Moving Target

Ned Rozell, Fairbanks Alaska

After 506 miles [814 kilometres] of walking, my dog Jane and I just hiked over the dashed line that encircles the top of every globe—the Arctic Circle. I'd like to pitch the tent precisely on the Arctic Circle. But it's not easy to pinpoint because this imaginary line is almost constantly on the move due to changes in Earth's axis called the Milankovitch Cycle. Serbian climatologist Milutan Milankovitch recognized that the tilt of Earth's axis shifted about 2.5 °C every 41,000 years which equals about 200 miles [322 kilometres] of movement in that time, or about 25 feet [8 metres] each year. It's like the Earth is a spinning top with a little wobble. This wobble confers variability on the Arctic Circle's location that may change as much as 50 feet [15 metres] every year. This makes it difficult to be a perfectionist when posing for pictures at an Arctic Circle highway stop or deciding exactly where to pitch your tent.

Loon Lakes in Canada) with trails leading north to large fishing lakes on the **Ramparts Plateau** and east up the **Tchaneta River** valley.

➤ Arm your bear bangers and don your party hat when you pass the big bend veering northward 15 kilometres downstream from Loon River. Congratulations! You've just crossed the **Arctic Circle** [WP260], that invisible line of latitude at 66°33' North, which marks the Arctic's southern limit. Here the sun will not rise on the winter solstice (December 21) nor set on the summer solstice (June 21). Only another 2,655 kilometres to the North Pole where, in the summer, the sun doesn't set for six months.

8

➤ An old **road scar** at the mouth of the **Tieda River** [WP261] harks back to the 1940s when the American army built a **military airstrip** on the flats above. This was part of a northern command-and-control network to counter a potential Japanese threat. The Tieda, another traditional route north,

creates a dramatic cleft in the **Ramparts Plateau**, revealing a similar but more subdued stature as the Ramparts above Fort Good Hope. Unusually steep banks on river-right accompany you for the next 20 kilometres.

➤ Near the north end of the **Askew Islands** [WP 262] on river-left are two well-maintained

In the footsteps of a very large grizzly

cabins and a charming two-holer outhouse belonging to Wilfred Jackson, a tourism entrepreneur in Fort Good Hope. Though this is a private camp, visitors are welcome. The Askew Islands are named not for their cock-eyed shape but after the pioneer boat-builder, George Askew, who constructed the mighty sternwheeler *Distributor* in 1921 at Fort Smith.

"Paying the water" with tobacco before pushing off

➤ 🙂 A cluster of log buildings once graced the empty limestone banks where **Andersons Landing** [WP263] is marked on older maps. Established in 1931, this was a busy trading post run for five years by one P.A. Anderson together with Gabriel Kakfwi of Fort Good Hope, who carried on the business until 1937 when the post was abandoned. Any lingering evidence of this settlement turned to ashes when an intense forest fire swept through here in 1998.

➤ 🙂 📖 🏠 **The Grand View** [WP264], a distinct widening in the river, begins near the outflow of the **Ontaratue River**. Just downstream on river-left is a wide-sloped clearing that leads to the homestead property of Fred and Irene Sorenson, who moved here from Norway in the 1950s and ran a sawmill and tourism lodge until the late 1990s. The family continues to use the well-equipped cabins, which were spared from the 1998 forest fire by aggressive water bombing. Camping is excellent on the pebble beach below the clearing, and visitors are welcome.

➤ 🙂 A little over 20 kilometres downstream from Grand View on river-right are **two cabins** [WP265], perched on a high, grassy bank like diehard sentinels from another era. As old as they must be—probably well over 50 years—they were solidly built,

Geoff after too many windbound hours

their roofs still supporting hundreds of kilograms of insulating dirt and sod now swathed in a tangle of wild roses.

> ⬚ 🏠 🌱 **Little Chicago** is located on top of a steep bank on river-right. This was the winter residence of a group of Chicago prospectors travelling to the Yukon's Klondike gold rush in the 1890s. It continued

---

Pierre Creek Picnics

Albert Ross, Tsiigehtchic

Everybody from town comes to Pierre Creek for picnics. We'll throw a net in the creek and—boom!—fifteen minutes later we'll catch some conny, whitefish, or maybe a pike for lunch.

---

as a Native community, trading post, and oil-drilling camp until destroyed by forest fires almost a century later. Though it still appears on most maps, all that remains is a humble plywood cabin, a tipi smokehouse, and an outhouse. A white cross just upstream from the cabin marks the location of a toddler's grave, lovingly adorned with coins, matches, rifle shells, and other gifts. Three larger crosses are visible as you paddle downstream. Just beyond the mouth of a nearby creek is a flat bench where the United States built another WWII airstrip, now home to an Environment Canada meteorological station. Bygone military debris still lines the bank. As a traditional meeting place steeped in history, Little Chicago retains its cultural importance for people in both Fort Good Hope and Tsiigehtchic. Plans for intensive oil and gas exploration in the vicinity of Little Chicago may soon change the character of this cherished place.

> ☠ ⬚ 🏠 🌱 The 150 kilometres between Fort Good Hope and Tsiigehtchic cover one of the longest, potentially loneliest stretches of unsettled river you will ever find on the Mackenzie. During the nine days it took us to paddle this section (and wait out the wind) we heard occasional ghostly wails, strange Loch Ness-type splashes, and eerie thuds in the night. Ironically, this stretch of the Mackenzie is one of the richest in terms of ongoing traditional use and cultural importance. The Gwichya Gwich'in of Tsiigehtchic so value the river corridor from **Thunder River** to **Point Separation** that, in 1998, they successfully es-

Alfred's bush skills pay off at Pierre Creek

8

tablished the **Nagwi-choonjik National Historic Site** in the heart of their traditional lands.

Sparkling path to the Lower Ramparts

➤ The mouth of the **Thunder River** [WP267] is a traditional source for siliceous argillite, a rare speckled black stone used to make spearheads and other stone tools. This traditional quarry site was used for thousands of years by Slavey, Gwich'in, and Inuvialuit alike. In Slavey it is called *Feetie Lushe*, in Gwich'in, *Vihtr'iitshik*, both names referring to the site's valuable stone for making tools. Archaeological evidence suggests that argillite from here was traded over vast distances across the western Arctic.

➤ One sign that you have entered the Arctic is that **grizzly bears** become more common. In over 30 years of northern fieldwork, the largest grizzly tracks I have ever seen were imprinted along the shore near Thunder River. From here onwards, be extra bear-aware when handling food or waste, and when entering thick foliage or noisy streamsides. You have also entered the realm of **arctic ground squirrels**, one of which chose to crawl under our tent floor while we slept, only to release a seismically loud shriek in the dead of night. Watch out for **golden eagles** and **peregrine falcons**, which nest and hunt along the **high riverbanks** that line this part of the Mackenzie. Dry, south-facing banks display a pleasing mix of open-grown spruce and sage-scented meadows (dubbed "hedgehog hills"), cut by short-lived but forceful streams. The impressive height and steep gradient of these banks contribute to landslides. Do not camp directly below any slope that looks the least bit unstable, especially in a heavy rain. The river narrows slightly, boosting the current, but lurking **sandbars** can still be a problem, particularly on river-left.

➤ Some older maps show a **trading post** at the mouth of the **Travaillant River** [WP269] (downstream side). Established in the early 1930s, all that remains is a large log-lined depression of what must have been the main post. Look also for a few vague pits, rotting boards, and garden beds associated with a busy settlement that sprang up around the post on both sides of the Travaillant River (there's a new cabin on the upstream side). This post saw brisk trade throughout the 1930s and early 1940s when both fur prices and competition were at an all-time high. The post was abandoned in the 1950s, but the site, called *Ghat'a Luwe Shee* in Gwich'in, remains an important fishing and recreation spot for people from Tsiigehtchic. The Travaillant River is one of the main traditional **trailheads** from the Mackenzie River to rich fish and wildlife resources at Travaillant Lake, or Khaii luk.

Enjoying comfort food on a blustery day

➤ 🏠 A **traditional fish camp** [WP271], known locally as "Gabe's camp," has been used for several generations by Tsiigehtchic's Andre family. The Gwich'in likely fished along this stretch of the Mackenzie thousands of years before the town even existed. When families started using dog teams during the early fur trade, traditional fish camps became even busier, because they had to catch and dry fish for their dogs as well.

➤ 🔄 An abrupt northwest bend [WP273] downstream from **Adam Cabin Creek** reveals a dramatic levelling in general topography and a dominance of stunted deciduous growth, signs that you are beginning your descent toward the Mackenzie Delta.

➤ ☠ 🏠 🔄 🐾 **Pierre Creek** [WP276] is the site of another traditional fish camp which, despite the dilapidated state of the cabins, is still regularly used today. Just a few hours paddle from our planned re-supply at Tsiigehtchic, our party was windbound here with virtually no food. After scrounging the long grass near the cabins, we found a rotten fish net that we gingerly repaired with dental floss. It held together long enough for us to catch two pearly whitefish for supper. We found out later that this is a popular hangout for bears. In the space of one month, one local fisherman was visited here by 11 black bears and one grizzly.

➢ At the **Lower Ramparts** [WP277], the shale walls of the Mackenzie narrow to 1 kilometre and rear almost 400 feet (122 metres) above the river. Though not as steep or as long as the Ramparts upstream of Fort Good Hope, the dramatic scenery is worth savouring especially when you consider that you are looking at the last real topographic relief this side of the Mackenzie Delta. Keep an eye and ear out for **peregrine falcons** that nest and hunt along these slopes.

Paddling in midnight sun above the Arctic Circle

➢ **Tsital Trein Creek**, or *Chidaltaii* [WP278], is another trailhead from which traditional Gwich'in trails fan out to backcountry lakes and wetlands rich with fish, ducks, and furbearing mammals. Owned by Rosa Andre, the **cabin** at the mouth of the creek was recently renovated, then almost knocked flat by a stupendous surge of spring ice in 2006. Breakup happened so fast that a nearby ice road that had been supporting heavy trucks on a Monday had disappeared by the following Wednesday.

8

APPROXIMATE DISTANCE 130 kilometres

HIGHLIGHTS
✳ Traditional community of Tsiigehtchic
✳ Point Separation, gateway to the Mackenzie Delta
✳ East Channel
✳ Diverse bird life in the Delta
✳ Campbell Hills
✳ Gwich'in traditional camp

OVERVIEW
Soon after leaving Tsiigehtchic you will enter one of the world's largest and most productive fresh-water deltas. The gateway to the Mackenzie Delta is Point Separation, named for the splaying of the river's flow into hundreds of web-like channels, the circulatory system of this world-famous ecosystem. The river widens sig-nificantly before breaking into

Neill Colin shares a rollicking story at Inuvik's Great Northern Arts Festival

smaller channels, potentially exposing you to big winds and waves before you duck into the intimate shelter of the East Channel. Not counting side trips or loaf-ing time, paddlers can expect to take at least three to four days to do this stretch, depending on the kinds of winds you encounter in the vicinity of Point Sepa-ration.

CAMPING TIPS
In spite of the Delta's ubiquitous mud, the occasional bar islands scattered along the East Channel are suitable for camping in low water conditions once you get above the wet fringe. Look for high, dry benches of sand on the inside of some of the more pronounced hair-pin curves.

Warning sign on dog cages, Inuvik

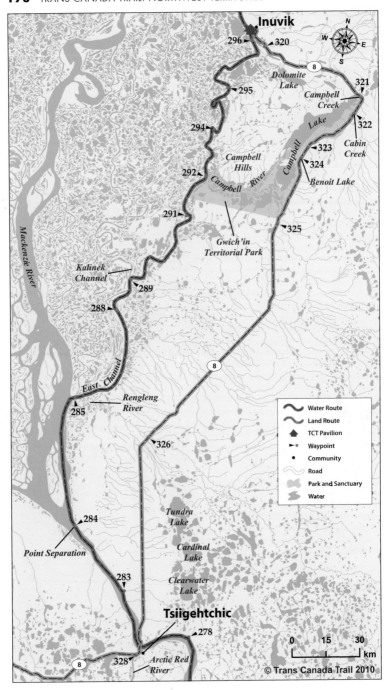

TSIIGEHTCHIC *(Gwich'in for "mouth of the iron river," formerly Arctic Red River)*
Population 185

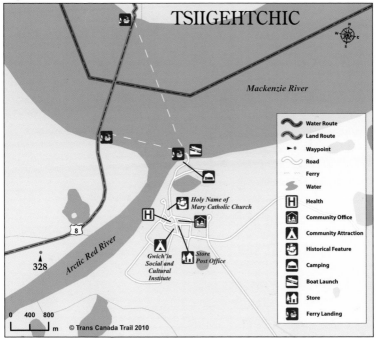

Community

❋ Tsiigehtchic is home to the Gwichya Gwich'in, one of the four Gwich'in communities in the Gwich'in Settlement Area. Originally a fishing camp, the Roman Catholics established a mission here in 1868 and a trading post soon followed. By 1940 only three permanent families lived in the settlement. However, the construction of the Dempster Highway attracted more residents. Today, tradition is alive and well in Tsiigehtchic with trapping, fishing, and hunting still central to many people's livelihoods. Tsiigehtchic offers access to the Arctic Red, a Canadian Heritage River that is

Doug Kendo of Tsiigehtchic rescues our canoe near Point Separation

navigable without portage for some 200 kilometres upstream. The Gwich'in Social and Cultural Institute is based here. Operation and maintence of the ferry crossing provides a few jobs and feeds local small businesses. The community is closely tied with Inuvik, located almost 100 kilometres north on the Dempster Highway.

Veteran spruce stump grounded in Mackenzie Delta muck

Visitor Info
✻ Hamlet Office, General Delivery, Tsiigehtchic, NT, X0E 0B0 (867-953-3201).

Things to Do
✻ Contact the Hamlet Office for information about tours of the Arctic Red River and local fish camps.
✻ Visit the Holy Name of Mary Catholic Church, if only for the great view of the confluence of the Arctic Red and Mackenzie Rivers.
✻ Tsiigehtchic is well known for its dryfish, a local delicacy that is often available for sale.

Accommodation
✻ None.

Camping
✻ No campground, but you can set up tents on the beach near the Tsiigehtchic ferry terminal. Inquire at the hamlet office about shower facilities.
✻ Camping is also permitted at the wayside

Camps Everywhere!

Peter Ross, former chief of Tsiigehtchic

I came up here from Aklavik in a steamer sixty-four years ago. There were cabins and fish camps spread out all along the river, maybe every five miles [eight kilometres] or so. When I came around the corner and saw Tsiigehtchic, the Flats was absolutely jam-packed with tents. There used to be big celebrations down there and they'd stick gamble for three days straight.

Point Separation

Lyn Hancock, *The Mighty Mackenzie*

Point Separation is the southern entrance to the Mackenzie Delta. Here the mighty river shatters into a million fragments. The three main channels and a myriad of lesser channels snake through a vast area of low-lying alluvial islands, ponds, lakes and peat bogs to stretch more than 240 kilometres to the Beaufort Sea.

park on the Dempster Highway across the river.

Outfitting/Hardware

✻ A grocery and dry goods store
operates intermittently.

Tips

✻ Look up local ethnographer
and author Alestine Andre of
the Gwich'in Social and Cultural Institute, and buy her excellent book on the Gwich'in
universe, *Gwichya Gwich'in
Googwandak: The History
and Stories of Gwichya*

A forest falls apart in the ever-shifting Mackenzie Delta

Gwich'in as Told by the Elders of Tsiigehtchic (867-953-3313).

✻ Canoe Days celebration is held in August with canoe races, community cook-
out, fiddling, and drum dances.

✻ Visitors are asked not to photograph or videotape the two cemeteries.

✻ This is a "dry" community, meaning that alcohol is prohibited.

Emergency

✻ Nursing clinic (867-953-3361).

✻ Inuvik hospital (867-777-8000).

✻ RCMP (867-952-1111 or 867-952-2251).

➤ 🎲 🛗 A steep climb up a high, rounded bluff straddled by two small
creeks brings you to the remains of
the original **Arctic Red River mission** [WP283], which dates back to
the 1860s. Wander through the
young spruce trees just back from
the brow of the hill and you'll find
the base of a stone chimney and, a
few metres away, a small rectangu-
lar pit delineating an unmarked

> **Liquid Highway to Inuvik**
>
> Peter Ross, former chief of Tsiigehtchic
>
> *The East Channel used to be our only highway. Be-
> fore the Dempster was built back in the early
> 1980s, we used to zip back and forth to Inuvik by
> boat all the time. In good weather it only took us
> about three hours. From here on you'll see camps
> all the way to town. Many are still used. Most of
> the older, abandoned cabins were occupied year-
> round. The river's taking a lot of them back.*

grave. Why the Roman Catholics chose this relatively unremarkable site is unknown. According to former Tsiigehtchic chief Peter Ross, "The missionaries had a good setup, but none of the locals wanted to come to church here so they shut her down. Everyone wanted to stay upriver where Tsiigehtchic is now." In spite of its unpopularity, this short-lived mission site offered a great view of the Richardson Mountains, which you can still enjoy today.

Inuvik Drummers and Dancers sing out at the Great Northern Arts Festival

➤ About 25 kilometres downstream from Tsiigehtchic is **Point Separation** [WP284], where the Mackenzie splits into countless streams and channels forming the Mackenzie Delta. Explorer John Franklin wrote of leaving a cache near this point back in the 1820s; it has yet to be discovered. The big islands beyond this point are popular among spring goose hunters from Tsiigehtchic. From here to the coast, in addition to more **geese, swans,** and **ducks**, you will likely see more mud, another hallmark of this dynamic delta ecosystem. Keep right to avoid mudbars and to stay on track for the crucially important East Channel.

> **Bush School, Gwich'in Style**
> Liz Hansen, traditional knowledge teacher, Inuvik
>
> *We talk with the kids about how things are done today compared to how their grandparents did things. We take them out on nature walks to set snares for muskrat. We teach them about drying fish and meat and about traditional clothing. Some parents can't afford to bring their children out to a camp such as this, so this gives the kids a great experience.*

➤ One glance at any map or satellite image of the Mackenzie Delta tells how easy it is to get lost there. The **East Channel** [WP285] offers a relatively sheltered, straightforward route to Inuvik. Marked with navigation buoys and beacons for barge traffic, its narrow entrance is about 16 kilometres from Point Separation. Even after

Alfred and Carrie revel in store-bought goodies from Inuvik

entering this channel, it's worth repeating this mantra to yourself—keep right!

➤ On river-right, 3 kilometres downstream of the East Channel entrance, is the mouth of the **Rengleng River**. Good access to the Mackenzie and local conditions favouring tree growth made this a prime timber-harvesting area during the construction of Inuvik in the late 1950s and early 1960s. You may hear rumours that this river offers a shortcut to paddlers wanting to bypass the notorious winds and waves around Point Separation and get a jump on the East Channel. Everything we heard suggests that the Renleng is virtually unnavigable due to multiple constrictions, beaver dams, and deadfall. Don't try it.

➤ In spite of the ubiquitous mud, the occasional **bar islands** [WP 288] scattered along the East Channel are suitable for camping in low water conditions once you get above the wet fringe. Because of the variety of wetland habitats in the

Spruce-bark shelter, Gwich'in traditional camp

Delta, there are generally more **waterbirds** here, many kinds of which—like terns, gulls, and ducks—prefer to breed or loaf on these islands.

➤ The East Channel swings abruptly eastwards where it meets **Kalinek Channel** [WP289], which continues due northeast. Hang a right here and stick to the Channel or you'll miss Inuvik.

➤ Though you won't see a welcome sign or fence posts when you reach the southern border of **Gwich'in Territorial Park** [WP291], you'll know you've arrived when you see an unusual outcrop of **dark limestone** on river-right near two cabins, one new and one old.

➤ As placid as the mouth of the **Campbell River** [WP292] may appear when you paddle by it on river-right, during most spring breakups this river presents a scene of grinding ice and surging meltwater that wield enough power to temporarily reverse the river's flow. At that time of year, the high, silt-choked waters of the Mackenzie back up as far as **Campbell Lake**, creating a unique **reversing delta** at the lake's southern end. Skirting the base of the

scenic **Campbell Hills**, the Campbell River is part of a two- to three-day paddling or boating trip that is popular with Inuvik residents who launch on Campbell Lake and paddle back to town via the East Channel.

➤ ⛵ 🏠 At the tip of a pronounced, right-hand **hairpin turn** [WP294] is a high,
dry bench of sand that offers excellent camping. The only drawback to this site
is that the neighbouring riverbanks are so active, your sleep may be disturbed
by occasional thunderous splashes as a dump truck's worth of mud ker-plunks
into the river.

➤ 🏚 🏕 About 17 kilometres upstream from Inuvik is a **Gwich'in traditional
camp**, called *Tithegeh Chi' vitaii* [WP295]. It consists of a ring of snug canvas
tents, several cabins, and two huge recycled buildings skidded here on an ice
road. The camp is used primarily by school children from Inuvik. Note the traditional spruce-bark lodge near the shore.

➤ 🚶 A **road** [WP296] within sight of Inuvik and just upstream of the grounded
ship MV *Mariner* provides access to a classy yet economical accommodation
option on the natural fringe of town, the **Arctic Chalet** (see Inuvik Accommodation).

9

APPROXIMATE DISTANCE

200 kilometres

HIGHLIGHTS

✳ Inuvik, the end of the road
✳ Caribou Hills
✳ Reindeer Station
✳ Treeline crossing
✳ Pingos
✳ Beluga whales
✳ Traditional whaling station
✳ Kitigaaryuit National Historic Site
✳ Tuktoyaktuk

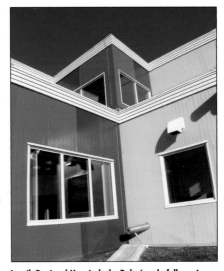

Inuvik Regional Hospital, the Delta's only full service health facility

OVERVIEW

On this, the last leg of the water route, you will cross over to several new worlds, from Gwich'in to Inuvialuit lands, from taiga to tundra, and from river to ocean. Standing on top of the Caribou Hills, you can literally put one foot in the forest and the other on bald tundra. Reindeer Station and its strings of camps along the river give you a tangible window into a unique era of arctic animal husbandry. Traditional whaling stations, past and present, convey the strong cultural ties that people here have with the sea. Natural wonders include waters alive with bobbing belugas and a landscape dotted with ice-filled pingos. In Tuktoyaktuk you can pose for pictures beside the northernmost trailhead of the Trans Canada Trail. Plan for at least four days to paddle this route. The last 30 kilometres across open ocean have kept more than one paddler windbound for a day or two.

CAMPING TIPS

As it slips toward the sea, the Mackenzie gets lower, and its banks muddier. Hurray for the East Channel, which takes you past some lovely sand beaches along the base of the Caribou Hills. You'll find more excellent campsites at the foot of Old Station, Kitigaaryuit, and Whitefish Station.

Father Matthew Ihuoma in the celebrated dome of Inuvik's igloo church

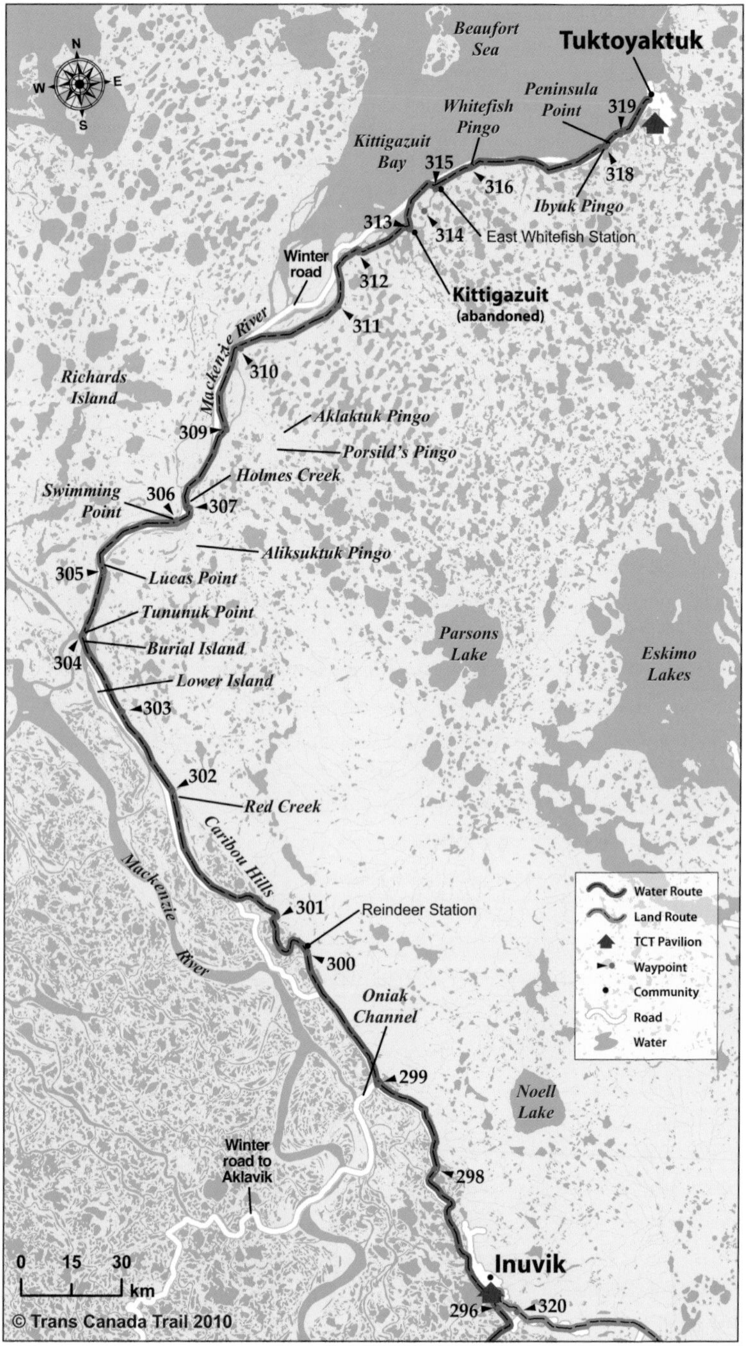

N W E S

Tuktoyaktuk

Beaufort
Sea

Peninsula
Point 319

Whitefish
Pingo

Kittigazuit
Bay 315
316 318

Ibyuk Pingo

313
314 East Whitefish Station

312

Kittigazuit
(abandoned)

311

310

Winter
road

Richards
Island

309

Aklaktuk Pingo

Porsild's Pingo

Holmes Creek

Swimming 306
Point 307

Aliksuktuk Pingo

305 Lucas Point

Tununuk Point

304 Burial Island

Lower Island

303

Parsons
Lake

Eskimo
Lakes

Mackenzie River

302

Red Creek

Caribou Hills

Mackenzie River

301 Reindeer Station

300

Oniak
Channel

299

Noell
Lake

298

	Water Route
	Land Route
▲	TCT Pavilion
▶•	Waypoint
•	Community
	Road
	Water

Winter
road to
Aklavik

Inuvik

0 15 30
km

296 320

© Trans Canada Trail 2010

10

INUVIK *(Inuvik, Inuvialuktun for "place of man")*
Population 3,586

Community

Inuvik was conceived in 1953 to replace Aklavik as the region's administrative centre because the latter was prone to flooding and had no room to expand. First called "New Aklavik," it was renamed Inuvik in 1958 because of confusion surrounding the Aklavik/New Aklavik split.

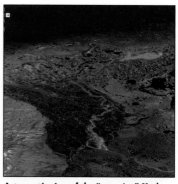

Astronaut's view of the "a-mazing" Mackenzie Delta (NASA)

Today Aklavik still stands, sporting a community motto of "Never Say Die!" The discovery of oil in the Beaufort Sea saw a big increase in the local population, but the 1986 closure of the Canadian Forces Base was a blow to the local economy. In recent years Inuvik has refocused on developing its Aurora College campus, and the tourism industry, with government jobs, oil and gas exploration, and a strong service sector making up the balance of the economy. For a town that is literally "at the end of the road," Inuvik is a colour-

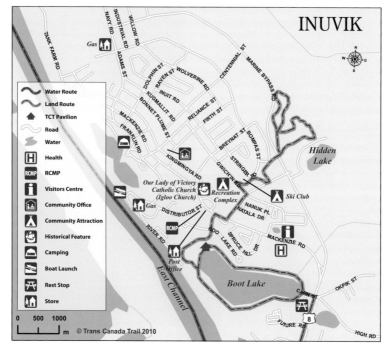

INUVIK

∿	Water Route
∿	Land Route
▲	TCT Pavilion
∿	Road
∿	Water
H	Health
RCMP	RCMP
i	Visitors Centre
⌂	Community Office
丸	Community Attraction
✍	Historical Feature
⌂	Camping
⛵	Boat Launch
⊼	Rest Stop
🏪	Store

0   500   1000   m   © Trans Canada Trail 2010

Our Lady of Victory Catholic Church (Igloo Church)
Recreation Complex
Ski Club
Hidden Lake
Post Office
Boot Lake
East Channel

ful, comfortable, and vibrant place where diverse cultures meet.

Sled full of flowers, Arctic Chalet, Inuvik

Visitor Information

✳ Western Arctic Regional Visitor Centre. Open June–Sept. Many interesting exhibits on regional ecology and culture with daily information on local tourism events and opportunities (867-777-7237, fax 867-777-7321, Travel_ Westernarctic@gov.nt.ca, www.iti.gov.nt.ca/parks/visitor_centres/inuvik).

✳ Town of Inuvik (www.inuvik.ca).

Things to Do

✳ Hike one of the many great trails in and around Inuvik, including the Boot Lake Trail (part of the Trans Canada Trail), the Treeline-Tundra Trail, Old Baldy, and Riverfront Walk. Ask at the visitors centre for a trail map and access details.

Inuvik Pavilion

✳ See the Trans Canada Trail Pavilion. Built in 2007, it is located at the corner of River Road and Duck Lake Street, overlooking the East Channel of the Mackenzie. It is also accessible via the Boot Lake Trail. It honours donors, fundraisers, and volunteers whose contributions have made the Trail a reality.

✳ Take a tour of the Inuvik Community Greenhouse, a creative project that converted an abandoned hockey arena into a northern Garden of Eden (867-777-3267, www.inuvikgreenhouse.com).

✳ Igloo Church, also known as Our Lady of Victory Catholic Church. Summer only; Mon, Wed, and Fri at 7 PM; Tues and Thurs at noon; Sun after church service. Phone to book

Drilling ship, MV *Mariner*, beached upstream of Inuvik

(867-777-2236).

∗ Boot Lake Park. A picnic area and sandy swimming beach. Paddlers can put in here to reach the East Channel.

∗ Climb the observation tower at Jak Park for a bird's-eye view of the Mackenzie Delta.

∗ Drive to the uttermost end of Canada's road system by heading north down Navy Road until it ends a few kilometres out of town.

∗ Visit the Inuvik Research Centre and enjoy its well-stocked library, free Internet access, and occasional evening talks.

Willy Simon expertly fillets a freshly netted whitefish, East Channel, Inuvik

∗ If you are ending your journey in Inuvik, consider taking a flight-seeing tour over the Mackenzie Delta or buzzing up to Tuktoyaktuk for a memorable day on the Beaufort coast. Ask at the visitors centre for tour package options.

Accommodation

∗ New or completely renovated hotels have mushroomed in Inuvik over the past few years. The town also offers several very attractive B & B options. See www.inuvik.ca/tourism/accommodations.html for a complete listing.

∗ Eskimo Inn (867-777-2801, fax 867-777-3234, Eskimo@permafrost.com).

∗ Mackenzie Hotel (867-777-2861, fax 867-777-3317, hotels@permafrost.com).

∗ Arctic Chalet Inn, easily accessed directly from the East Channel just upstream from town centre (867-777-3535, fax 867-777-4443, judi@arcticchalet.com, www.arcticchalet.com).

Camping

∗ Happy Valley Campground, on a bluff overlooking the East Channel of the Mackenzie. Nice views of the Richardson Mountains. RV and tent park with 19 powered and 8 non-powered sites (867-777-3652).

∗ Jak Park Campground. RV and tent park with 6 powered and 32 non-powered sites, observation

Celebrating a rare patch of bone-dry sand in the mucky Mackenzie Delta

tower, and trails. On highway toward airport (867-777-3613).

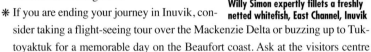

* You can pre-book campsites at Jak Park and Happy Valley campgrounds by visiting www.camping nwt.ca.

Outfitting/Hardware
* Central Mackenzie Road has a wide range of stores offering groceries, camping equipment, maps, books, and hardware.

Amenities
* Accommodation, restaurants, stores, bank, bank machine, visitor information, pharmacy, medical services, police, airport, gasoline, diesel, propane, automotive service.

Unwinding on the beach at Inuvik's Boot Lake

Tips
* Inuvik hosts the Great Northern Arts Festival, usually the last two weeks of July, an exciting gathering of artists and musicians from across the Northwest Territories.
* For those who are driving or biking out, current highway conditions and ferry schedules are available (867-777-2678 or 1-800-661-0752).

> **Divine Current**
>
> Carrie McGown, Mackenzie River guide
>
> *In my trip journal, I describe the presence of current in the Mackenzie Delta like the presence of God in our lives. You're not aware of the current until you try to paddle against it.*

Emergency
* Hospital/Clinic (867-777-8000).
* RCMP (867-777-1111).

➤ Though there are over 25,000 productive **ponds and lakes** [WP298] in the waterscape called the Mackenzie Delta, you won't see many unless you find some high ground or get a peek

Unwinding on the beach at Inuvik's Boot Massive underground ice lens revealed after a landslide, Mackenzie Delta

through a break in the riverbank like the one here on river-right.

➤ 🏠 🛶 🔍 🎣 At about the point where you get your first clear view of the **Caribou Hills**, you will see the opening of **Oniak Channel** [WP299] on river-left. It is here where boaters from Aklavik would hang a left on their return trip from Inuvik. On river-right you may spot a faded green and red sign that declares you are 97 miles (156 kilometres) from Tuktoyaktuk. Between here and Reindeer Station is a lovely rapier-straight stretch of river that skirts the base of the Caribou

Sled dog or wolf? The distinction seems to blur the farther you go north

Hills and features bald, dry grasslands, ribbons of spruce, and unusual outcrops of red and orange sediment.

➤ 🏠 🐾 In the early 1900s, wild caribou, a crucial food source for the Inuvialuit, became scarce. The federal government transplanted a herd of domestic reindeer from Alaska to this region and encouraged Inuvialuit to become herders. **Reindeer Station** [WP300] was built as a base for this new endeavour. Called

Qun'ngilaat by most Inuvialuit, this station was once a village, with houses, a school, a trading post, workshops, and warehouses. It was closed in the late 1960s when the base of reindeer husbandry operations was moved to Inuvik. The most prominent structure still standing is the station manager's two-storey house, built in the 1930s, and a lively gathering place for all-night square dancing and fiddling among local herders (in Gwich'in, it is referred to as *Vadzaih degaii zheh*, for "caribou white house"). A few cabins are maintained for trapping, hunting, fishing, or plain old relaxing on the land.

Edwin Rogers and Snoopy hang out at Whitefish Station

10

➤ 🏔 💬 🏞 Five kilometres before the East Channel widens out on its last leg to the Beaufort Sea, look for a distinct **trail** [WP301] up a wide tundra-covered valley. This was one of several traditional winter routes to important hunting areas east of the Delta and beyond, to the Husky Lakes (or Eskimo Lakes) area. It was also popular with reindeer herders, who did their work on dog sleds. Trek up this valley and you will behold the vast tundra plateau beyond the Caribou Hills. You may also catch a glimpse of the **Ikhil gas plant**, which supplies local fossil fuel energy to Inuvik.

Jamie in *muktuk* school, Whitefish Station

➤ 🛏 🚶 🏢 The East Channel comes closest to the **Caribou Hills** (WP302) just downstream from the outflow of **Red Creek**. A wide sandy beach at the base of a bald hill makes an excellent lunch spot or campsite. It's an easy climb to the top where you may literally have one foot in the taiga forest and one on the **arctic tundra**. Along the way, discover the diverse flora and time-polished pebbles in shades of milk-white, orange, and jade. Take a moment to enjoy the spectacular views of the Mackenzie Delta.

The Original Reindeer Station

Inuvialuit Land Administration

These four log buildings are what remain of the first reindeer station. The buildings were constructed in 1931–1932 and herders referred to this site as the "Old Station" once the new Reindeer Station was built about 100 km further up the Mackenzie River. Visitors are cautioned that the walls of the buildings and surrounding soils contain the pesticide DDT.

10

➤ 💬 About 1 kilometre south of **Lower Island** [WP303] are three distinct humps on river-right called the **Three Shahmans' Graves**. In the winter, folks from Tuktoyaktuk will stop here on their way to Inuvik and toss a loonie

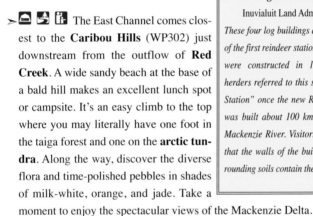

Fresh cut *muktuk* drying in the midnight sun

on the ice road for good luck.

➤ 🖥 🏔 🌀 During the Beaufort-Macken-
zie oil exploration boom of the 1970s and
1980s, Imperial Oil operated a staging
base for its field operations at **Tununuk
Point** [WP304]. *Tununuk* means "at your
back" and is aptly named since the many
channels leading out from here all leave
this point behind you. Also called **Bar C**,
it is strategically located on the most
southerly point of **Richards Island** where
the East Channel meets major western
Delta channels. Before industry moved in,
this point had been a traditional hunting
and fishing camp used by local Inuvialuit.

Diseases Ravage Kitigaaryuit
Canada's Western Arctic

*American whaling ships arriving in the
1890s brought with them unfamiliar diseases, and measles, diphtheria and flu epidemics ravaged the community [of
Kitigaaryuit]. According to estimates, of the
2,500 Inuvialuit alive in 1850, only 259 re-
mained by 1905. The Inuvialuit were fright-
ened by the terrible plague that devastated
their community. Eventually Kitigaaryuit
was abandoned and families moved to Tuktoyaktuk. This once sacred place turned into
a town of ghosts and sad memories.*

Just off the point is **Burial Island**, or *Qikiqtaaryuaq*, a traditional Inuvialuit
cemetery now pincushioned with buoy alignment markers. It is said that so
many Inuvialuit used to gather at Tununuk Point each spring that they could
stand in a circle around Burial Island and all join hands.

➤ 🐾 🦌 To the north of Tununuk Point on river-left you will get your first good
view of an ice-cored **pingo**. Though you are still about 60 kilometres from the
Beaufort Sea, don't be surprised to see **beluga whales** swimming upstream.
Something magical happens once you turn
your back on Tununuk Point: you leave all
trees behind you. Welcome to the arctic
tundra.

➤ 🖥 🏔 **Lucas Point** [WP305] is named
after a local trapper who made his base
camp here long before hydrocarbon exploration facilities were established in the
1970s. Since then it has become a staging
area for ice road construction.

➤ 🖥 🏔 ☠ Like Tununuk and Lucas
Point, the oil and gas industry moved to
Swimming Point [WP306] in the 1970s,

Mackenzie Turns Back
Alexander Mackenzie ponders the ice-
choked Beaufort Sea, July 12, 1789

*My men express much sorrow that they are
obliged to return without seeing the Sea,
in which I believe them sincere for we
marched exceeding hard coming down the
River, and I never heard them grumble;
but on the contrary in good Spirits, and in
hope every day that the next would bring
them to the Mer d'Ouest, and declare
themselves now and at any time to go with
me whenever I choose to lead them.*

10

constructing a barge landing, fuel storage facilities, a work camp, a helipad, and an airstrip. These facilities have been largely mothballed since the mid-1980s, pending construction of some megaproject like the proposed Mackenzie Valley gas pipeline. The name is derived from the tradition of herding reindeer across this relatively narrow gap in the Mackenzie from their winter range east of the Caribou Hills to their summer range on Richards Island. Look south of Swimming Point for the great bulbous mound

> **Paddle to "The End of the World"**
>
> Lyn Hancock, *The Mighty Mackenzie*[126]
>
> *Following in the wake of Mackenzie come pleasure-seekers in ever increasing numbers—in canoes and kayaks, motor cruisers, rubber dingys and plastic tubs, the wealthy and the poor alike. They come from places as far distant as England, Florida and Australia, to paddle, sail, motor or float to what literally is the end of the world, the ice-swept Arctic Ocean.*

of **Aliksuktuk Pingo**. Though by now you know how unpredictable the winds can be on this river, people in Tuktoyaktuk speak of this area being windy most of the time, so prepare to be windbound—as we were for several restful hours.

Two kilometres downstream from Swimming Point on river-right just south of the **Holmes Creek** outlet are the two **log cabins** [WP307] used by herders that may date as far back as the 1920s, when reindeer were first introduced into the region.

Whether it's windy or not, hang a right at what is locally known as **Peach Creek** [WP309] to see a more intimate side of the Mackenzie River's arctic face. As you go through this sheltered, scenic channel, look right for **Aklaktuk Pingo**, meaning "having bear" and, about 1 kilometre south, **Porsild Pingo** named after arctic botanist A.E. Porsild. Near the north end you'll see half a dozen cabins and tent frames that are used all year as hunting and fishing base camps.

Much like Point of Separation north of Tsiigehtchic, there is a sudden **widening in the Mackenzie** [WP310] as you approach **Kittigazuit Bay** and

> **The Great Ibyuk**
> Inuvialuit Place Names
>
> *The Inuvialuktun word pinguryuaq refers to a hill with a core of ice. Pingos, as they are known in English, are formed in areas of permafrost when ponds or lakes are drained. When the wet lake bed freezes, the ice below expands and is forced upwards. The land near the mouth of the Mackenzie River is low lying. Some pingos, like Ibyuk, are important to Inuvialuit because they are good landmarks to use when travelling. Big pingos make great lookouts. Ibyuk and Split Pingo are part of Tuktoyaktuk's community emblem.*

10

ultimately the Beaufort Sea. Beware of feisty winds and weird waves. Continue to take the far right channel, but watch for shallow water, especially along the mainland shore. This is a very scenic stretch with high, dissected banks reminiscent of the Welsh and Irish coasts. Some of these banks show pronounced **thermal slumping** due to the melting of underlying permafrost — a tell-tale sign of arctic climate change. As we paddled by one major thaw-slope, we could literally hear it falling apart.

Bar-3 DEW line station framed by caribou antlers, Tuktoyaktuk

As the river swings north again, look for an attractive **beach** [WP311] complete with lots of firewood and a clear-running stream. Besides offering a good rest stop or campsite, this site is rich with history related to the earliest days of reindeer herding. A short hike up the nearby trail takes you to the original reindeer station cabins or "**Old Station**." Once you have respectfully looked around the cabins, continue up the hill behind them for your last bird's-eye view of the amazing Mackenzie Delta and your first hello to the **Beaufort Sea**!

Stone Caribou

Inuvialuit Place Names

Tuktuuyaqtuuq, or Tuktoyaktuk as it is more commonly spelled today, takes its name from an Inuvialuit legend. Felix Nuyaviak told this story in Inuvialuktun in the 1970s. "The name Tuktuuyaqtuuq comes from a legend about a girl who was forbidden to look at some caribou that were swimming across the harbour. She disobeyed and the caribou turned to rock. Several large rocks can still be seen from the point at the north end of the town when the water is low."

Keep right through the sheltered, scenic **channel** [WP312] that spills out into **Kittigazuit Bay**.

Kitigaaryuit [WP313] (or Kittigazuit as it is shown on some maps) is the name of an abandoned Inuvialuit village on

Boogie Pokiak of Ookpik Tours tells stories about his beloved Tuktoyaktuk

river-right where the Mackenzie meets the sea. For at least 500 years, as many as 1,000 Inuvialuit gathered here each summer to hunt beluga whales in skin kayaks in the shallow nearshore waters. Whalers, traders, and missionaries brought schooners that allowed the Inuvialuit to hunt whales farther afield.

Driftwood windscreen at Kitigaaryuit whaling camp, a national historic site

They also brought new diseases that devastated the local population. Most of the survivors of the epidemics moved to Tuktoyaktuk in the 1930s. The immense historical value of Kitigaaryuit was recognized in 1978 when the Government of Canada declared it a **National Historic Site**. Besides ancient graves and ruins of large traditional Inuvialuit houses, there are tangible reminders of more recent history, such as a log cabin from a Hudson's Bay Company post and the foundation of an Anglican church. Many of these artifacts are extremely fragile. If you explore the area, please tread lightly on this sacred ground, and take nothing but pictures. And beware of large barrels sunk in the ground and veiled by bushes. They were used to store muktuk (whale skin) and whale oil—you don't want to fall into one!

A narrow opening south of the more recent structures at Kitigaaryuit (including a Quonset hut frame and wind-wall of vertically stacked driftwood) leads to a peaceful **inside channel to the Beaufort coast** [WP314]. To find the channel, hug the southern tip of Kitigaaryuit, then immediately swing north. From here you've only got another 6 kilometres to the coast. There are attractive sandy stretches along the way, suitable for camping or resting as you say goodbye to anything resembling a river.

Beluga or "whitefish" *muktuk,* **a staple Inuvialuit food for centuries**

➤🏠☠😊🎒 At the mouth of the channel you will see an orderly row of tent frames and plywood cabins built on a long gravel spit. Welcome to **East Whitefish Station** [WP315], traditionally known as *Nalruriaq*, meaning "to go around." Inuvialuit have lived here for centuries, although today it is used mainly as a seasonal camp by beluga hunters from Inuvik. "Whitefish" is a term some locals use for beluga whales. The spit was once at least 30 metres wider with room for two rows of camps. Visit soon before this beautiful site is reclaimed by the sea! The sheltered

Spelunking in the frozen catacombs beneath the streets of Tuktoyaktuk

bay behind the spit once offered safe harbour for whaling schooners. If you arrive during prime whaling season, from mid-June to July, many of the camps will be occupied. Visitors are generally welcome. Chances are you will have to stop here to wait for optimal wind conditions before dashing for Tuktoyaktuk, so why not learn how to make muktuk or hear a few whaling stories in the meantime? To reach Tuktoyaktuk, you must cross **30 kilometres of wide open ocean** along a shore that, should the wind come up, offers little protection and few safe beaching sites. Pick your traverse time carefully and *heed the advice* of any locals you may meet at Whitefish Station. Count on four to five hours to make the crossing.

➤🏠☠🏊🦌 A few kilometres east of Whitefish Station you will paddle past **Whitefish Pingo** [WP316], the first of several pingos close to shore along the next 10 kilometres. Watch for the spouts and risings of **beluga whales** along this stretch. During a late-July crossing, we were escorted by

Colossal cement slabs line Tuktoyaktuk's fragile shore to keep it on the map

10

a pod of about 50 belugas, blowing and breaching all around us. One of the silver herrings they were chasing jumped into the bow of our canoe! Watch for driftwood **muktuk racks** along the shore, which have been used by several generations of whale hunters. If you see a dead beluga on shore, stay well away. For one thing, they smell bad. For another, that smell is honey to **grizzly bears**, seven of which showed up to feed on one dead whale as we paddled by.

➤ ⛷ 🔲 **Ibyuk Pingo** [WP318] is one of the largest pingos on the planet. *Ibyuk*, meaning "thick" or "sod," is one of about 1,350 pingos in the Inuvialuit Settlement Area. It forms the centrepiece of the **Pingo Canadian Landmark**, an

area near Tuktoyaktuk that was established to protect Ibyuk and several other pingos. You can approach the pingo from the water by heading through the gap just south of **Peninsula Point**. Please respect the sensitive vegetation that insulates this sod-covered cone of ice. As of June, 2007, Ibyuk is all the more sensitive

Paddling from Whitefish Station to Tuktoyaktuk, 30 km of wide open ocean

due to a runaway campfire that scorched over two hectares of insulating cover. Study your map carefully and you'll discover the maze-like inland route that takes you to Tuktoyaktuk.

10

➤ ⛷ At the northeast end of Peninsula Point [WP319] is a **collapsing pingo**—what local people call a "half pingo"—and a **slumping shoreline** that exposes glistening chunks of ground ice, vivid evidence of a warming arctic climate.

TUKTOYAKTUK *(Tuktuujaqrtuuq, Inuvialuktun for "place where there is something that looks like a caribou")*
Population 990

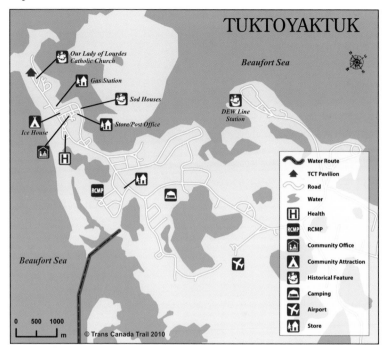

Community

Tuktoyaktuk, or Tuk as many call it, is the largest Inuvialuit community and is considered a centre for Inuvialuit culture. This site was originally a hunt camp for *tuktu*, or caribou. In 1931, a transport camp was built here to take advantage of its protected natural harbour. A few years later, a general store and trading post opened to serve the few families that lived here. Once known as Port Brabant, the community was renamed in 1950 as part of an ongoing trend to revive traditional names. During the 1970s and 1980s oil and gas boom, Tuk grew as a staging area for

Delta braid lines the hem of homemade parka, Tuktoyaktuk

drill ships, tug boats, icebreakers, and building materials. A slump in the late 1980s was followed by a recent spike in gas exploration associated with the proposed Mackenzie Valley pipeline. Whether in boom days or bust, supply tugs and barges continue to stage here, supplying essential goods to arctic communities along the coast. Here, at the northern terminus of the Northwest Territories Trans Canada Trail, you will be some 50 kilometres above the treeline, 40 kilometres from the Mackenzie River, and 136 air kilometres from Inuvik.

Hanah Lucas with Deh Cho and Bambi, Tuktoyaktuk

Visitor Information

✳ Tuk hamlet office (867-977-3221).

Things to Do

✳ Visit Tuk's Trans Canada Trail pavilion. Officially opened in 2001, it is located past the Town Hall en route to the shore of the Beaufort Sea. The Trans Canada Trailhead Monument, which marks the spot where water was drawn to begin the Relay 2000 events, is to the immediate right. The pavilion inscriptions acknowledge the fundraisers, supporters, and volunteers for their essential role in the development of the world's longest recreational trail.

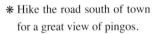
Tuk Pavilion

✳ Hike the road south of town for a great view of pingos.

✳ If you haven't visited Ibyuk, contact local tour operators or Inuvik's Parks Canada office for a tour.

✳ Walking tour of Tuk. Follow the signs around the edge of town.

✳ Traditional sod house.

✳ Guided town tours are available, exposing you to the local history, culture, and

10

food. Some tours include a visit to the famous community freezer, a cavernous chamber built below the streets of Tuktoyaktuk.

2:00 a.m. sunset over East Whitefish Station whaling camp

* Visit local soapstone carvers. Just ask around.
* Fishing tours are available from local operators.

Accommodation
* Tuk Inn, Box 193, Tuktoyaktuk, NT, X0E 1C0 (867-977-2381).
* Pingo Park Lodge, 95-TDC, Bag 6000, Tuktoyaktuk, NT, X0E 1C0 (867-977-2155).

Camping
* Basic camping off Beaufort Drive. Ask at hamlet office.

Outfitting/Hardware
* Northern Store (867-977-2211).

Amenities
* Accommodation, restaurant, store, bank machine, medical services, police, airport, gasoline, automotive service.

Tips
* Traditional Inuvialuit arts and crafts from the Nautchiaq Fur Shop (867-977-2118).

Emergency
* Nursing station (867-977-2321).
* RCMP (867-977-1111).

10

—

OVERLAND ROUTES

APPROXIMATE DISTANCE

315 kilometres

HIGHLIGHTS

✳ Caen Lake fire tower
✳ Birdwatching at Caen Lake
✳ Mackenzie Bison Sanctuary
✳ Chan Lake
✳ North Arm Park and Tower Hill
✳ Behchokò community
✳ Stagg River
✳ Canadian Shield scenery
✳ Yellowknife, capital of the Northwest Territories

Psyched for the 315 km ride from Fort Providence to Yellowknife

OVERVIEW

Some people call the road from Fort Providence to Behchokò "Bison Alley" since there are few places on earth where the likelihood of seeing a wild bison is as great. The landscape changes dramatically just a few kilometres west of Behchokò as you cross the geological divide between the flat taiga plains and the rolling, lake-studded Canadian Shield.

For information on Fort Providence, see pg. 107.

CAMPING TIPS

Though the Caen Lake fire tower is a bit off the road, visitors are welcome and the camping, view, and local culture are great. Chan Lake picnic area is an adequate place to camp, but black bears will hang around here when sloppy tourists have left goodies for them. There are numerous gravel or sand pits along this route that, though not aesthetically overwhelming, offer flat ground in a relatively bug-free setting.

BIKERS BEWARE!

According to Department of Transport surveys, traffic counts along Highway 3 peak in the summer at around 500-600 vehicles per day. This isn't much compared to some southern roads you may have cycled, but

Jamie chronicles the day's bike journey near Caen Lake

11

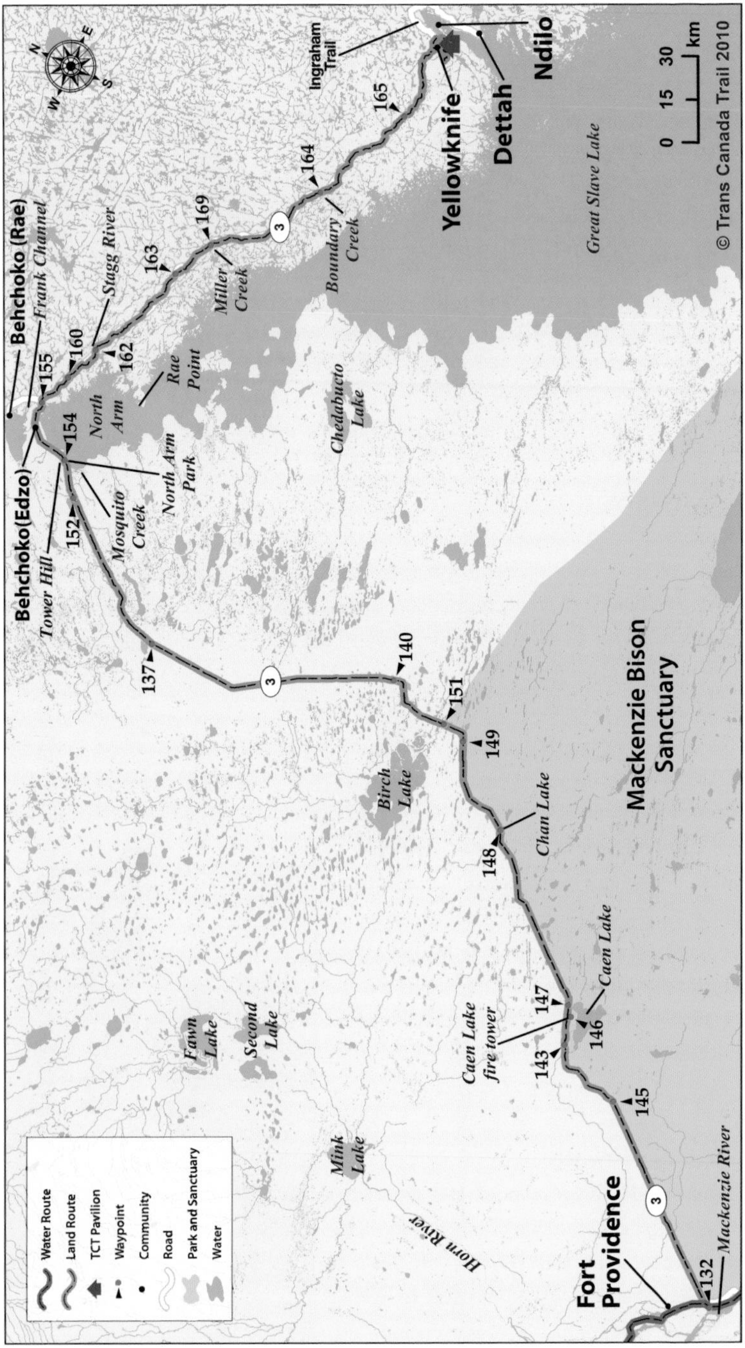

Ingraham Trail

Ndilo

Dettah

Yellowknife

Great Slave Lake

165

164

169

163

Boundary Creek

Miller Creek

Behchoko (Rae)

Frank Channel

Stagg River

160

155

162

Rae Point

North Arm

154

Chedabucto Lake

Behchoko (Edzo)

Tower Hill

152

North Arm Park

Mosquito Creek

137

140

3

151

149

Mackenzie Bison Sanctuary

Birch Lake

Chan Lake

148

Fawn Lake

Second Lake

Caen Lake

147

146

Caen Lake fire tower

143

Mink Lake

145

Horn River

Fort Providence

3

132

Mackenzie River

km

0   15   30

© Trans Canada Trail 2010

Legend
- Water Route
- Land Route
- TCT Pavilion
- Waypoint
- Community
- Road
- Park and Sanctuary
- Water

11

light traffic can make you less vigilant and therefore more accident-prone. Even with the recent upgrades, shoulders can be narrow and gravelly, offering little leeway for a safe, fast exit when spooked by a vehicle. To help with orientation, the following description includes kilometre distances derived from roadside posts (where visible) topped with blue mileage indicators.

➤ Note that at [WP145/km 66] km zero of Highway 3 begins south of the Mackenzie River where it intersects with Highway 1, the Mackenzie Highway.

➤ At [WP145/km 66] you arrive at the first real curve ending a flat, **laser-straight stretch of highway** over 35 km long. Make sure you're awake for it!

➤ There is a **pullout** on the west side of the highway at [WP143]. A 150-metre gravel road south of the garbage container leads to a small lake where you can make a quiet, level camp for the night.

There's Nothing Better than Bikes

Edith and Norm Mair, septuagenarian cyclists

Edith and Norm Mair have been long-distance cyclists since 1980, starting in their native Great Britain and, over the next quarter century, have covered much of Scandinavia, western Europe, New Zealand, and Australia. In their late sixties, they crossed the entire breadth of Canada over three summers. Five years later they set out from their Yellowknife home to bicycle to Edmonton, over 1,500 kilometres due south. Here are their impressions of the Trans Canada Trail portion of Highway 3 between Yellowknife and Fort Providence.

A lot of people would stop and ask if we were okay. Others would wave or honk at us. Sometimes we knew them, sometimes not, like the trucker who stopped on his way to Yellowknife. He jumped out of his big semi with a couple tins of juice and a snack for us. He spotted us again on his way back south. This time he had some oranges for us. When we pulled into a restaurant down the road the waitress announced that this anonymous trucker had already paid for a coffee and a piece of apple pie for us both. He was such a kind young man.

In all the biking we've done all over the world, this was the first time we'd ever cycled past a bear right on the roadside. He came out and looked at us, disappeared into the woods, then popped his head out again for another look. Of course we saw a lot of buffalo along that stretch too. We scooted past three or four big groups. Wolves too. One big one appeared out of nowhere just a spit and a throw from our tent.

Cycling gives you such a sense of freedom. You don't have to worry about phones or gas stations, just a new scene everyday. There's nothing better than bikes to enjoy a road like that. You miss so much in a car.

➤ 🏕 🏠 🚣 ⛰ 🚻 At the crest of a hill 65 kilometres from Providence is a gravel road on the east side of the highway that leads to the **Caen Lake fire tower** [WP146/km 86.5]. This scenic road winds 800 metres over a high, poplar-lined ridge and, though primitive, is easily negotiated with loaded bikes. Territorial government fire crews stationed at the tower

Jamie and Alfred ready to roll after a rest stop at Chan Lake picnic area

welcome visitors—with a big sign to prove it. Enjoy the dry open meadow, colourful trails, and vegetable gardens lined with rocks painted pink and blue by firefighters with apparently lots of time on their hands. This is an excellent picnic or camping spot, complete with picnic tables, outhouse, and friendly locals. As for climbing the tower, don't try this unless invited and supervised by one of the crew.

➤ 🚣 An added treat at this site is the **kilometre-long hill** just beyond the fire tower road that will catapult you into the next chapter of your journey. With fully loaded bikes you can break 30 kilometres per hour, no problem.

➤ 🚵 🚣 ⛰ Two kilometres beyond the fire tower road is another gravel road, also on the east side, which leads to **Caen Lake** [WP147/km 89] a biological magnet for water birds. This warm, shallow lake is typical of the **Great Slave Lake Plain ecoregion**, where wetlands dominate 50 percent of the landscape. Productive aquatic plant growth and lush marshes rimming the lake support abundant ducks, geese, and shorebirds as well as a large colony of black terns at the northernmost edge of their range. This lake makes for a bird-rich paddle if you have kayak or a canoe in tow.

➤ 🏠 🦌 The **Chan Lake picnic area** at [WP148/km 122] is

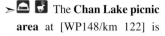

A golden hike up Tower Hill, North Arm of Great Slave Lake

Corralled by Bison!

Mike Keizer, interpreter, Wood Buffalo National Park

Many years ago, on a hot June day, I was out on patrol on Parson's Lake Road, a wilderness strip road through the park. I came into a big bison herd and stopped the truck. It was an old truck with no air conditioning. I was having a great time watching the adults stomp around and the calves frolicking.

After a few minutes I decided to back up and turn around but by that time they had circled around me. I was totally surrounded by bison. I couldn't move. So I turned the truck off—it was running out of gas—and sat there watching them for a while. It was a big brown truck that seemed to soak up the sun. I was getting pretty hot so I rolled down the windows.

Have you ever been in the middle of a bison herd? Can you imagine how many bugs they carry around with them? I said to myself, "Whoah!" and rolled the windows up, trying to kill every bug in the truck. I was trapped. I couldn't open the windows. It was getting hotter and hotter. An hour went by. An hour and a half. I'd eaten the orange I brought with me. I'd drunk my Coke. I took my shirt off. I took my shoes and socks off. I opened up my pants. I was slowly dying in the truck saying, "Oh God, somebody move!"

Finally the herd opened up and I was about to move when a tourist came towards me in another vehicle. It was then that I realized I was sitting in a Park truck basically wearing nothing but my underwear. I slammed on the brakes, pulled my pants up from around my knees, threw on my uniform and waved out the window. "Hi!" I said as nonchalantly as possible. "How's it going? There're a few bison back there. You might want to turn around."

That was my big bison encounter.

locally known as the rough halfway mark between Fort Providence and Behchokò (Rae-Edzo). This Territorial "park" offers a large kitchen shelter, picnic tables, a woodstove, a large grass clearing, and outhouses. If you choose to camp here, keep in mind that black bears looking for goodies occasionally trash this site. The small lake behind the picnic shelter is a popular feeding spot for **sandhill cranes**. Seven kilometres beyond Chan Lake you cross the northern boundary of the **Mackenzie Bison Sanctuary**. Don't worry, you have not seen your last bison. Twenty years ago, they rarely strayed much beyond Behchokò. Recently, they have been observed almost as far east as Yellowknife, due perhaps to an

Chris patiently doctors a third flat tire

expanding population and our changing north-ern climate.

➤🏕 About 15 kilometres beyond Chan Lake [WP149/km 138] is a **rest area**. A short gravel road at its east end leads to several good tent sites and fire rings beside a small lake. We dubbed it Rosebud Lake, having found a lone red rose mysteriously placed by the shore.

> **Talk to the Animals**
>
> Ruth Rolfe, cyclist
>
> *Why do I like cycling on northern roads? Because I can. There's something spiritual about cruising down the road in this wild country. You can talk to the animals and birds. There is this huge sense of peace.*

➤🏕 🏊 📷 You've seen one **gravel pit**, you've seen them all—right? Not so with the one at [WP151/km 143]. This pit offers a great eastern view over a wide swath of taiga forest and bison meadows. There is a variety of high, dry tenting options and lots of water nearby from the creek that flows out of **Birch Lake**. We called this the Birch Lake Bluffs.

➤🦌 🏊 By the time you reach [WP140], you should have a visceral sense of what the **taiga plains** are all about. In case you don't, stay tuned for some of the flattest landscape you'll find this side of the prairies. For the next 40 kilo-metres you will cross only one contour line. The combination of even, grassy terrain interspersed with willow shrublands and open forests make for excellent **bison habitat**.

➤ 🏕 🏛 😊 Most maps show "**Mile 129 Mackenzie Highway**" at [WP137/km 196]. This was once a major construction camp and airstrip when Highway 3 was being built back in the late 1950s and early 1960s. Though your map may show that this site is abandoned, don't expect to find a ghost town here. Scars from old cat trails and a rough trail to a small lake just west of the road are the only signs visible from the road. Basic camping at the lake is an option if you can't make it to North Arm Park roughly 50 kilometres down the road. A major trail lead-ing north is used by local hunters on quads and snowmobiles. Unless you are especially fond of muskeg and bogs, this trail is not suit-able for mountain biking.

> **On the Road to Heaven**
>
> Mike Mitchell, cyclist
>
> *I thought we had died and gone to heaven when, after miles and miles of flat, we finally came to the first decent hill since Providence and dropped down to Mosquito Creek. What a rush that was!*

➤ 🏊 ⛰ 🦌 A distinct limestone **roadcut** thick with marine fossils at [WP152/km 226] marks the crest of the biggest hill on Highway 3. The hill drops down to Mosquito Creek which was once a popular pickerel (walleye) spot until overfishing resulted in regulations imposing a daily catch limit and possession limit of 3 and 5 fish respectively. The season on this species is closed during the spawning period between May 1 and June 30. There is a well-used **hiking and fishing trail** from the highway bridge to Great Slave Lake along the east bank of the creek.

> ▢ ▢ ▢ ▢ You get your first full-blown roadside view of Great Slave Lake from the **North Arm Park**, a Territorial picnic area that offers a large kitchen

> ### Tower Hill Treasures
> Dave Siemens, Behchokò resident
>
> *I bet not one tourist in a hundred goes up Tower Hill, yet it's got to be the most impressive natural highlight in the three hundred kilometre stretch between Fort Providence and Yellowknife. It's parked smack on the boundary between the young sediments and the ancient Canadian Shield rock. One of the best things about living here is that I can keep one foot in each landscape. I can go one kilometre west of my home and go fossil hunting. One kilometre in the other direction and I can go look for quartz crystals.*

shelter, picnic tables, firewood, a woodstove, and outhouses [WP154/km 233]. A primitive track leading west from the entrance and paralleling the highway takes you to **Stevens' cabin**, a log structure built by a Mr. Stevens, the well-regarded manager of Fort Rae's Hudson's Bay Company post in the 1950s. Keep walking down the trail and discover a lovely pocket beach—so-called **Wellington Beach** for the street sign erected there (borrowed from the Hull, Québec, headquarters of Indian and Northern Affairs Canada).

Signatures of Shield Country
Jamie Bastedo, *Shield Country*

The pilot begins our final descent over the Yellowknife River. An endless tapestry of familiar images unfurls below the plane: bald rock outcrops spattered with multi-coloured lichens, azure waters dotted with bobbing gulls, spires of spruce punctuating a crystalline sky—for me, these are signatures of shield country.

Near the north shore of Great Slave, we spot a bald eagle, gliding in tandem with the plane for a few moments as if to guide us home.

In these moments with the eagle, the charm and mystery of this country sink into me just a little deeper. I reflect on the time it takes to befriend this sometimes overwhelming landscape. An occasional bird's-eye view certainly helps. The apparent chaos of bedrock and bush on the ground falls into patterns which begin to make sense from the air. Things seem to fit together in an elemental unity of rock, water, fire and life. Gazing at the stark beauty of my favourite landscape below, I feel I am looking straight down into Nature's face.

11

➤ ☖ ⚑ The access road to **Tower Hill** (also called **Crystal Mountain**) is located immediately across the highway from the North Arm Park. A gentle 2 kilometre trail contours through lovely poplar stands and lifts you 100 metres above Great Slave Lake for a superb view of the taiga plains to the west and the taiga shield to the east. This

Casing out a campsite en route to Behchokò

trail is easily biked or hiked. If you find any tempting quartz crystals, please leave them in place for others to enjoy.

➤ ⛏ If you have even a mild interest in geology, you may want to get off your bike and walk across the **Frank Channel Bridge** [WP155/km244] to avoid being overcome with awe and falling into the lake. It takes you across a remarkably precise divide spanning roughly two billion years of geological time. Behind you to the west are sedimentary limestones, shales, and sandstones laid down during the Paleozoic era, which began about 570 million years ago. Ahead of you to the east is the ancient bedrock of the great Canadian Shield, which covers two-thirds of Canada and averages about two-and-a-half billion years old. This geological divide runs invisibly down the centre of Great Slave

---

An Endless Maze of Islands

Damian Panayi, canoeist 2003

We have just spent a second night on a lonely island, one of millions in this stretch of shield country. Both behind and ahead of us is an almost endless maze of rocky islands, stunted spruce, swamps, and open lake. We started in Rae, at the very northern tip of the North Arm of Great Slave Lake. We are paddling home. To Yellowknife.

After spending 20 hours tent-bound during a storm, the wind finally lifted. Early in the morning, two of us dipped a canoe into the water to scout the paddling conditions around the corner from Trout Rock. The wind looked favourable, a nor'wester off the land and slightly at our backs. The swells were large, but manageable and diminishing.

After a hearty breakfast, we struck off, two families and one dog in three canoes. We chose to stay close together and were at first a little nervous in the post-storm swells. But after a few strokes, we soon relaxed, letting our hips roll in the waves, and resuming our count of eagle nests along the wild shore.

11

Lake's North Arm, revealing itself along opposite shores of the Frank Channel.

St. Michael's Catholic church built in 1926, Behchokò

➤ 🚶 🏔 One way to celebrate your arrival in shield country is to paddle the **North Arm of Great Slave Lake** from the Frank Channel to Yellowknife, roughly 150 water-kilometres away. This trip takes you past **Rae Point**, the original site of **Old Fort Rae**, and through a constellation of pristine islands forged billions of years ago from Precambrian granites and volcanics. The best place to put in is at the Territorial government dock just north of the bridge. Allow at least five days for this journey as there are two 10-kilometre stretches of unprotected shoreline that may leave you wind-bound—at **Trout Rock** and **Yellowknife Bay**.

Behchokò *(Rae-Mbehchò Ko, Dogrib for "big knife place") Edzo, (named after Edzoo, a beloved Tlicho Chief)*
Population 1,867

Community

Behchokò is actually two communities, Fort Rae and Edzo. A 19-kilometre access road off Highway 3 leads to Fort Rae. Located on scenic Marion Lake, it is the largest Tlicho community and the headquarters for the Tlicho government. The scenic older section of Rae sits on the rolling shoreline of Marion Lake at the western limit of the Canadian Shield. The historic church was once part of a much larger Roman Catholic Mission based here.

> **Looking After Each Other**
> Father Pochat, O.C., Behchokò
>
> *When I arrived here in 1956 as a young priest from France, I saw my role as helping to care for the needs of the people of Rae. Now, in my old age, these beautiful people are taking care of me—even building me a new house! If you want to know this community, talk to the people. They will be happy to tell you their stories.*

Fort Rae was named after Dr. John Rae, an Arctic explorer and Hudson's Bay Company trader who, in 1852, established a trading post now called Old Fort Rae, 8 kilometres to the south on the North Arm of Great Slave Lake. Edzo, 24 kilometres away by road and 6 by water, is largely a residential community and is home to the Chief Jimmy Bruneau High School. Edzo is named for the historical Tlicho leader who brought peace between the Tlicho—formerly

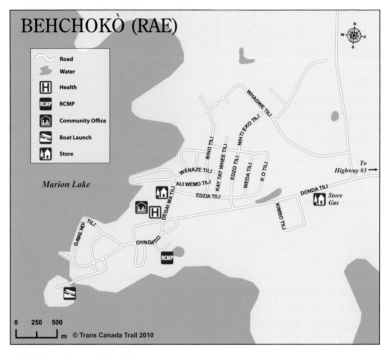

BEHCHOKÒ (RAE)

Road
Water
Health
RCMP
Community Office
Boat Launch
Store

Marion Lake

WHAGWE TILI
NIH TI EKO TILI
BINO TILI
EDZO TILI
KAY TAY WHEE TILI
WEDA TILI
K-O TILI
WENAZE TILI
ALI WEMO TILI
DEGAI MA TILI
EDZIA TILI
DONDA TILI
GAME NDI TILI
KIMBO TILI
OHNDA TILI

To
Highway #3 →

Store
Gas

RCMP

0   250   500

m   © Trans Canada Trail 2010

called Dogrib—and the Chipewyan. Edzo was started in 1965 as a federal government brainchild to attract Rae residents away from what were judged to be poor living conditions, but many opted to stay put. Edzo is in fact named after the very chief who opposed it! Traditional craftwork such as beaded jackets, mitts and slippers, and reproductions of traditional Dene tools are made by families in both communities. Between the two is Sah Naje Kwe, a traditional Dene camp and wilderness spa that is well worth a visit. Many residents are employed with the Tlicho government or related businesses, or work on rotation at diamond mines some 300 kilome-

---

Big Knife Place

David Siemens, Behchokò

The town site of present-day Behchokò was bare Canadian granite until an American trader built a few humble buildings there at the beginning of the twentieth century. The Tlicho people called that trading post Beh-cho-ko meaning "big-knife-place" for the American traders who first began operations at the rocky peninsula in 1902. In the 1800s, American soldiers were widely known among North American Native tribes as Beh Cho (Big Knives) for the large bayonets that they were issued with. Among [local] Native people ... the name Beh Cho gradually came to mean all Americans and the town site was quite naturally named Behchokò or "American Place" for the American trading interests that began there in 1902.

tres to the north. Hunting, trapping, and fishing are still mainstays of the economy and lifestyle.

Visitor Information

✳ Hamlet office, in the Nishi Kohn Centre, PO Box 68, Behchokò, NT, X0E 0Y0 (867-392-6500, hamlet@arcticdata.ca).

Canoes lie in wait for annual Tlicho trip from Gameti to Behchokò

Things to Do

✳ Hire a local guide to go touring or fishing on Great Slave Lake or Marion Lake. Inquire at band office.

✳ Hire a boat to visit the historic site and traditional camp at Old Fort Rae, which is called *Nishi Kohn* in Tlicho, meaning "houses among the hills."

✳ Hike the 1-kilometre loop trail behind Edzo's high school. Originally conceived as a suburban ring road that now features abandoned fire hydrants in the woods.

The Birchbark Canoe Builders

Peter Baker, An Arctic Arab

I was told by some Indian old-timers … that long before the Hudson's Bay Company, French or other white men came to trade commodities for furs, close to present-day Yellowknife, there was a settlement on Old Fort Island …The Hudson's Bay Company moved north about sixty miles (97 kilometres) and established a trading post on a hillside flat on a point on the north arm, about sixteen miles [26 kilometres] from Marion Lake, above Frank Channel where the present Fort Rae (Behchokò) is. That was a very prosperous trading post, for a big band of Dogrib Indians inhabited the very rich hunting area. The people were tough and good workers, and excellent hunters. The pelts of mink, lynx, marten, fox, and white fox, beaver and muskrat were of a high quality, and the country was noted as a hunting paradise for woodland caribou, barrenland caribou, moose and muskox.

The Dogribs are the birchbark canoe builders. I remember, in 1923, I came to Fort Rae with an outfit of my own, in a scow with motor and sail, carrying a load of merchandise. When I landed in Rae in the month of July I saw every man with a well-built canoe. In the 1800s they used to go to various parts of the country in their birchbark canoes with their families, trapping and hunting for game to provide themselves with dry meat and fats. This made a ready meal for anybody, very nourishing and delicious. I still crave for some.

Good blueberries by mid-summer.
* Visit historic St. Michael's Roman Catholic church built in 1926.
* Hike Tower Hill.
* Relax on a secluded sand beach a few minutes walk west of the North Arm Park campground.
* Pamper yourself with a clay bath, a healing cultural ceremony, or a meal of freshwater ceviche at the idyllic Sah Naji Kwe Lodge

Students at Chief Jimmy Bruno High School, Edzo – all "strong like two people"

(meaning "Bear Healing Place" in Tlicho). Groups preferred. Call ahead to confirm availability (867-371-3144).

Accommodation

* Tli Cho Motel, centrally located with clean, basic rooms, Box 8, Behchokò, NT, X0E 0Y0 (867-392-6333, fax 867-392-6260)
* Sah Naji Kwe Lodge, a unique "Wilderness Spa and Meeting Place." Access road is 700 metres west of the Frank Channel, Box 98, Behchokò, NT, X0E 0Y0 (867-371-3144, fax 867-371-3155, jrabesca@ lincsat.com

Camping

* There is an abandoned campground just off Highway 3 on the east side of Edzo. While there are no facilities, it does offer decent tent sites in a quiet, somewhat scruffy setting.
* The nearest Territorial campground is the North Arm Park, a few kilometres west of Edzo.

Outfitting/Hardware

* Northern Store (867-392-6301).
* FC Services, gas bar and convenience store (867-392-6955).

Amenities

* Accommodation, restaurant, store, bank machine, medical services, police, gasoline, diesel, propane, automotive service.

Jamie after a mudbath on Marion Lake

Tips

✱ Regular bus service connects to Yellowknife. Ask at hamlet office.

✱ Trapper's Hideaway restaurant on the road out of Rae offers great food and hospitality, open 9 AM – 8 PM, Mon to Fri (867-392-6868).

Emergency

✱ Nursing station (867-392-6075).

✱ RCMP (867-392-1111).

Edzo entrpreneur David Siemens with wife Mary and lab Shadow

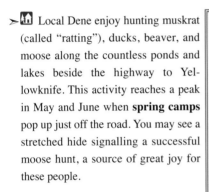 Local Dene enjoy hunting muskrat (called "ratting"), ducks, beaver, and moose along the countless ponds and lakes beside the highway to Yellowknife. This activity reaches a peak in May and June when **spring camps** pop up just off the road. You may see a stretched hide signalling a successful moose hunt, a source of great joy for these people.

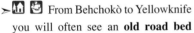 From Behchokò to Yellowknife you will often see an **old road bed**

> ### Caribou Column at Old Fort Rae
> Frank Russel, *Explorations in the Far North, 1898*
> *They were often killed from the buildings, and throughout the winter might be found near the post. In 1877 an unbroken line of caribou crossed the frozen lake near the fort; they were fourteen days in passing, and in such a mass that, in the words of an eyewitness, "daylight could not be seen" through the column.*

weaving north or south of Highway 3 [WP160]. This is the original route that was punched into the north woods by winter "cat trains" — bulldozers pulling supplies on skids — headed for Yellowknife back in the 1940s. The first cat drivers dodged every hump of granite that got in the way, of which there were hundreds. Behind them they left a sinuous trail that later was upgraded to an all-season gravel "highway" by 1962. It quickly became one of the scariest roads in the country. Frequent traffic accidents and a sharp increase in industrial trucking to service a booming mineral industry prompted an aggressive road-straightening campaign in the mid-1990s. Enjoy the road. It cost Canadian taxpayers about one million dollars per kilometre to straighten it through one of the most challenging terrains on earth! The huge **rock-crushing quarries** you will see along the way added significantly to this cost, since gravel is perhaps rarer than diamonds in this glacially scoured landscape.

11

➤ 🏠 🦌 🏕 The collection of cabins, tent frames, a small schoolhouse, and fenced graves attest to the cultural importance of the **Stagg River** [WP162]. This site is a traditional base camp for the Tlicho of Behchokò who travel up and down the Stagg to fish, hunt, and trap. In spite of the immense cultural importance of

A window on Great Slave Lake's North Arm

this river, it was officially named after a British meteorologist in 1927. The Stagg is also a draw for non-Native hunters, especially for waterfowl and moose. A short paddle downstream brings you to an expansive **marshland** loaded with ducks. Keep paddling and you will soon reach a sample of the countless whale-backed, spruce-topped islands typical of the North Arm where you can take your pick of campsites. The Stagg can also be paddled in the opposite direction to quiet upstream backwaters with ample camping. From the highway north, the river follows a major geological fault for 17 kilometres, then swings 90 degrees to the east into **Stagg Lake**, a large secluded lake in the heart of shield country.

➤ 🏕 🦌 🏠 About 10 kilometres south of the mouth of the Stagg River is a strange round lump of Proterozoic sediment glued onto the Precambrian Shield of Great Slave Lake's north shore. This is **Rae Point**, the site of **Old Fort Rae**, built in 1852 by the Hudson's Bay Company and named for Chief Factor John Rae, an intrepid member of John Franklin's first Arctic expedition. This became a central provisioning hub for other fur-trading posts from Lake Athabasca to the lower reaches of the Mackenzie Valley. Abandoned in the early 1900s after a trading post was established at Behchokò, the site has been re-established as a Métis cultural and historical site complete with a spacious lodge and several comfortable cabins.

> **Build a Road, Save the Fish**
> Road sign beside the Stagg River
>
> *Fish habitat adjacent to the Stagg River was developed to replace habitat lost due to highway construction between Frank Channel and the Stagg River. The replacement habitat was designed to provide spawning and rearing habitat for northern pike. In 1999, two ponds were constructed and connected to a natural pond close to the Stagg River. To allow for free movement of fish between the ponds and the river, channels were constructed connecting the natural pond and the constructed ponds to the Stagg River.*

For more information, contact the North Slave Métis Alliance in Yellowknife (867-873-9176).

➤ 🦌 The Stagg River is among several important fish habitats along the realigned highway that were affected by construction. But thanks to Fisheries and Oceans' strict policy of "no net habitat loss," environmental impacts to fish were minimized. The series of constructed **pike ponds southwest of the Stagg River bridge** demonstrate this commitment.

> **Tough Times**
>
> Gabriel Denetre, Fort Providence[141]
>
> *I was born quite a ways out of Fort Rae (Behchokò), in the bush. We lived in tents in those days and it was very cold that winter. My mother died giving birth to me, before I had even nursed. You couldn't go and buy milk then so I was fed flour mixed with water ... We were real people in those days.*

➤ 🏕 🚻 🦌 The prominent **communications tower** at [WP 163/km 275] marks the approximate halfway point between Behchokò and Yellowknife. The high bedrock knob on which it sits can be accessed via a stretch of original roadbed that begins just west of the tower. The hilltop itself or the lakeside peatlands and meadows offer good spots for picnicking or wildlife watching. The marsh-lined lake dotted with small islands of vegetation is often alive with ducks, muskrats, beavers, and the occasional moose. Though maintained only to the base of the tower, the old road continues on for another 2 kilometres until it reconnects with the highway. If you don't mind lifting your bike over one soil roadblock and negotiating your way through a few potholes, this is a scenic side trip that will give you a taste of the "old road" and how it once nestled into the shield landscape.

➤ 🏕 🦌 🎿 **M i l l e r Creek** [WP 169/km 282] is one of a handful of major stream courses flowing south to Great Slave Lake across Highway 3. Like the Stagg River, all of these empty into large shallow bays that support productive wetland complexes brimming

Bike parade en route to Yellowknife

with wildlife. They were also used as traditional year-round travel routes from Great Slave to interior hunting and fishing grounds. Though less than 3 kilometres to the mouth of Miller Creek, plan a day for this side trip to allow stress-free negotiation of fallen trees, beaver dams, or other obstruc-tions in the upper part of the

Chris and Alfred at home on the Trail, Highway 3

creek. Your sweat equity will not have been wasted, as Miller Creek widens significantly downstream into an almost pastoral stream reminiscent of rural Scotland. The creek eventually spills into an island-studded bay, featuring **Trout Rock**, a time-honoured gathering place for local Dene, which should be marked on most maps. Note that this creek is navigable only during the spring high-water season, which usually lasts from mid-May to the first week of June. You won't find the name "Miller Creek" on any map but that's what all the lo-cals call it.

➤ Approximately 18 kilometres southeast of Trout Rock is the **En-odah Wilderness Lodge**, a popular tourism destination catering to fishermen. Set among the wild rocky islands of the North Arm, it offers a well-equipped main lodge plus several attractive four-person cabins. A Hudson's Bay Com-pany outpost was located near the lodge site from 1922 to 1927. For more information, contact lodge owner Ragnar Wesstrom (867-873-4334, info@ enodah.com, www.enodah.com).

➤ After the Stagg River, **Boundary Creek** [WP164/km 305] is the second largest stream course flowing into Great Slave Lake. The creek's name is de-rived from the meeting of two Dene territories in this vicinity, the Dogrib and the Yellowknives. Though a lot more water flows down Boundary Creek than Miller Creek, it too may present you with a few obstructions along its narrower stretches. Spring or early summer passage is recommended while water levels are high. It is approximately an 8 kilometre paddle downstream to Great Slave Lake. This creek takes you through a pleasing variety of small lakes and ponds before reaching the 4 kilometre marsh-rimmed bay that opens to Great Slave Lake.

➤ 🏠 🔁 Just before [WP165/km 324] you will see the first of several signs which read "Entering Scientific Reserve." This indicates that you have entered the **Yellowknife Seismic Observatory**, which measures and studies not stars but seismic events deep in the earth's crust, using an array of seismometers stretched over the land. Since Yellowknife is located on one of the most seismically stable parts of the planet, it is well suited as a baseline monitoring station for seismic disturbances elsewhere, for example, detecting a tsunami or nuclear weapons

Sah Naji Kwe Wilderness Spa, Edzo

test on the other side of the planet. If this kind of scientific investigation interests you, contact the Natural Resources Canada office in Yellowknife (867-766-8519, Lorne.McNeice@nrcan-rncan.gc.ca) to arrange a visit to this unique station.

Niven Lake—Urban Oasis for Wildlife

Jamie Bastedo, *Blue Lake and Rocky Shore*

Throughout the great Canadian muskeg, there are thousands of shallow peat-bottomed lakes and ponds, most of them nameless. What makes Niven Lake special is the ecological diversity it offers so close to downtown Yellowknife and its biologically enriched state because of its former role as a sewage lagoon. Named after John McNiven, one of Yellowknife's first mayors, this lake was selected as a lagoon soon after Yellowknife moved up the hill from Old Town in 1947. It received over 30 years of sewage which had a tremendous fertilizing effect on the entire ecosystem. Since its closure as a lagoon in 1981, the lake has returned to a relatively natural state. Numerous water and sediment studies indicate a remarkable level of rejuvenation, so much so that in March 1994, the Department of Health declared the area free and clear of health concerns. The lake has been saved along with the most productive wetland habitats around it. Encircling the lake is a splendid new trail system which offers many scenic vistas and opportunities for wildlife viewing.

11

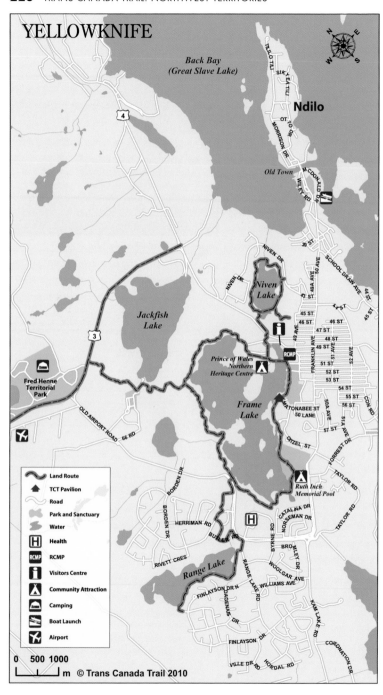

YELLOWKNIFE

Back Bay
(Great Slave Lake)

Ndilo

Old Town

Niven Lake

Jackfish Lake

Fred Henne Territorial Park

Prince of Wales Northern Heritage Centre

Frame Lake

Ruth Inch Memorial Pool

Range Lake

Land Route
TCT Pavilion
Road
Park and Sanctuary
Water
Health
RCMP
Visitors Centre
Community Attraction
Camping
Boat Launch
Airport

0   500 1000
        m   © Trans Canada Trail 2010

11

Yellowknife *(Sombak'e, Tlicho for "Money Place")*
Population 18,700

Community

Yellowknife is an urban island surrounded by a sea of subarctic wilderness. Its name originates from the copper-wielding Aboriginal people who lived along the northern shores of Great Slave Lake. The town sprang up after a 1936 gold strike along the eastern shore of Yellowknife Bay. Over the next decade, Yellowknife grew into a full-fledged mining town of more than 3,000, most of whom were crammed into what is now called Old Town. With no room on the rock and another gold mine — Giant — going into full production, the town's growth was directed up the hill to "New

Nimisha and Jamie cast for supper on the Marion River

Town." Over half a century and hundreds of underground tunnels later, gold mining has since wound down, while nearby diamond mining now fuels the local resource economy. Within living memory, this town, whose "gold is paved with streets," has grown from a loose collection of prospectors' tents to a bustling, and culturally diverse capital city of close to 19,000 people.

Visitor Information

✳ Northern Frontier Visitors Centre, #44807 49th St., Yellowknife, NT, X1A 3T5 (867-873-4262, toll free in North America 877-881-4262, fax 867-873-3654, info@northernfrontier.com, www.northernfrontier.com).

✳ Yellowknife City Hall, PO Box 580, Yellowknife, NT, X1A 2N4 (867-920-5600, info@city.yellowknife.nt.ca, www.yellowknife.ca).

Things to Do

✳ Northern Frontier Visitor's Centre, the place to start your exploration of Yellowknife. Interpretive displays on local land, culture, and attractions. Piles of information and brochures.

✳ Prince of Wales Northern Heritage Centre. Territorial government museum featuring cultural and natural history displays, historical and anthropological archives (867-873-7551, fax 867-873-0205, pwnhcweb@learnnet.nt.ca, www.pwnhc.ca).

✳ Old Town has a charm all its own, with great eating, quaint ambiance, water

11

views, historic buildings, and bush planes on floats or skis to take you back to the early days of the city and of northern flying.

* Wildcat Café. Unique Old Town restaurant offering first class northern dining in 1937 log building. Regular jam sessions and performers. May long weekend to Labour Day. (There is an exact, life-size model of the café in Ottawa's Museum of Civilization.)

* Bullock's Bistro. Folksy, friendly, fun place to enjoy fresh fish pulled from Great Slave Lake (867-873-3474).

* Bush Pilot's Monument, top of "The Rock" in Old Town. Yellowknife's version of Toronto's CN tower with 360-degree view of Old Town and Yellowknife Bay. A favourite for aurora watching on dark nights.

* Frame Lake and Niven Lake Trails. Part of the Trans Canada Trail. Remarkably

Yellowknife pavilion

wild and picturesque trails just minutes from downtown—urban oases for wildlife. Trails on tamer eastern side of both lakes are fine for casual biking.

* The largest of the Northwest Territories' Trans Canada Trail pavilions is found along the Frame Lake Trail. The closest major intersection is Matonabee and 50th Avenue. From there, follow Matonabee to the lake.

* Legislative Assembly. Shaped like a traditional snowhouse and almost hidden in a natural stand of spruce and jackpine, this is the scenic focus of the capital region. The Assembly's unique circular chambers recall the traditional northern approach to government and encourage an unusual consensus-style government.

* Tours and fishing excursions on Great Slave Lake. Inquire at visitors centre about local operators.

* Cameron Falls, the most visited natural attraction in the Yellowknife region. A rolling 1 kilometre trail is accessed from the Ingraham Trail about 50 kilometres east of town.

Ecotheatre on the rocks, Tin Can Hill, Yellowknife

Accommodation

✳ Visit the Northern Frontier Visitors Centre Web site (www.northernfrontier.com) and follow the visitor services and accommodation links to find the best listing of the many hotel, inn, and B & B options in town.

Camping

✳ Fred Henne Territorial Park, across from the airport on Long Lake, is a popular recreation area for locals and visitors. Excellent swimming beaches, playground equipment, hiking trails, interpretive kiosks, picnic areas,

Canoe regatta on the Yellowknife River

kitchen shelters, showers, and over one hundred campsites, half of which are powered. Pre-booking recommended for July and August (867-920-2472, www.campingnwt.ca).

Outfitting/Hardware

✳ You will find all you need in the grocery and hardware stores spread between downtown and a retail strip south of Frame Lake beyond the hospital.

✳ Overlander Sports. Wide range of quality outdoor gear (867-873-2474, fax 867-920-4079, sales@overlandersports.com, www.overlandersports.com).

✳ Weaver and Devore. One-of-a-kind outfitting store in the heart of Old Town. A must visit (867-873-2219).

Amenities

✳ Accommodation, restaurant, store, bank, bank machine, visitor information, pharmacy, medical services, police, airport, gasoline, diesel, propane, automotive service.

Tips

✳ Folk on the Rocks, a two-day folk-blues festival held in mid-July in a beautiful sandy amphitheatre on the shores of Long Lake. Local and national performers, workshops, kids events.

✳ Yellowknife International Airshow. Bi-annually, usually in late July.

✳ Float Plane Fly-In features great flying, pilot reunions, bush pilot story-telling. Bi-annually in late June or July.

11

✳ Midnight Sun Golf Tournament. Tee off at midnight on the longest day of the year.

✳ See the books *Shield Country, Blue Lake and Rocky Shore* and *Reaching North* by Jamie Bastedo for details on local natural and human history, as well as the region's best hiking and camping destinations.

Emergency

✳ Hospital (867-669-4111).

✳ RCMP (867-669-1111).

➤🦶🏔🚻☠ **Cameron Falls by foot.** A lovely 20-minute hike to the falls takes you through a diverse mix of forests and over a fascinating showcase of sedimentary rocks that record many of the geolog-

Xanthoria lichen on 2.6-billion-year-old sedimentary rock (Tessa Macintosh)

ical stresses that shaped this landscape. This trail offers a pleasant family adventure and an excellent opportunity to take in the best of subarctic scenery. The Cameron Falls parking lot is located 2.3 kilometres from the **Powder Point boat launch** at the east end of Prelude Lake, or 48 kilometres from Yellowknife. This 1 kilometre trail is suitable for children, but extra caution should be taken along its steeper portions, especially around the cliffs above the falls.

➤🦶🏔🚻 **Cameron Falls by water.** If you are equipped with a canoe or kayak, you can park at Powder Point and paddle an easy hour or so up the Cameron River. Once you reach the base of the falls, take the portage on the north side of the river to a good viewing ledge above the falls. Or, you can launch your watercraft upstream of the main falls near the **Cameron River bridge**, 10 more kilometres down the road from the Cameron Falls parking lot. Park in the sandy area on the west side of the bridge and look for a trail heading north from the sand. This takes you around a smaller, though still very beautiful, falls. Including this portage, it will take you a leisurely half-day to paddle downstream, past the main falls, and back to Powder Point (where you should have arranged road transportation back to your vehicle at the bridge).

11

12 DEMPSTER HIGHWAY: INUVIK TO THE YUKON BORDER

APPROXIMATE DISTANCE 260 kilometres
HIGHLIGHTS
* Campbell Lake
* Gwich'in Territorial Park
* Tsiigehtchic and "Georgetown"
* Fort McPherson
* Peel River crossing
* Midway Lake
* Richardson Mountains
* Yukon–Northwest Territories border

OVERVIEW

Lookout tower at Jàk Park, Inuvik

The Dempster Highway, stretching from Inuvik to Dawson City, takes you through some of the most beautiful scenery in the world, traversing several mountain chains, pristine rivers, subarctic forests, arctic tundra, and traditional Native communities. This guide describes a route that, for the majority of travellers, would represent only a segment of a longer journey. Make sure you do your homework on connecting legs of your trip to get the most out of it and to travel safely through this remote environment. For additional details on some of the sites described in this guide, visit http://explorenorth.com/articles/dempster.html and follow the links to "Driving the Dempster."

CAMPING TIPS
Territorial campgrounds or wayside parks are conveniently scattered along much of this portion of the Trans Canada Trail. Several informal camping options along the way include the Rengling River and Frog Creek.

BIKERS BEWARE!
As celebrated as the Dempster Highway is as a wilderness travel corridor, it is by no means a biker's paradise. A lack of shoulder, guard rails, and fencing plus an abundance of loose gravel, potholes, dust, steep banks, and rapid elevation changes make this one of North America's most challenging bike routes. Add huge trucks or

Ehjuu Njik Wayside Park, Dempster Highway

12

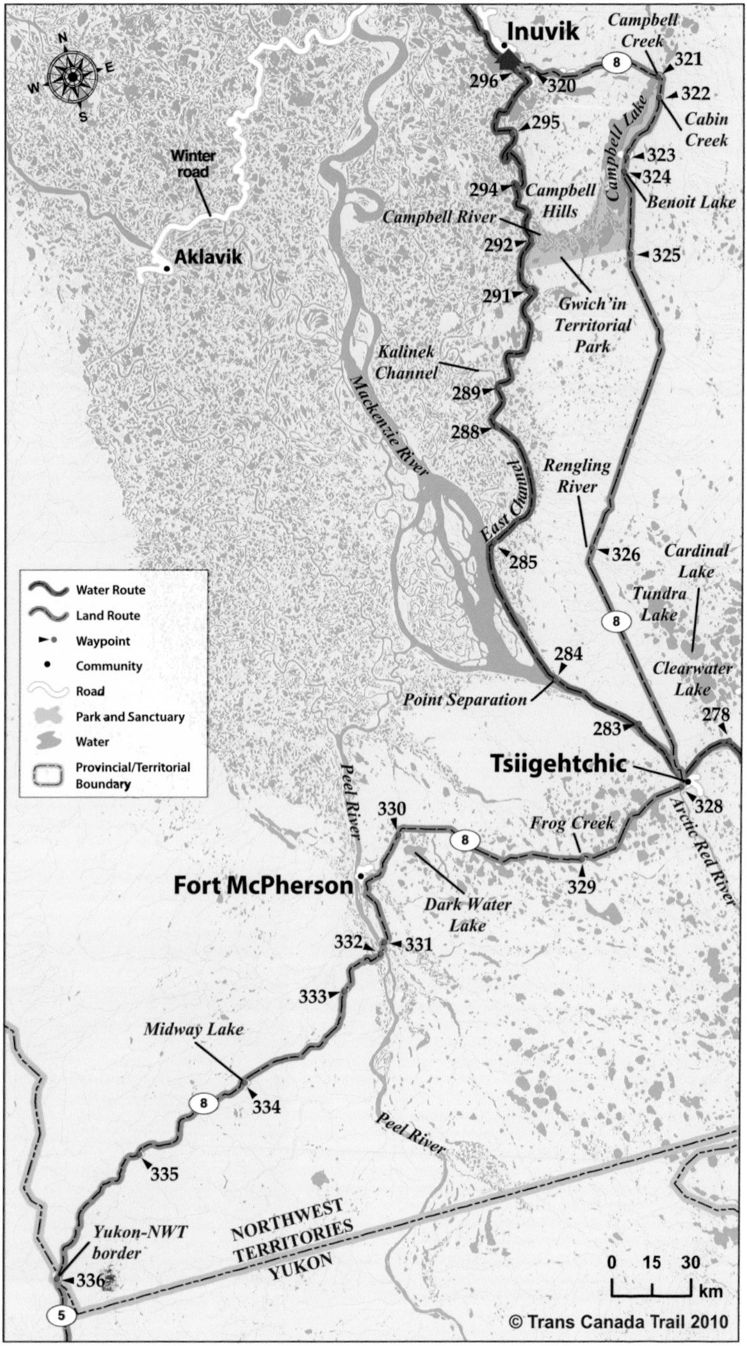

Inuvik

Campbell Creek

296
320
321
8
322
Cabin Creek
295
323
324
294
Campbell Hills
Benoit Lake
Campbell River
292
325
Winter road
291
Gwich'in Territorial Park
Aklavik
Kalinek Channel
289
288
Rengling River
Mackenzie River
285
East Channel
326
Cardinal Lake
Tundra Lake
8
284
Clearwater Lake
Point Separation
283
278
Tsiigehtchic
328
Arctic Red River
330
Frog Creek
Peel River
329
8
Fort McPherson
Dark Water Lake
332
331
333
Midway Lake
8
334
335
Peel River
Yukon-NWT border
NORTHWEST TERRITORIES
YUKON
336
5

Legend:
- Water Route
- Land Route
- Waypoint
- Community
- Road
- Park and Sanctuary
- Water
- Provincial/Territorial Boundary

N W E S

0 15 30 km

© Trans Canada Trail 2010

12

sleepy Winnebago drivers to this mix and the biking hazards become extreme. So be very careful out there. When in doubt, pull over. Take no chances. Beware of strong winds, especially in alpine areas, which could blow you off the road or over some precipice. Dust or no dust, assume drivers may not see you, having driven long hours on this beautiful but occasionally mind-numbing road. To help with orientation, the following description includes kilometre distances derived from roadside posts (where visible) topped with blue mileage indicators.

> **Doing the Dempster**
>
> Bumper sticker on dust-caked van
>
> *DEMPSTER HIGHWAY*
>
> *Winding in*
>
> *And winding out*
>
> *Fills my mind*
>
> *With serious doubt*
>
> *As to whether the lout*
>
> *Who built this route*
>
> *Was going to Hell*
>
> *Or coming out!*

> ⬛ ⬛ ⬛ About 5 kilometres south of Inuvik on the Dempster Highway is **Jak Territorial Park** (formerly Chuk Park) [WP320/km 266], a full-service Territorial government campground. Besides a short interpretive trail featuring interesting natural and cultural details of the

landscape, the highlight of Jàk Territorial Park is the 10-metre **lookout tower** that offers great views of the Mackenzie Delta and Richardson Mountains with excellent interpretive signs. And don't forget the berries. *Jàk* means "berries" in the Gwich'in language, after the area's plentiful cranberries, cloudberries, currants, and blueberries (867-777-3652).

Campbell Lake, Gwich'in Territorial Park

> ⬛ ⬛ ⬛ Besides serviced campgrounds, Gwich'in Territorial Park offers several wayside parks, the first of which out of Inuvik is the **Nihtak Day Use Area** [WP321/km 247] (formerly Campbell Creek). *Nihtak* is Gwich'in for "a divide," referring to the large valley between **Campbell Lake** and the huge **Sitidgi Lake** to the northeast. There are eight picnic sites on the north side of the road next to **Campbell Creek**. On the south side is a boat launch that is a local fishing spot, especially in the spring when large

> **It's a Long Road**
>
> Highway sign near Jàk Territorial Park
>
> *Tsiigehtchic 114 km*
>
> *Fort McPherson 172 km*
>
> *Yukon border 257 km*
>
> *Eagle Plains 356 km*
>
> *Dawson 767 km*
>
> *Whitehorse 1220 km*

numbers of spawning **whitefish** migrate up the creek.

Reversing delta, Campbell Lake, viewed from Tithegeh Chi'Vitaii Park

➤ 🏕 🦌 **Ehjuu Njik Wayside Park** [WP322/km244] (formerly Cabin Creek) is located on the banks of **Cabin Creek**, which is known for good **arctic grayling** sport fishing. *Ehjuu Njik* is Gwich'in for "tall trees creek." (Remember, you are in the Arctic.) This basic site offers two picnic areas, barbecue pits, firewood, and toilets. Cranberries are plentiful here in late August and September.

➤ 🏕 ⛺ **Gwich'in Territorial Park** [WP323] includes 12 open, relatively bug-free campsites, a kitchen shelter, and toilets. Because of upstream beavers and the risk of giardiasis ("beaver fever"), water taken from the creek should be boiled or treated. A westbound road through the campground takes you to the gravel shores of **Campbell Lake** where you can skip stones and enjoy impressive **Campbell Hills** across the water.

➤ 🏕 🏊 🚻 A 300-metre **hiking trail** at the **Tithegeh Chi' Vitaii Day Use Park** [WP324/km 232] (also known as **Benoit Lake**) takes you westwards to the edge of an impressive cliff that overlooks the south end of Campbell Lake. From the lookout deck you can see the unique **reversing delta** at the lake's southern end, formed by spring backwash from the **Campbell River**.

➤ 🏕 ⛺ 🏔 **Vadzaih Van Tsik Campground** [WP325/km 221] is a 12-site campground that sits on the inside of a pronounced oxbow of **Caribou Creek** and is protected from the elements by a dramatic cliff on the north side. For a few weeks each spring, Caribou Creek offers paddlers an exhilarating fastwater run from the campground to Campbell Lake where you can portage back to the highway.

➤ ⛺ 🚻 🦌 The scenic **Rengling River** [WP326/km173], with its dramatic limestone backdrop, is a popular spot to fish for **arctic grayling**. There are no facilities here, but if you're looking for a basic campsite, you will find it on the south side of the road by the river. While crossing the river, enjoy the stowaway **cliff swallows** who nest on the good ship *Louis Cardinal*.

➤ 🏠 🔍 You may not be the first person confused by the routing of the **Tsiigehtchic ferry**. It operates among three points: the Inuvik side of the Mackenzie, Tsiigehtchic, and the Fort McPherson side of the Mackenzie. Just wait a few minutes and it will find you.

➤ 🏠 You won't find it on any map, but just up the hill from the

George Niditchie and grandchildren relax at his home in "Georgetown"

McPherson side of the ferry crossing is what locals refer to as "**Georgetown**" [WP328/km142], named after George Niditchie, a retired deckhand who refuses to move to Tsiigehtchic even after his scenic homestead had been assaulted by fierce flooding and ice jams over many years.

➤ 🛏 🏠 🛫 🚽 And just up the same hill from Georgetown is **Theetah K'yit Park**. *Theetah k'yit* is the Gwich'in word for "portage." Facilities at this wayside park include a lookout tower, a kitchen shelter, picnic tables, barbecue pits, toilets, and interpretive displays. This is a good spot to photograph the confluence of two great northern rivers, the **Arctic Red** and the **Mackenzie.**

➤ ☠ 🧭 **Tsiigehtchic to Fort McPherson** [km 143 to 86]. Whether you are on two wheels or four, drive with extra care between these towns because there are often long dusty sections with loose gravel. As you head westward, you'll notice the **taiga forest thinning** and the trees getting shorter and scrawnier. Still, it's amazing that there are any trees this far north. In the Delta, the treeline stretches as far as 69°C north latitude thanks to the Mac-kenzie River's positive effects on local climate and soils.

➤ 🛏 ☠ 🛫 🚤 🚽
Viewed from high above along the highway, **Frog Creek** [WP329] presents a pretty picture of sparkling ponds and clear running

Gravesites of the Lost Patrol, Fort McPherson

waters. A side road east of the creek leads you into the heart of this scene, an informal camping, picnic, and/or fishing spot. Exercise extreme caution near the **loose, steep banks** lining the elevated stretch of road spanning Frog Creek valley. There are no guard rails or fencing to stop you from careening over the edge if you're startled by a big truck or disoriented by thick dust.

➤ 🏃 ℹ️ Just after the last major turn toward Fort McPherson, as the Dempster veers to the southwest, take time to admire a sampling of the Mackenzie Delta's 25,000 lakes, including **Dark Water Lake**, [WP330] a couple of kilometres south of the road. The **unusual rolling hills** nearby are pin-cushioned with surprisingly robust spruce trees for this latitude, some of which are "veterans" that survived the last wave of forest fires to sweep through this region.

> **Memory Trails**
>
> Mary Snowshoe, Fort McPherson
>
> *I started travelling with dog teams when I was twelve years old. Where the Dempster Highway is now—that was one of our main trails. We usually left town January 10 and would follow the caribou up into the mountains. We travelled, sometimes 15 or 20 families together. We wouldn't come back till Easter. Though that trail is a road now and I travel through it in a truck, it always brings back a lot of memories. When I see that land it's all so familiar. I know where all the old camps are. I can point them out from the road. What I remember most is where people held service. I can remember them singing Gwich'in hymns. That never leaves me.*

FORT MCPHERSON *(Tetlit Zheh, Gwich'in for "house at the head of the waters")*
Population 878

Community

Sitting on a bluff above the Peel River, the site of Fort McPherson and the surrounding area have been home to the Gwich'in people for thousands of years. The Hudson's Bay Company created a post here in 1840, later naming it after Murdoch McPherson, the company's chief trader. The Anglicans moved in 20 years later and started a mission. The RCMP followed in 1903, building a post and regularly conducting patrols from Fort McPherson to

Calvin Francis embroiders at the Fort McPherson Tent and Canvas Company

12

Dawson City. In 1911, Inspector Fitzgerald and three others of the famous "Lost Patrol" perished in the Mackenzie Mountains. The Gwich'in have maintained a traditional lifestyle based on hunting and fishing that continues today. This community was rarely visited by tourists until the Dempster Highway connected it with the rest of the world in 1979. Fort McPherson is the home of Wally Firth, who became Canada's first northern Aboriginal member of Parliament in 1972, and John Tetlichi, who in 1967 became the first Aboriginal member of the Northwest Territories Legislative Assembly. The Fort McPherson Tent and Canvas Company is a unique, home-grown business that sends tipis and tents to customers around the world.

Trail to Peel River flats, Fort McPherson

> **The Lost Patrol**
>
> Grave markers, Fort McPherson
>
> *Inspector Fitzgerald 43*
> *Constable Taylor 29*
> *Constable Kinney 28*
> *Special Constable Carter 41*

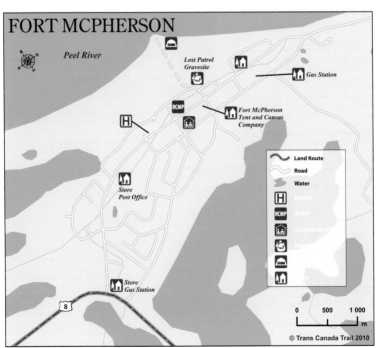

FORT MCPHERSON

Peel River

Lost Patrol Gravesite

Gas Station

RCMP

Fort McPherson Tent and Canvas Company

H

Store Post Office

Store Gas Station

8

Land Route
Road
Water
H Health
RCMP RCMP
Community
Store
Store

0   500   1 000
m

© Trans Canada Trail 2010

Visitor Information

✳ Hamlet of Fort McPherson, PO Box 57, Fort McPherson, NT, X0E 0J0 (867-952-2428, 867-952-2330, hamlet@internorth.com, blue-painted Annie G. Robert building).

Things to Do

✳ Lost Patrol gravesite near the base of the flag-pole in the local cemetery.

✳ Walking trail behind the church parallels the Peel. Nice views of the river and floodplain. Connects with gravel road to riverbank.

✳ Replica of the "Mad Trapper's" (aka Albert Johnson) cabin just south of the cemetery.

Tabetha Nerysoo shows off her dryfish in Fort McPherson

Note the bunker-like design and holes on the side for his rifle barrel.

✳ Fort McPherson Tent and Canvas Company, produces high-quality canvas bags, packs, and tipis. Tours available (867-952-2179, fax 867-952-2718, fmtent@netcom.ca, www.permafrost.comm).

✳ Boat tours and fishing expeditions on the Peel and Rat rivers. Inquire at the band office.

✳ Shildii Rock and Stone

Boardwalk path through the heart of Fort McPherson

Scraper Creek, two sacred sites that can be visited with a local guide.

✳ Fort McPherson Language Centre. John Tetlichi Building across from the Hamlet office. Carries Gwich'in stories, photographs, and books.

✳ Tl'oondih Healing Camp. Secluded traditional camp with charming cabins on the Peel River. Inquire at the Language Centre or hamlet office.

12

> **Tipis Anyone?**
>
> Erwin Kamenz, Fort McPherson Tent and Canvas Company
>
> *Tipis? Why I've sent them to Brussels, Germany, Holland, Australia. They go out of here like crazy. Specialty ones too, for weddings, conventions, massage parlours, dining rooms, five-star wilderness resorts. We can make anything out of canvas that you can think of. You name it, we've made it. We're known for our quality worldwide.*

Accommodation

✳ Tetlit Hotel. Accommodates 16 guests in 8 rooms, groceries. Box 27, Fort McPherson, NT, X0E 0J0 (867-952-2417).

✳ Tetlichi B & B. Accommodates 2 guests in 1 room,, laundry facilities available. Box 101, Fort McPherson, NT, X0E 0J0 (867-952-2356).

Camping

✳ No campground, though camping possible on the Peel River flats. Inquire at hamlet office.

Outfitting/Hardware

✳ Northern Store (867-952-2366).

✳ Tetlit Co-op (867-952-2417).

Amenities

✳ Accommodation, restaurant, store, bank machine, medical services, police, gasoline, diesel, propane, automotive service.

Tips

✳ Midway Lake Music Festival. Annual music festival 30 kilometres southwest of town, July or August.

✳ Canoe Daze. Canoe races, tea boiling, and other fun contests and entertainment, early August.

Emergency

✳ Nursing clinic (867-952-2586).

✳ RCMP (867-952-1111).

➤ 🖵 ⛺ 🎪 🚻 Nine kilometres south of Fort McPherson and 1 kilometre north of the Peel River ferry crossing is the **Nitainlaii Territorial Park**

> **Music Town**
>
> Lawrence Robert, Midway Lake[145]
>
> *You wouldn't believe this place when the music festival starts. Every tent and cabin is full up. More than a thousand people come from all over, as far away as Alaska. We get big-name musicians, locals, and everything in between. It's like a little town springs up here for just three or four days a year.*

French biker, Célia Tauzin, getting high on the Dempster Highway

> **It's All Good**
>
> Célia Tauzin, biker from Grenoble, France, near the Northwest Territories–Yukon border
>
> *We planned five weeks from Whitehorse to Inuvik. I am amazed by the immense green spaces. People are so nice. They will step out of their cars to make sure that we are okay. My legs hurt when I go up these hills but it's all good. It's a treat for us to bike the Dempster. I've enjoyed it all the way.*

12

[WP331/km 76]. *Nitainlaii* is Gwich'in for "flowing out in all directions." Perched on a cliff overlooking the river, this peaceful campground includes the **Johnny D. Charlie Visitors Centre** (open 9 AM to 9 PM, seven days a week, from June 1 to Sept. 1), 21 campsites, firewood, and a kitchen shelter. The visitors centre is worth a stop for

Lawrence Robert (L) and friend set the stage for the Midway Lake Music Festival

its excellent displays on traditional Gwich'in life. The centre's logs were cut locally from the banks of the Peel. For more information on this park call 867-777-3652.

➤ 🚶 💬 🏠 One of Canada's few cable ferries, the *Abraham Francis,* will meet you at the **Peel River crossing** [WP332/km 74]. The ferry is free and operates from 9 AM to 12:30 AM daily from early June to mid-October. You may see tents and cabins set up along the river near the crossing. Locally, this site is called "Eight Miles" after the distance to Fort McPherson. This is a bush settlement where traditional activities such as catching and drying whitefish, trapping, and hunting are continued year-round.

➤ 🏕 🚣 🚻 As you leave the taiga forest behind and start seriously climbing westward, take a break at **Tetlit Gwinjik Wayside Park** [WP333/km 71] on a hilltop overlooking the Peel River Plateau. From the interpretive platform you will get a magnificent view of the Richardson Mountains, the Mackenzie Delta, and Fort McPherson. *Tetlit Gwinjik* is the Gwich'in name for the Peel River. In

---

Land of Ancient Trails

Trans Canada Trail sign at the Northwest Territories–Yukon border

You are now entering the NWT. The people of the NWT invite you to enjoy the natural beauty and blessings of this part of the Trans Canada Trail. The NWT is a land of ancient trails woven through a landscape of incredible natural beauty and diverse geography. We are a place rich in culture with strong links to the natural rhythms of the land. We thank our ancestors who travelled before us on these trails, whose gentle footprints remain to guide us safely on our journey. We honor those who show humility and walk softly on our land. We welcome you to explore and enjoy the beauty of our Territory.

late July and August, strings of vehicles on the side of the road tell you that locals have fanned out over the land to pick **blueberries** and **cloudberries** (also called akpik or knuckleberries).

➤ 🏠 🏔 Nestled into a scenic curve of the Dempster, **Midway Lake** [WP334/km

Hilltop lookout at Tetlit Gwinjik Wayside Park

44] is the site of the annual Midway Lake Music Festival. Generally held over the long weekend in early August, this grassroots celebration was started by Fort McPherson Chief James Ross in 1986 as a way to have a good time out on the land with no drugs or alcohol. The event now attracts country musicians, fiddlers, jiggers, and fans from across northwestern Canada and Alaska, creating a temporary town of over two thousand people along an otherwise deserted stretch of the Dempster. For more information on the festival, contact the Fort McPherson Band Council at 867-952-2330.

➤ 🏔 🏠 Whether you're biking or driving, it's a colossal climb up to the base

of a **peak crowned with a communication tower** [WP335]. If you're not completely tuckered out by the time you get there, consider hiking up the gated road leading to the tower for an awesome view from the Richardson Mountains' eastern frontier.

➤ 🧍 🏠 Congratulations! You've

Yukon-NWT border!

reached the **Yukon border** [WP336], 270 kilometres west of Inuvik. Looking east from the top of this continental divide you can see a vast mountain-rimmed plain. Don't forget to set your watch back an hour if you are continuing into the Yukon. Only another 507 kilometres to Dawson City!

12

APPENDICES

Jamie and Tassie check out a recently
vacated black bear den near Bechokò

APPENDIX A
COMMON PLANTS OF THE GREAT SLAVE–MACKENZIE REGION

Lichens

Iceland Moss	*Cetraria islandica, C. nivosa* and others
Leaf Lichens	*Peltigera rufescens, P. aphthosa; Nephroma arcticum*
Reindeer Lichen	*Cladina rangiferina, C. stellaris* and others
Rock Tripe	*Umbilicaria* spp., *Lasallia* spp.
Tree Hair	*Alectoria sarmentosa; Usnea* spp.; *Bryoria* spp.
Trumpet Lichens	*Cladonia coccifera, C. chlorophaea, C. pyxidata* and others
Shrubby Lichens	*Cladonia uncialis, C. cornuta, C. amaurocraea* and others

Mosses

Bog Mosses	*Sphagnum* spp.; *Drepanocladus* spp.; *Aulacomnium* spp.
Dryland Mosses	*Polytrichum juniperinum, P. piliferum; Hedwigia ciliata*
Feathermoss	*Hylocium splendens; Pleurozium shreberi*

Ferns

Fragrant Shield Fern	*Dryopteris fragrans*
Parsley Fern	*Cryptogramma crispa*
Polypody	*Polypodium vulgare*
Rusty Woodsia	*Woodsia ilvensis*

Lower Plants

Horsetails	*Equisetum arvense, E. palustre, E. sylvaticum, E. scirpoides*
Marsh Horsetail	*Equisetum palustre*
Spike-moss	*Selaginella selaginoides*
Water Horsetail	*Equisetum fluviatile*

Submerged and Emergent Plants

Bur-reed	*Sparganium angustifolium, S. minimum*
Buckbean	*Menyanthes trifoliata*
Cattail	*Typha latifolia*
Duckweed	*Lemna* spp.
Mare's Tail	*Hippuris vulgaris*
Pondweed	*Potamogeton gramineus, P. Richardsonii*
Water Arum	*Calla palustris*
Water Milfoil	*Myriophyllum exalbescens, M. verticillatum*
Water Smartweed	*Polygonum amphibium*
Yellow Pond Lily	*Nuphar variegatum*

Grasses and Sedges

Bentgrass	*Agrostis scabra*
Blue Grass	*Poa glauca*
Bulrush	*Scirpus cespitosus*
Cotton Grass	*Eriophorum angustifolium, E. Scheuchzeri*

Marsh Sedge	*Carex aquatilis, C. rostrata, and others*
Reed Bentgrass	*Calamagrostis canadensis*
Wild Rye	*Elymus innovatus*

Trees

Balsam Poplar	*Populus balsamifera*
Black Spruce	*Picea mariana*
Jack Pine	*Pinus banksiana*
Paper Birch	*Betula papyrifera*
Tamarack*	*Larix laricina*
Trembling Aspen	*Populus tremuloides*
White Spruce	*Picea glauca*

Tall to Medium Shrubs

Dwarf Birch	*Betula glandulosa*
Grey or Hoary Alder	*Alnus incana*
Mountain Alder	*Alnus crispa*
Red Osier Dogwood	*Cornus stolonifera*
Willows	*Salix Bebbiana, S. myrtillifolia, S. planifolia, S. glauca, S. serissima, S. arbusculoides, S. alaxensis,* and others

Low Shrubs and Ground Cover

Bearberry	*Arctostaphylos rubra*
Blueberry	*Vaccinium uliginosum*
Bog Laurel	*Kalmia polifolia*
Creeping Juniper	*Juniperus horizontalis*
Crowberry	*Empetrum nigrum*
Gooseberry	*Ribes oxyacanthoides*
Ground Juniper	*Juniperus communis*
Highbush Cranberry	*Viburnum edule*
Kinnickinnick	*Arctostaphylos uva-ursi*
Labrador Tea	*Ledum decumbens, L. groenlandicum*
Leatherleaf	*Chamaedaphne calyculata*
Mountain Cranberry	*Vaccinium vitis-idaea*
Red Currant	*Ribes glandulosum, R. triste*
Shrubby Cinquefoil	*Potentilla fruticosa*
Soapberry	*Shepherdia canadensis*
Sweet Gale	*Myrica gale*
Wild Raspberry	*Rubus strigosus*
Wild Rose	*Rosa acicularis*

Herbs and Flowers

Bog Star	*Parnassia palustris*
Bunchberry	*Cornus canadensis*
Calypso Orchid	*Calypso bulbosa*
Cinquefoil	*Potentilla nivea*

* *Official symbol of the Northwest Territories*

Cloudberry	*Rubus Chamaemorus*
Lady's Slipper Orchid	*Cypripedium passerinum, C. guttatum*
Large-flowered Wintergreen	*Pyrola grandiflora*
Marsh Five Finger	*Potentilla palustris*
Miterwort	*Mitella nuda*
Mountain Avens*	*Dryas octopetala*
Northern Bog Orchid	*Habernia obtusata*
Northern Comandra	*Geocaulon lividum*
One-flowered Wintergreen	*Moneses uniflora*
Pale Corydalis	*Corydalis sempervirens*
Pink Rubus	*Rubus acaulis*
Prickly Saxifrage	*Saxifraga tricuspidata*
Red Dock	*Rumex occidentalis*
Water Parsnip	*Sium suave*
Wild Onion	*Allium Schoenoprasum*
Wild Strawberry	*Fragaria virginiana*

Large-flowered

Bur Marigold	*Bidens ceruna*
Indian Paintbrush	*Castilleja Raupii*
Labrador Lousewort	*Pedicularis labradorica*
Northern Yarrow	*Achillea nigrescens, A. sibirica*
Pussytoes	*Antennaria rosea, A. nitida*
Skullcap	*Scutellaria galericulata*
Twinflower	*Linnaea borealis*

Narrow-leaved

Goldenrod	*Solidago decumbens, S. multiradiata*
Groundsel or Ragwort	*Senecio lugens*
Hawkweed	*Hieracium scabriusculum*
Sweet Coltsfoot	*Petasites sagittatus*

APPENDIX B

COMMON MAMMALS OF THE GREAT SLAVE–MACKENZIE REGION

American red squirrel	*Tamiasciurus hudsonicus*
American beaver	*Castor canadensis*
American black bear	*Ursus americanus*
American marten	*Martes americana*
American mink	*Mustela vison*
Barren-ground caribou	*Rangifer tarandus*
Bison (or Buffalo)	*Bison bison*
Ermine or Short-tail weasel	*Mustela erminea*
Grey wolf	*Canis lupus*
Least weasel	*Mustela nivalis*
Lynx	*Lynx lynx*
Moose	*Alces alces*
Muskrat	*Ondatra zibethicus*

* Official symbol of the Northwest Territories

North American porcupine	*Erethizon dorsatum*
Northern red-backed vole	*Clethrionomys rutilus*
Red fox	*Vulpes vulpes*
River otter	*Lontra canadensis*
Snowshoe hare	*Lepus americanus*
Wolverine	*Gulo gulo*
Woodland caribou	*Rangifer tarandus caribou*

APPENDIX C

COMMON BIRDS OF THE GREAT SLAVE–MACKENZIE REGION

Loons and Grebes
Common Loon
Horned Grebe
Pacific Loon
Red-necked Grebe
Red-throated Loon

Swans and Geese
Canada Goose
Tundra Swan
White-fronted Goose

Wading Birds
Sandhill Crane

Ducks
American Wigeon
Blue-winged Teal
Bufflehead
Canvasback
Common Goldeneye
Common Merganser
Greater Scaup
Green-winged Teal
Lesser Scaup
Mallard
Northern Pintail
Northern Shoveller
Red-breasted Merganser
Ring-necked Duck
Surf Scoter
White-winged Scoter

Hawks, Falcons and Eagles
American Kestrel
Bald Eagle
Gyrfalcon*
Merlin

Northern Goshawk
Northern Harrier
Osprey
Red-tailed Hawk
Sharp-shinned Hawk

Grouse, Ptarmigan
Rock Ptarmigan
Rough Grouse
Sharp-tailed Grouse
Spruce Grouse
Willow Ptarmigan

Shorebirds
Least Sandpiper
Killdeer
Lesser Yellowlegs
Pectoral Sandpiper
Red-necked Phalarope
Semipalmated Plover
Sora
Spotted Sandpiper
Wilsons Snipe

Gulls and Terns
Arctic Tern
Black Tern
Bonaparte's Gull
California Gull
Caspian Tern
Herring Gull
Mew Gull
Ring-billed Gull

Kingfishers
Belted Kingfisher

Swallows
Barn Swallow
Cliff Swallow

Tree Swallow

Goatsuckers
Common Nighthawk

Owls
Boreal Owl
Great Gray Owl
Great Horned Owl
Northern Hawk Owl
Short-eared Owl

Woodpeckers
Hairy Woodpecker
Northern Flicker

Jays, Crows, Magpies
American Crow
Black-billed Magpie
Common Raven
Gray Jay

Flycatchers
Alder Flycatcher
Eastern Kingbird
Eastern Phoebe
Least Flycatcher

Chickadees
Black-capped Chickadee
Boreal Chickadee

Thrushes, Kinglets
American Robin
Gray-cheeked Thrush
Hermit Thrush
Ruby-crowned Kinglet
Swainson's Thrush
Varied Thrush

Waxwings
Bohemian Waxwing

* official symbol of the Northwest Territories

Warblers
- Black and white Warbler
- Blackpoll Warbler
- Canada Warbler
- Northern Waterthrush
- Orange-crowned Warbler
- Palm Warbler
- Tennessee Warbler
- Yellow-rumped Warbler
- Yellow Warbler

Vireos
- Blue-headed Vireo
- Red-eyed Vireo

Blackbirds
- Common Grackle
- Red-winged Blackbird
- Rusty Blackbird

Finches
- Common Redpoll
- White-winged Crossbill

Sparrows
- American Tree Sparrow
- Chipping Sparrow
- Dark-eyed Junco
- Fox Sparrow
- House Sparrow
- Lincoln's Sparrow
- Savannah Sparrow
- Song Sparrow
- Swamp Sparrow
- White-crowned Sparrow
- White-throated Sparrow

APPENDIX D

COMMON FISH OF THE GREAT SLAVE–MACKENZIE REGION

Arctic grayling	*Thymallus arcticus*
Burbot (maria, ling)	*Lota lota*
Emerald shiner	*Notropis atherinoides*
Inconnu	*Stenodus leucichthys*
Lake chub	*Couesius plumbeus*
Lake trout	*Salvelinus namaycush*
Lake whitefish	*Coregonus clupeaformis*
Ninespine stickleback	*Pungitius pungitius*
Northern pike	*Esox lucius*
Spottail shiner	*Notropis hudsonicus*
Slimy sculpin	*Cottus cognatus*
Trout-perch	*Percopsis omiscomaycus*
Walleye (pickerel)	*Stizostedion vitreum*
White sucker	*Catostomus commersoni*

APPENDIX E

FIELD GUIDE TO NORTHERN WETLANDS

Wetland

A wetland is any area of generally low, flat land that holds water during at least part of the year. This water may be at, near, or above the ground surface. Wetlands are by far the most biologically productive ecosystems in northern Canada.

Pond

Ponds are well-defined basins up to several hectares in size that are filled with still or slow-moving water. Most ponds are shallow with an average depth of less than four metres. Fed by rainwater, snowmelt, or small streams, many ponds owe their existence to the handiwork of beavers. Yellow pond lilies may cover their surface. Cat-tails, horsetails, or other reedy plants often fringe their shores.

Bog

Bogs are poorly drained areas covered by mats of moss, the most common species of which is

Sphagnum. Because of high acidity and low levels of oxygen, biological decomposition in bogs is very slow, creating thick underlying layers of peat. As peat piles up over many years, bogs often take on a raised or plateau-like appearance. Low shrubs such as Labrador tea plus scattered black spruce, tamarack, and willows are the most common plants on northern bogs.

Fen

More water flows through fens than through bogs, which promotes the growth of a thick carpet of sedges, their characteristic plant. You can tell sedges from true grasses by their triangular stems. Spin a sedge stem between your fingers and you will know why botanists say that "sedges have edges." Fens also support some mosses, grasses, willow shrubs, and occasional tamarack trees.

Marsh

Marshes are productive areas usually found along the shore of a river or lake, which gives them a typically linear shape. Their most characteristic plants include cat-tails, horsetails, and other reedy species. Marshes are subject to wide fluctuations in water levels and may dry out completely by late summer.

Swamp

A swamp is simply a marsh that supports trees and tall shrubs. Still or gently flowing water covers most of the land surface during the wetter periods of the year. Swamps are found most commonly along major rivers in the western arctic. Typical plant species include balsam poplar trees or alder and willow shrubs.

APPENDIX F

OUTFITTERS, TOURS, AND EQUIPMENT RENTALS

For a more complete listing, see www.spectacularnwt.com

SOUTH SLAVE AND UPPER MACKENZIE

Canoe Arctic Inc.
Box 130
Fort Smith, NT
X0E 0P0, Canada
Tel: 867-872-2308
Email: alex@canoearctic.com
Web site: www.canoearctic.com

Canoe North
47 Studney Drive
Hay River, NT
X0E 0R6, Canada
Tel: 867-874-6337
Fax: 867-874-3866
Email: info@canoenorth.ca
Web site: www.canoenorth.ca

Det'an Cho Tourist Camp
Box 145
Fort Resolution, NT
X0E 0M0, Canada
Tel: 867-394-4411

Taiga Tour Company
Box 852
Fort Smith, NT
X0E 0P0, Canada
Tel: 867-872-2060
Fax: 867-872-2401
Email: taigatour@northwestel.net
Web site: www.taigatour.com

M&M River Taxi
Wrigley, NT
X0E 1E0, Canada
Tel: 867-582-3416

Wrigley's Wonders
Wrigley, NT
X0E 1E0, Canada
Tel: 867-581-3678

NORMAN WELLS & TULITA

Mountain River Outdoor Adventures
Box 245
Norman Wells, NT
X0E 0V0, Canada
Tel: 867-587-2697
Fax: 867-587-2697
Email: info@mountainriver.nt.ca

INUVIK & TSIIGEHTCHIC

The Arctic Chalet
Box 1099
Inuvik, NT
X0E 0T0, Canada
Toll Free: 1-800-685-9417
Tel: 867-777-3535
Fax: 867-777-4443
Email: judi@arcticchalet.com
Web site: www.arcticchalet.com

Arctic Nature Tours
Box 1190
Inuvik, NT
X0E 0T0, Canada
Tel: 867-777-3300
Fax: 867-777-3400
Email: reservation@arcticnaturetours.com

TUKTOYAKTUK

Ookpik Tours & Adventures
Box 131
Tuktoyaktuk, NT
X0E 1C0, Canada
Tel: 867-977-2170
Fax: 867-977-2399

Bushmasters Catering
PO Box 37
Tulít'a, NT
X0E 0K0, Canada
Tel: 867- 588-3503
Fax: 867- 587-2375
Email: bushmasters@ssimicro.com

Heritage Tours c/o the Blake family
Box 67
Tsiigehtchic, NT
X0E 0B0, Canada
Tel: 867-953-3171
Cell: 867-678-5093
Email: blake_christensen92@yahoo.ca

Timber Island Enterprises
Tsiigehtchic, NT
X0E 0B0, Canada
Tel: 867-678-2998
Email: timberisland@yahoo.ca

Western Arctic Adventures & Equipment
Box 1554
Inuvik, NT
X0E 0T0, Canada
Tel: 867-777-2594
Fax: 867-777-4542
E-mail: canoenwt@permafrost.com

Arctic Tour Company Ltd.
Box 325
Tuktoyaktuk, NT
X0E 1C0, Canada
Tel: 867-977-2230
Fax: 867-977-2276
Email: atc@permafrost.com

YELLOWKNIFE

NARWAL Northern Adventures
Box 11072
Yellowknife, NT
X1A 3X7, Canada
Tel: 867-873-6443
Fax: 867-873-2741
Email: outdoors@narwal.com
Web site: www.narwal.ca

Omega Marine
4801 School Draw Ave
Yellowknife, NT
X1A 2K6, Canada
Tel: 867-873-3770
Toll Free: 800-873-5104
Fax: 867-873-3693
Email: omegamarine@theedge.ca
Web site: www.omegamarine.ca

Overlander Sports
Box 964
Yellowknife, NT
X1A 2N7, Canada
Tel: 867-873-2474
Fax: 867-920-4079
Email: sales@overlandersports.com
Web site: www.overlandersports.com

SOUTH OF 60

Black Feather—The Wilderness Adventure Company
250 McNaughts Road
RR#3, Parry Sound, ON
P2A 2W9, Canada
Tel: 705-746-1372
Toll-Free: 888-849-7668
Fax: 705-746-7048
Email: info@blackfeather.com
Web site: www.blackfeather.com

Stan Stevens Mackenzie Mountain Outfitters
Box 175
Dawson Creek, BC
V1G 4G3, Canada
Tel: 250-786-5118
Fax: 250-786-5404
Email: mmostanstevens@gmail.com
Web site: www.mmo-stanstevens.com

APPENDIX G
WAYPOINTS USED IN THIS GUIDE

Waypoints #	Longitude	Latitude	Waypoints #	Longitude	Latitude
013	-112.089437	60.024103	088	-113.765119	60.996685
020	-111.890397	60.016529	091	-114.033627	60.982254
023	-112.235586	60.107317	092	-114.048300	60.967040
024	-112.240878	60.135712	095	-114.253349	61.012058
025	-112.295437	60.202677	096	-114.288841	60.997830
032	-112.698930	60.355848	097	-114.333079	60.994029
033	-112.686838	60.367414	098	-114.350257	60.989167
034	-112.556954	60.371454	099	-114.392403	60.968033
035	-112.524739	60.369135	101	-114.518188	60.946062
036	-112.438263	60.403675	105	-114.582878	60.942173
037	-112.495118	60.463302	106	-114.826965	60.931473
040	-112.572373	60.550758	109	-115.043938	60.882662
041	-112.598752	60.545978	110	-115.344928	60.839253
044	-112.651921	60.553612	111	-115.369795	60.833398
045	-112.685190	60.554174	112	-115.505455	60.828537
046	-112.770603	60.583514	113	-115.531032	60.831074
047	-112.829217	60.628947	114	-115.623622	60.830645
049	-112.875909	60.735116	116	-115.973068	60.841322
050	-112.899845	60.749206	117	-116.121651	60.891416
053	-112.915677	60.800853	119	-116.314137	60.917025
055	-113.050913	60.777207	121	-116.265905	60.913035
057	-113.146674	60.760591	125	-116.582061	61.021978
059	-113.203437	60.814455	127	-116.743933	61.042950
060	-113.257927	60.844960	128	-116.858097	61.048608
061	-113.273387	60.903264	130	-117.414156	61.235772
062	-113.230638	60.966951	132	-117.606511	61.299303
064	-113.190597	60.990695	135	-116.908018	61.134372
066	-113.135871	61.062302	137	-116.483274	62.489634
067	-113.219712	61.091186	140	-116.255921	62.134455
068	-113.151621	61.184923	143	-117.059825	61.670973
069	-113.226103	61.185001	145	-117.152321	61.566799
070	-113.160699	61.229246	146	-116.971803	61.680140
071	-113.126713	61.227257	147	-116.941770	61.690318
072	-113.293441	61.237080	148	-116.536465	61.894848
073	-113.329854	61.246977	149	-116.335179	62.001028
074	-113.403282	61.261568	151	-116.313787	62.038783
075	-113.510657	61.255077	152	-116.176340	62.684638
076	-113.512325	61.253281	154	-116.081696	62.718917
077	-113.617077	61.228930	155	-115.946764	62.784001
078	-113.652189	61.231819	160	-115.840863	62.764749
079	-113.668995	61.219676	162	-115.724288	62.743598
081	-113.722740	61.198760	163	-115.401779	62.682860
082	-113.760869	61.188368	164	-114.970528	62.534933
086	-113.742062	61.083930	165	-114.640652	62.467074
087	-113.777454	61.006488	169	-115.272233	62.652858

Waypoints #	Longitude	Latitude	Waypoints #	Longitude	Latitude
172	-118.034963	61.455286	237	-126.604360	65.237118
173	-118.405922	61.390075	238	-126.839679	65.278552
176	-118.680131	61.295447	239	-126.955600	65.250793
177	-118.680334	61.295920	242	-127.446484	65.435014
178	-119.035290	61.232640	243	-127.886464	65.566644
180	-119.208445	61.227195	247	-128.283021	65.617415
181	-119.215629	61.227050	248	-128.570670	65.620188
182	-119.799263	61.296042	249	-128.796869	65.665841
183	-119.993089	61.341984	251	-129.148627	66.030901
186	-120.682104	61.555983	252	-129.121567	66.070515
187	-120.679560	61.578988	253	-128.926367	66.176227
188	-120.696248	61.782707	254	-128.845073	66.222100
190	-120.792642	61.813870	255	-128.794999	66.223526
191	-120.975530	61.837380	256	-128.627854	66.293821
192	-121.170572	61.844640	258	-128.746341	66.387535
193	-121.578337	61.926413	259	-128.973141	66.471076
194	-121.802550	61.987738	260	-129.215519	66.550011
195	-122.176948	62.084684	261	-129.327897	66.630386
196	-122.536786	62.136892	262	-129.573676	66.696807
197	-122.992582	62.155477	263	-129.898998	66.736828
198	-123.174103	62.223090	264	-130.075233	66.771508
199	-123.311000	62.236152	265	-130.159855	66.960879
200	-123.369514	62.283694	267	-130.909064	67.476254
202	-123.250053	62.448790	269	-131.494491	67.465124
203	-123.167340	62.577777	270	-131.966700	67.369776
204	-123.125045	62.699056	271	-132.531387	67.292113
206	-123.220535	62.943656	273	-132.997253	67.219601
207	-123.239179	62.981009	276	-133.357415	67.331929
208	-123.307326	63.131244	277	-133.518145	67.386287
209	-123.610307	63.266446	278	-133.573494	67.477727
210	-123.620024	63.293809	283	-133.855535	67.528189
211	-123.697776	63.467387	284	-134.087418	67.608869
212	-123.743915	63.533690	285	-134.171033	67.792637
216	-124.204082	63.955256	288	-134.066880	67.927290
217	-124.271032	63.969529	289	-134.027612	67.973844
218	-124.420622	64.099281	291	-133.851258	68.077429
219	-124.403091	64.182951	292	-133.800289	68.136156
220	-124.520666	64.287003	294	-133.799193	68.205872
221	-124.795957	64.416357	295	-133.771883	68.266846
223	-124.891381	64.622664	296	-133.705411	68.338129
226	-125.122450	64.755420	298	-133.844134	68.475471
227	-125.139446	64.869456	299	-133.976388	68.559439
228	-125.403386	64.897795	300	-134.135857	68.688352
229	-124.894981	64.685440	301	-134.206394	68.723983
231	-124.777185	64.449351	302	-134.459136	68.849594
233	-125.698514	64.907420	303	-134.575082	68.927620
235	-125.849518	64.933050	304	-134.665503	69.002329
236	-126.311265	65.136508	305	-134.593986	69.057161

Waypoints #	Longitude	Latitude
306	-134.389652	69.099001
307	-134.350805	69.109084
309	-134.235568	69.176982
310	-134.178898	69.250147
311	-133.912257	69.280218
312	-133.847209	69.327351
313	-133.707927	69.344111
314	-133.665422	69.359496
315	-133.631809	69.378526
316	-133.533276	69.395019
318	-133.169803	69.402962
319	-133.128205	69.413322
320	-133.655310	68.333280
321	-133.251496	68.285785
322	-133.265935	68.261647
323	-133.423459	68.202790
324	-133.442338	68.186580
325	-133.491400	68.088661
326	-133.859584	67.754327
328	-133.767240	67.438496
329	-134.152720	67.384670
330	-134.724270	67.475070
331	-134.858500	67.350400
332	-134.880220	67.337370
333	-135.030500	67.304470
334	-135.433070	67.227700
335	-135.835170	67.175850
336	-136.202179	67.051531
337	-119.374240	61.222406

REFERENCES

Andre, Alestine, Alma Cardinal, Micheal Heine and Ingrid Kritsch. 2008. *Gwichya Gwich'in Googwandak – The History and Stories of Gwichya Gwich'in as Told by the Elders of Tsiigehtchic*. Tsiigehtchic and Fort McPherson, Northwest Territories: Gwich'in Social and Cultural Institute.

Andre, Alestine, Alma Cardinal, Micheal Heine and Ingrid Kritsch. 2008. Gwichya Gwich'in Googwandak – The History and Stories of *Gwichya Gwich'in as Told by the Elders of Tsiigehtchic*. Tsiigehtchic and Fort McPherson, Northwest Territories: Gwich'in Social and Cultural Institute.

Anonymous, no date. 1962 *Dogrib Tea Dance*. Audio CD produced in Yellowknife by Dogrib Treaty 11 Council with assistance from the Prince of Wales Northern Heritage Centre and the Department of Education, Culture and Employment, Government of Northwest Territories.

Avens Associates Ltd. in conjunction with Cygnus Consulting, EDA Collaborative, and Hanks Heritage Consulting. 1995. *Highway #3 Reconstruction: Initial Situation Analysis*. Yellowknife: Avens Associates Ltd.

Baker, Peter. 1976. *An Arctic Arab: The Story of a Free-trader in Northern Canada*. Saskatoon: Yellowknife Publishing Company.

Bastedo, Jamie. 1994. *Shield Country: Life and Times of the Oldest Piece of the Planet*. Calgary: Red Deer Press.

—— 1996. *Blue Lake and Rocky Shore: A Field Guide to Special Natural Areas in the Yellowknife Region*. Yellowknife: Artisan Press. (Reprinted in 2008 as *Yellowknife Outdoors*)

—— 1998. *Reaching North: A Celebration of the Subarctic*. Calgary: Red Deer Press.

—— 2004. *"Hey Nah-Nah Hearne Hoh."* Song prepared for a living history presentation on the history of Yellowknife, *YK Tales*, at the Prince of Wales Northern Heritage Centre, Yellowknife.

—— 2006. *On Thin Ice*. Calgary: Red Deer Press. (A novel about polar bears and arctic climate change. Sequel released in 2009 under the title, *Sila's Revenge*)

Bell, W.H. (Bill). 1998. *Beyond the Northern Lights*. Surrey, British Columbia: Hancock House Publishers, www.hancockhouse.com.

Camsell, Charles. 1954. *Son of the North*. Toronto: Ryerson.

Canadian Red Cross Society. 1998. *Wilderness and Remote First Aid*. Calgary: The Canadian Red Cross Society.

Canadian Wildlife Service. no date. *Slave River Delta*. Ottawa: Environment Canada. (Poster)

Canfield, Jack, Mark Hansen, and LeAnn Thieman. 2004. *Chicken Soup for the Caregiver's Soul*. Deerfield Beach, Florida: Health Communications.

Carrière, Suzanne. Ecosystem ecologist, Energy and Natural Resources, Government of Northwest Territories. Personal interview. Yellowknife. 15 Jan. 2006.

CBC archives. Guest, Frank T'Seleie. "My nation will stop the pipeline." CBC Television News. http://archives.cbc.ca/IDC-1-73-295-1549/politics_economy/pipeline/clip5

Collins, Eileen. 1999. *I've Been Here Ever Since: An Informal Oral History of Hay River*. Hay River: Town of Hay River.

Davies, Raymond. "Fort Smith: Capital of the Northwest Territories." *Saturday Night*. 27 Nov. 1943.

Dixon, Franklin W. 1963. *The Viking Symbol Mystery. The Hardy Boys Series, Vol. 42*. New York: Grosset and Dunlap Inc.

Donham, Parker Barss. 1990. "Storm on Great Slave." *Reader's Digest,* May. pp. 62– 67.

Evans, Earl D. Cabin owner near Cunningham Landing, Slave River. Personal interview. 8 Aug. 2005.

Fredrickson, Olive A. 2000. *The Silence of the North*. Markham, Ontario: Fitzhenry & Whiteside.

Gage, S.R. 1990. *A Walk on the Canol Road: Exploring the First Major Northern Pipeline*. New York: Mosaic Press.

Gough, Barry. 1997. *First Across the Continent: Sir Alexander Mackenzie*. Toronto: McClelland & Stewart.

Gray, Larry. 1999. *Other Voices*. Fort Smith: Dome Productions and Shadowland Records. (audio CD)

Green, Jim. 1995. Summer on the Water." *Up Here,* July–Aug. 1995, 21–23 (includes contributions from Jim's wife, Juneva Green)

Grono, Shawn, producer and director. 2001. *Slave to the River.* Edmonton: Split Fork Productions. (video)

Gwich'in Social and Cultural Institute. 1997. *"That river, it's like a highway for us.": The Mackenzie River through Gwichya Gwich'in history and culture*. Tsiigehtchic and Yellowknife: Historic Sites and Monuments Board of Canada, Unpublished agenda paper.

Hancock, Lyn. 1974. *The Mighty Mackenzie: Highway to the Arctic Ocean*. Saanichton, British Columbia: Hancock House Publishers, www.hancockhouse.com.

Harrison, David. no date. Physical Geography of the Hay River Area. Hay River: Unpublished classroom notes. (See his PhD. thesis: Harrison, David. 1984. *Hay River, NWT. 1800-1950: A Geographical Study Of Site And Situation*. Edmonton: University of Alberta.)

Hewitt, Mike. 1968. "Fort Smith Landslide: Houses swept away, one killed." *News of the North*, Fort Smith, 15 Aug. 1968. Vol 26, no. 33, 1.

Indian and Northern Affairs Canada. 2006. "Backgrounder: Dehcho (Mackenzie River) Bridge." http://www.ainc-inac.gc.ca/ai/mr/nr/j-a2004/02486bk-eng.asp

Keizer, Mike. Manager, Communications and Visitor Services, Wood Buffalo National Park. Personal interview. Fort Smith. 6 Aug. 2005.

King, John. "Strong roots in the snow." *News North,* Yellowknife: Northern News Services, March 27, 2006, p. 1.

Kitto, F.H. 1920. *Report of a Preliminary Investigation of the Natural Resources of Mackenzie District*. Ottawa: typescript.

Klein, Clayton, and Verlen Kruger. 1985. *One Incredible Journey*. Toronto: Wilderness House Books.

Krebs, Charles, ed. 2001. *Ecosystem Dynamics of the Boreal Forest*. Oxford: Oxford University Press.

LaTour, Vicky. 1999. "A Brief History of the Port Town of Hay River." Hay River: Unpublished manuscript prepared for the Tourism Advisory Committee of the Town of Hay River.

Maldaver, Sharone. no date. *As Long As I Remember: Elders of the Fort Smith, Northwest Territories region talk about bush life and changes they have seen*. Fort Smith: Cascade Graphics.

McCreadie, Mary. 1995. *Canoeing Canada's Northwest Territories: A Paddler's Guide*. Hyde Park, Ontario: Canadian Recreational Canoeing Association.

McGown, Carrie. 2006. "Mackenzie River Itinerary." Unpublished report. (available through Blackfeather—The Wilderness Adventure Company, info@blackfeather.com)

McGuffin, Gary and Joanie. 1988. *Gulf of St. Lawrence to the Beaufort in Two Seasons*. Erin, Ontario: Boston Mills Press.

Natural Resources Canada. 2007. Permafrost, landslides and slope stability. http://gsc.nrcan. gc.ca/permafrost/landslides_e.php?p=1 (includes excellent images of landslides near Old Fort Point and Tulít'a)

Northwest Territories Tourism Committee. 1979. *On the Banks of the Slave: A History of the Community of Fort Smith, Northwest Territories*. Yellowknife: Department of Education, Government of the Northwest Territories.

Parks Canada. no date. *Wood Buffalo National Park*. (video presentation for park visitors)

Prince of Wales Northern Heritage Centre. 2007. *"Remembering Reindeer Station," Inuvialuit Place Names: Qun'ngilaat*. Yellowknife: Government of the Northwest Territories. http://pwnhc.learnnet.nt.ca/inuvialuit/placenames/reindeerremembering.html

Richardson, John. 1984. *Arctic Ordeal: The Journal of John Richardson, Surgeon-Naturalist with Franklin, 1820–1822*. Kingston and Montreal: McGill–Queen's University Press.

Russel, F. 1898. *Explorations in the Far North*. Des Moines: University of Iowa.

Seton, Ernest Thompson. 1911. *The Arctic Prairies: A Canoe journey of 2,000 miles in search of the caribou being the account of a voyage to the region north of Aylmer Lake*. New York: International University Press.

Siemens, David. 2005. "From the Dogrib of Fort Rae to the Tlicho of Behchokò." Unpublished manuscript.

Stastny, Paul, and Andrea Lorenz. "Delta Details." *Oilweek Magazine,* Jan. 2007. (http://www.oilweek.com/articles.asp?ID=345)

Thom, Margaret M., and Ethel Blondin-Townsend, eds. 1987. *Nahecho Keh: Our Elders*. Fort Providence, NWT: Slavey Research Project.

Weber, Bob. "Firm plans to strip-mine coalfield for gasification: Pipeline spurs West Hawk proposal." *Vancouver Sun*. 21 Mar. 2006, p. 4.

Western Arctic Handbook Committee. 2002. *Canada's Western Arctic, Including the Dempster Highway*. Inuvik: Western Arctic Handbook Committee.

Van Pelt, Jacques. Tourism outfitter and naturalist. Personal interview. Fort Smith. 6 Aug. 2005.

INDEX

Jamie Bastedo's work is all about taking science to the streets. Whether hosting lively nature shows on the radio or writing about his northern home, Jamie spreads a contagious enthusiasm and love for the land. Well established as a popular science writer in his books *Falling for Snow: A Naturalist's Journey into the World of Winter*, *Shield Country: The Life and Times of the Oldest Piece of the Planet*, *Reaching North: A Celebration of the Subarctic and Blue Lake and Rocky Shores*, he writes to inform and inspire, telling a "story of place." He also has written over 30 natural history features in magazines, including *Up Here*, *Backpacker*, and *Winter Living*. When not out on the land, he hangs his hat in Yellowknife, Northwest Territories, where he lives with his wife and two daughters.

He also brings his environmental message to his young adult novels including *Tracking Triple Seven*, *On Thin Ice*, and *Sila's Reveng*e.

For More Information About The Trans Canada Trail

Join the thousands of Canadians from every province and territory who are helping build the world's longest recreational trail. Find out how you can support the Trail at:

www.tctrail.ca
1-800-465-3636